'This is a full life story from the fish's own mouth: his jokes, his sauce, and detailed revelations from his criminal past. Devilfish is a master storyteller and this book is broad, funny, northern and poetic'
Guardian

'You will be in clover if you want to be rousingly entertained by a man who will tell you that "if you live slap bang between a fish warehouse and an abattoir, you're happy when you catch a cold". Devilfish is the soul of poker. And he has a massive heart' Victoria Coren, *Observer*

'I haven't laughed so hard in ages. If you look back on your own life and think of all the times you've wished you said this and wished you'd done that, know that Ulliott's the sort of bloke that said it and did it, and a hell of a lot more besides. Boy does he have some stories to tell! In a world full of self-pitying cardboard cutout celebs, Ulliott is a stand-up, stand-out 3D superstar. This'll become a poker classic' Roger Cook, *Daily Star*

'A rollicking good read . . . amusing, honest and compelling' *Blonde Poker*

Devilfish

The Life and Times of a Poker Legend

THE AUTOBIOGRAPHY

DAVE 'DEVILFISH' ULLIOTT
with MARCUS GEORGIOU

PENGUIN BOOKS

PENGUIN BOOKS

Published by the Penguin Group
Penguin Books Ltd, 80 Strand, London WC2R ORL, England
Penguin Group (USA), Inc., 375 Hudson Street, New York, New York 10014, USA
Penguin Group (Canada), 90 Eglinton Avenue East, Suite 700, Toronto, Ontario, Canada M4P 2Y3
(a division of Pearson Penguin Canada Inc.)
Penguin Ireland, 25 St Stephen's Green, Dublin 2, Ireland (a division of Penguin Books Ltd)
Penguin Group (Australia), 250 Camberwell Road, Camberwell, Victoria 3124, Australia
(a division of Pearson Australia Group Pty Ltd)
Penguin Books India Pvt Ltd, 11 Community Centre, Panchsheel Park, New Delhi – 110 017, India
Penguin Group (NZ), 67 Apollo Drive, Rosedale, Auckland 0632, New Zealand
(a division of Pearson New Zealand Ltd)
Penguin Books (South Africa) (Pty) Ltd, 24 Sturdee Avenue, Rosebank, Johannesburg 2196, South Africa

Penguin Books Ltd, Registered Offices: 80 Strand, London WC2R ORL, England

www.penguin.com

First published by Viking 2010
Published in Penguin Books 2011

1

Copyright © Dave Ulliott, 2010

The moral right of the author has been asserted

Set in Garamond MT
Typeset by Palimpsest Book Production Limited, Falkirk, Stirlingshire
Printed in Great Britain by Clays Ltd, St Ives plc

A CIP catalogue record for this book is available from the British Library

ISBN: 978–0–141–04753–9

www.greenpenguin.co.uk

To my sister Janet, my brother Paul, my mother Joyce, my father Stanley. And to my best mate Pete Robinson, and, of course, to Rob Gardner, who made all this possible. And finally to my ex-wife Mandy – the sweetest, kindest woman I've ever known. Without you I would be dead or in prison.

Contents

Contents

Introduction: Unlucky Lucky F**ker

You keep your luck – I'll keep mine

I've never been lucky at cards. It doesn't say 'poker player' on my passport, it says 'unlucky fucker'. That might seem like an odd thing to say for someone like me who travels the world playing poker, lives in a big house, has a Ferrari and a Hummer in the garage and a two-hundred-grand watch on my wrist, all of it paid for by poker. But it's true. Everyone in poker knows I'm not lucky at catching cards or outdrawing other players when I'm behind.

But I don't mind.

OK, maybe a few of the players I've beaten wouldn't say I'm unlucky. But that's because poker players tend to be a bunch of bitter twisted fuck-ups.

I'm only kidding – they're all a lovely bunch.

Of bastards.

It's funny how things have changed. At the beginning, whenever someone asked you what you did for a living, you'd never even think of saying you were a professional poker player. It didn't even exist as something to be. Then it got to the stage where if someone asked you that question you *could* actually say 'poker player', but they'd just look at you as if you were daft – as if you'd said 'skydiving burglar' or 'underwater car thief'. It's only recently that it's become acceptable to tell someone you're a professional poker player without them calling a mental-health charity or *Crimewatch*.

In the past, if someone was asking me how I got hold of my money, my usual reply was, 'No comment. And where's my solicitor?' (But that's the police for you – nosey bastards.) Nowadays it's accepted that people play poker for a living: it's on TV and the Internet and in pubs.

I'm only an unlucky fucker professionally, not personally. Although I might have been unlucky with cards, I've always been very lucky in life. And I'd much rather have it that way round. You can always walk away from bad luck at the card table but you can't always walk away from the hand life deals you.

I cheated death in the very first minute I was born; I twice escaped being beaten to death, survived prison, am an undamaged ex-boxer, walked away from a plane struck by lightning, and I'm still sane after two marriages. No amount of card-luck on earth would get you through all that.

Even though when I get a bad beat at poker I can moan and bitch for England, the reason I say I don't mind being unlucky at cards is because I sometimes think that if I started getting *lucky* at cards, it might mean I started getting unlucky in life – as if I'd have to switch one luck for the other. Now that would be a bad exchange.

I might walk away from a card table after getting another bad beat but I do at least get to walk away, and I walk away healthy. What's the point of being lucky at cards if, when you get up from the table, you walk outside and get flattened by a bus? No royal flush *on the planet* is gonna make up for that, son.

So . . . if I'm the unlucky fucker in a penthouse suite in Las Vegas, sitting in a jacuzzi with a young, cute blonde who's turned on by bubbles – so be it. In that case, thank fuck I never got lucky.

I started from nothing, and when I die I'll go back to nothing. We all know where we're going in the end, and it's not to have a picnic with Jesus, two clouds down from God. It's to a big black hole in the ground or a little metal urn under the stairs – that's where I'll be ending up. So if I'm going to leave this world empty handed, I might as well have a bloody good time while I'm here. I've certainly tried to.

Like they say – *you can't have everything*. For a start, where would you keep it? No one's got a garage that big.

OK, let's play . . .

1. Starting at the Bottom and Working My Way Down

The worst thing you can do is win

On 1 April 1954 I knew I'd been born when a midwife smacked me on my arse. We hadn't even been introduced. I always thought that I was a born gambler because when that midwife slapped me I didn't cry. I yelled: 'Deal me in, love.'

That same year the first hydrogen bomb was tested at Bikini Atoll – the place the bikini was named after. So I can't even say that my birth was the most important thing that happened that year, although I like to think my mother would disagree.

I was born at home, as most babies were then. That was fine if the birth went OK but not so good if it didn't. Mine was one of the not-so-good births, a breech, and so the midwife called for help. I don't know what was going on inside that was so good it made me want to stay in – maybe I'd started up a card game and was ahead. Whatever the reason, I wasn't coming out easily. Probably word had got back to me that I was about to be born in Hull, not Hawaii. But then again, it *was* April Fool's day, so maybe it was my idea of a joke.

The doctor finally arrived, which must have been a relief to my mother, Joyce, because the only other person

1

available was the local vet. When I finally popped out I was black all over. And dead. Or so they thought. I looked still-born, and I was about to be thrown on the fire – that's what they did with stillborns then, just disposed of them. But the midwife took out this tube that she had in her pocket, put it between my lips and breathed life into me. That's when she smacked me on the arse and I started yelling. Well, wouldn't you, after that?

Because of all the people since then that I've annoyed, punched, pissed off, out-played or broke at cards, in the interests of that midwife's safety I'm not going to name her. She deserves to live quietly without being tracked down by a mob carrying burning torches.

I found out recently that I was also born nine years to the month after Hitler had shot himself and his dog (not in that order). My dad, Stanley, did his bit during the war – he was in the Paratroopers. He was a tough guy, my dad, hands like shovels. You wouldn't want to feel the back of them, but because I was a naughty little fucker I often did.

My sister Janet was a bit jealous when I came along – she threw my baby clothes on the fire. Fortunately I wasn't in them. (That was the second burning I'd escaped in a matter of days.) Janet was only two years old, and later we'd become really close because we were the only kids in the house. It would be another five years before my brother Paul was born. Janet took me under her wing and looked out for me. Our house was only two-bedroom so we grew up sharing a room.

We lived in a council-house terrace on Trinity Street in

Hull. It was so small we had to paint furniture on the walls. My mam's parents, Billy and Olive, lived round the corner in Stanley Street. Their back door was opposite ours – the houses backed onto each other with just an alleyway between – so we were always in my gran's house. You always get better treatment from your grandparents because they can hand you back at the end of the day.

We didn't have much; we were a typical working-class family. My mother would send me to Tom the butcher's for a sheep's head and say, 'Ask him to the leave the legs on.' We ate so much mince when we were kids that if somebody cracked a whip we'd have galloped off to the nearest field. And I used to have a Wagon Wheel biscuit for my breakfast. I don't know why. Later on, when I realized that large quantities of Wagon Wheels weren't doing me much good, I changed to a hot buttered bread cake. That was luxury.

One time that sticks in my mind was when a policeman knocked on the door. I was about five years old. That was the first time I'd heard a policeman's knock but it wouldn't be the last. Janet and me had just been to get fish and chips, which was a rare treat for us, and we were at the table tucking in like it was the last meal we'd ever have. The copper removed his helmet and asked my mam to sit down. I now know that is a sign that bad news is on its way, but the only bad news I could see was on the greasy newspaper that I was eating my fish and chips off.

The policeman told my mam that my dad's mother had drowned. He asked if my dad could go and identify the body. Dad was upstairs, and when he came down to put on his coat me and Janet were delighted because we had his fish and chips to fight over. That sounds odd, but my dad's parents lived miles away in Broomfleet and we hardly saw them. When you're a kid you need constant contact with the people that come to mean something to you. Kids can be pretty oblivious to the pain of grown-ups if it doesn't affect them directly.

One of the weird things about being a kid is that you can take death in your stride because you don't really know what it means. I guess it's nature's way of protecting you until you can cope. When bad things happen all it means is that adults cry in other rooms. And you and your sister get all the fish and chips to yourselves.

Obviously I was a lot closer to my mam's mam and would have been a lot more shocked if I'd heard that she had drowned. Especially as there was bugger-all water near where we lived, for one thing, and no one could afford to fill a bath deep enough to drown in, for another.

The day of the policeman's knock, I might have become the world's first fatality from a fish and chip overdose if Janet hadn't helped me out and saved me from bursting. I could see the headlines: 'LOCAL BOY IN COD 'N' CHIP CALAMITY! ~ Mother says he died with a smile on his face ~ Father says, "It's how he would have wanted to go."'

If I hadn't exploded with fish and chips, though, I might easily have been blown up for real by a German bomb. Trinity Street was in an area bordered by the cemetery, the hospital and the railway station. This was Hull's version of the Bermuda Triangle, where people and fish and chips disappeared without a trace. Opposite our house were some bombed-out houses that had been given a makeover by the Luftwaffe during World War II and left that way ever since. I guess there was no money around to rebuild them.

Because it was an important seaport near to Europe, Hull was the most bombed city outside of London during the Blitz. Most of the city centre was flattened. If you read now about the tons of shit and shrapnel that Hitler dropped on Hull, you'd be shocked that anything survived. As well as the ordinary bombs there were parachute bombs, landmine bombs, incendiary bombs, flying bombs, butterfly bombs and oil bombs. I'd be surprised if you couldn't find a picture of a German bomber dropping kitchen sinks.

We loved to explore in the bombed-out houses. We didn't have tree houses – we didn't have trees – or adventure playgrounds, so we made our dens and hideouts in the bomb site. The buildings were death traps, really, and should have been condemned. But at that age you have no sense of danger – you go everywhere. Which is why so many kids got accidentally killed everywhere, I guess. Summer wasn't summer unless some local kid turned up dead in a reservoir or fried halfway up an electricity pylon. Still, our gang were different, we were invincible. So after school we couldn't wait to play in the shells of these falling-down houses.

One day we were very lucky. We were playing in one of the houses and we were about to explore the living room. Half the ceiling was missing, and the house roof above that was ripped off too, so sunlight came down into the room, or rain or snow. It could all have come crashing down at any time. We'd played in the house before, though, and it was no worse than it had always been, but for some reason we just didn't fancy it that day and went off somewhere else.

That afternoon we heard some adults talking about how some other kids had gone into the living room of that house and found a guy who had hanged himself. He'd been there for a while and his body was blown up with maggots. That might have put even *me* off my fish and chips.

The first thing I ever stole was when I was five, from a chemist's on Spring Bank called Abba's. I twagged off school one day with this little older villain who was about nine. He decided to show me how to steal. We went into Abba's to steal a bar of soap. I was hardly Public Enemy Number One in the making because the first thing I did was take my bar of Camay home to my mother. She grabbed hold of my ear and marched me right back to the chemist. My father knocked seven shades of shite out of me that night. Shame I didn't have the soap to clean myself up.

At school they sold biscuits to the kids at break time, a chocolate finger biscuit or a round digestive – and all the lucky kids would line up with their pennies. One day I got in the queue, I don't know why because I had no money. Deep down I must have known what I was going to do. When I got two from the front I made a dart for the tins of biscuits, grabbed a handful of each and ran. I'd moved up from being the Phantom Soap Bar Thief to committing Grand Theft Biscuit. I was obviously ambitious, even then.

I thought it was a big joke until I was marched to the headmaster's office and standing there looking down on all three-foot-six of me was a policeman. He was obviously there on some other business – I don't think Hull's finest had a Rapid Response Biscuit Recovery Squad – but the headmaster decided to make me think he'd been called out just for me. The copper gave me a ticking off and the school sent a letter to my parents. Knowing that letter was going to arrive was the worst feeling. If I hadn't already scoffed the biscuits I probably wouldn't have been able to stomach them. There's nothing worse than that dread you feel when you're a kid waiting for something bad that you know is going to happen. Sure enough, when the letter arrived, my old man gave me another bloody good hiding.

Also when I was five, my brother Paul was born. Paul was my dad's favourite, but so are a lot of youngest children, so no big deal. I always liked being independent, anyway, even when I was very young.

From an early age I was a bit of a rogue with an eye for making a quick buck. Stealing brought too much grief, so I decided there must be a better way to money-make and get my thrills. One day a chance presented itself. In an abandoned shop I found a box of old gravy powders and they looked exactly like a sweet called Toffolux that all us kids really liked. When I first saw this big box I felt like

I'd stumbled on a secret treasure chest of sweets. Then I tasted one and spat it straight out. Still, if I thought they looked like Toffolux, why wouldn't anyone else? So I took them to school and sold packets of this stuff to other kids at half the shop price. They were happy with the bargain – until they ate it. I realized I hadn't really thought it through, but by then I was being chased all over the school and across the playing fields and down the street by a gang of kids who all had *exactly* the same expression on their faces – the one you get when you eat gravy powder.

My little scam had been doomed from the off, but the risk seemed worth it at the time. I remember being scared as I ran away from the gangs – every breath was double-deep and every beat of my heart was triple-loud – but I also remember the thrill of it. And the money in my pocket. Most of all, though, it was the buzz.

As well as being a little hustler in the making, I was also advanced in other ways. I started taking an interest in girls at about seven or eight. There was a local girl called Catherine who used to lie in the long grass by the bomb site and, with a gang of about eight of us watching, she used to take her drawers off. One time I did get Catherine by herself. Or, more accurately, she got me. Between our street, Trinity Street, and my gran's street behind, there was Witches Alley. Catherine took me by the hand and led me down the alley. We were there against the wall, messing about, when one of the neighbours saw us, put a hose pipe over his wall and blasted us down the alley like a couple of dogs in heat.

I used to get sent for my hair cut at a barber's down Derringham Street run by this dodgy-looking bloke who all us kids thought was a bit weird. We made up stories about him having a collection of kids' ears on a rope in the back of the shop. But the big attraction was the magazines that he had for his customers. Some of these magazines were worth risking getting your ear cut off for because they had nude centre-spreads and we'd never seen any pictures of naked women before. I definitely had more haircuts than I needed. I'm surprised I had a hair left on my head.

Those pages didn't stay in the magazines for long because while I was waiting for my turn in the chair I'd carefully tear them out. I'd try to disguise the noise with a lot of coughing. But if there were a few magazines lying round I'd end up sounding as if I was on forty fags a day. I was known as the eight-year-old with really fast-growing hair and a terrible smoker's cough.

I sneaked the centre-spreads home and hid them under my mattress. Soon my bed was only six inches away from the bedroom ceiling – I had to get into it with a ladder and jump out of it with a parachute; if I laid on my belly, the light bulb would burn my arse. One day my mother found them all when she changed my sheets. I couldn't look her in the eye for a few days. And she couldn't hold my hand for a week. I don't know if she told Dad, and I didn't want to know, but I noticed he gave me a few more smiles than he used to. It was good to get a reaction from him that didn't include a hiding. When my own kids were young I made sure I was always grabbing hold of them and kissing them and telling them I loved them. But that wasn't how things were when I was young. My dad's dad was the same with him, and it's easy for that kind of thing to get passed down.

If I used the word 'she' when referring to my mother, as in 'she said this', I'd get a backhander and be on the floor. But Paul, being younger, could get away with more. Maybe because my dad started to mellow a bit. Later on, he loved his grandkids to death and was really good with them.

My dad had run away from home when he was seventeen and joined the army. Since there was a war on at the time, that doesn't say a lot for his home life. It's not that I got smacked any more than any other kid – it's just that, like a lot of men at that time, he was quite strict and he didn't have that much time for us. Children were to be seen and not heard. And preferably not even seen that much.

Because my dad worked long hours driving lorries, and my mam worked hard as a cleaner, we were able to afford a few luxuries. My old man saved like mad and bought a Ford Consul. Now we were among the few kids on the street whose parents owned a car. It was Dad's pride and joy and he polished it until it gleamed. It was black, but could have ended up silver by the time he'd polished it to the metal. He kept it in an old garage that looked like it had taken a direct hit during the Blitz. He was lucky it didn't fall down and crush the car, which would have probably been safer in the street.

'It'll give us a bit of freedom,' he said. Not that we saw much of it. Before we had the car, we'd never been further than Bridlington, a little seaside place about thirty miles away. The first day trip we took in the car was to . . . Bridlington. You'd have thought we'd at least have got there quicker, but with no train to catch, by the time my dad had finished his routine of putting Brylcreem in his hair it was two o'clock in the afternoon before we set off.

We were all standing outside in the sunshine waiting for him – not daring to lean on the car in case we smudged it. When he finally emerged, the sun struck his Brylcreemed head and sent a beam of light across Hull that was so bright it was mistaken for a sign of the Second Coming. By the time we set off for Brid, cars were passing us the other way full of families coming back. Drivers were shielding their eyes from the Brylcreem searchlight. I swear I saw three cars swerve into a ditch.

We thought that was bad until one year Dad announced that we were going to Cornwall. That seemed more exciting until we realized it would take fifteen hours to get there. Coming back was worse because the fourth gear of the car was knackered so we had to crawl home in third. I think I hit puberty round about Sheffield.

Kids today don't think they've been on holiday unless they've been on a plane. Well we didn't think we'd been on holiday unless we'd been waiting by the car for two hours, travelled a few miles to a boring seaside town, got a clip round the ear for asking for an ice cream, listened to my dad arguing with someone and doing his best to tip the penny avalanche machine in his favour, and then driven home in silence. Then we'd round off the day playing in a derelict building full of unexploded bombs and a corpse hanging in the living room. Happy, happy days.

Actually, I do think I had a happy childhood. Owning expensive things never makes you happy if the things that count aren't there. I knew that my mam and dad loved me, I had a great brother and sister, good grandparents, aunties and uncles, and lots of mates. I had fish and chips and a stash of porn under my mattress that a mountain goat couldn't jump.

Funny, then, that I went on to become such a naughty little bastard.

Hull Fair is famous – one of the biggest funfairs in Europe. For a kid it's the best thing on earth. There were more rides and stalls and roller-coasters and games and prizes and girls and lights and noises than I'd ever seen or heard. There seemed to be more smells in one place there than you could ever get anywhere else. Not all of them good. The sound of the fairground organs playing together could be heard all over Hull. The fair was huge – like a big spaceship of lights that had suddenly dropped out of the sky onto your doorstep.

We never had enough money to go on many rides or buy as many toffee apples as we'd like, but we'd go down the fair anyway, just to be there. One time I went down with a penny in one pocket and a two-bob bit in the other. There was a game where you had to throw your penny and try to get it to land on a plate. I fished out my penny and threw it, but when it landed I saw that I'd gone into the wrong pocket and thrown the two-bob bit, worth twenty-four times as much. I asked the stallholder to give it back to me so I could play again with my penny but the greasy old sod just picked it up and pocketed it. I couldn't believe he wouldn't give me it back. It was all I had.

I went back to the stall five minutes later and tried the game again, but this time I didn't use a penny, I used a big rock that I'd found. I flung it right in front of the stall owner and it smashed about half a dozen plates. The great thing about the fair was you could easily get lost if someone was chasing you.

My mother's brothers were trawlermen and they were all as hard as nails. My Uncle Jim was a great fighter, so when the Hull Fair came he'd go along to the boxing booths. These were big tents with a ring inside, where people paid to watch the booth fighters take on anyone from the audience who fancied their chances. Uncle Jim always fancied his chances and, more often than not, he knocked down the boxing-booth champion. That always went down well with the crowds but not so well with the booth owners. They took the threat away by hiring Uncle Jim to fight for them.

We lived in Trinity Street until it was decided that our houses were going to be knocked down. The council offered us a house on a new housing estate called Orchard Park. My mam and dad decided 'Orchard Park' sounded quite posh; they weren't the only ones to be fooled by the name. It was about as rough an estate as you could get. Shithole Park would have been more accurate, but I suppose if they'd called it that then no one would have gone there.

The estate was in north Hull, on the edge of the city, as if it had been put there to keep it away from everybody else. To me, after being slap bang in the centre of town, it felt like I was in the middle of nowhere.

Another example of fancy naming was the school on the estate, which was called the Sir Leo Schultz High School. There was nothing fancy about it whatsoever, believe me. My first day at the school was strange because there were only about two classes. It had just opened and I was one of the first kids in. I also wanted to be one of the first kids out. I figured that my chances of leaving the school by the end of the day through a window were higher than me going out through the front door. Maybe that was just because I was a breech birth.

As in most schools in the sixties, corporal punishment was common at Leo Schultz, but this was the first time I'd seen pupils inflicting it on the teachers. I'd never before seen a chemistry teacher set on fire. He burned quite well for a skinny bloke. Amazing how many kids it took to put him out, though – they just didn't have enough piss between them. But I did get six lashes of the cane on both hands for accidentally throwing a dart into the caretaker's daughter's arse.

You've never seen such a rough lot of kids in your life. Or at least I hadn't. And I lived in Hull – I hadn't been sheltered. They were right rough bastards. And that's coming from me, someone who wasn't exactly Little Lord

Fauntleroy. This school was like a cross between St Trinian's and Alcatraz.

At this time my best mate was Arthur Lusher – Archie. We'd have some right laughs: dodging petrol bombs in the corridors, swerving knife fights in the playground, tripping up over shallow graves on the running field.

I don't know why, but my best subject was maths. I just never had a problem with numbers and calculations, though I'd no way then of knowing how important this would be in the future.

The best thing I got out of the school was that I discovered my love of music and also my ability to play instruments. I learned to play the guitar and started playing in the school band. I guess the teachers thought if our hands were busy we couldn't burn the place down or string up teachers from the goalposts. (We did that as well, but we just had less time to do it in.) So that saved a few lives.

I found that I had a natural ability for playing the guitar, which I'm still really grateful for. It's a good thing to be able to whip out a six-string and impress the birds. And unlike the other thing I liked whipping out to impress girls, I could play the guitar in public.

The school band was definitely a good aid to pulling. I'd already started off young with Catherine, so by the time I got to fourteen I was a randy bastard. But you had to use the power of rock wisely or you might come a cropper. I found this out one Christmas during the school concert. I did my usual act on stage, singing and playing guitar, which went down a storm. But when I got off the stage, there was a gang of girls waiting for me. I didn't like the look of things, so made a dash for it – and they started chasing me. Now I didn't mind one or two selected groupies, but not a random mob. I was outnumbered, and some of these girls were not the lightest fairies off the tree.

I ran into the teachers' toilets and closed the door. Outside it went really quiet. I stood on the loo and looked out the glass at the top of the door and they were all just standing there like a bunch of half-starved hyenas. You might think, 'Why was he running away from girls?' but you know what happens to a wish bone when people fight over it . . .

One of the girls I really used to fancy in those days was called Marilyn Ferriby. But I had no chance with her because she was going out with some older guy. I might have missed that one, but one ride I *did* catch was over the local fields . . . on a cart horse. It was in Palmer's Field, opposite Orchard Park, which was a place we used to go exploring in summer. I don't know where this horse had come from or who it belonged to; there were some gypsies near by and it might have wandered off from them. It was a big bastard though, and it took a running jump for me to get on it. Archie then had the bright idea of whacking it on its arse with a stick. It reared up and shot off at a hundred miles an hour with me clinging on to its neck for dear life. It ran around until it threw me off head first and then smashed my hip in with its hoof. I guess that was revenge for the smack on the arse. Luckily, it galloped off without stamping my head into the ground.

I didn't go to hospital but I probably should have done because I was in a pretty bad way. I didn't have the strength to kick Archie for trying to turn me into Lester Piggott. Archie helped me stagger home and collapse into bed. I asked Archie if he thought I'd ever dance again.

'You couldn't never even dance before, twat,' he said.

Nice to have friends.

My gran also moved from her house in Stanley Street to live in Orchard Park – we lived at 22 Fell Dane and Gran was at 26. So that made it feel more like home because I was used to living within escaping distance of my gran's. She moved because they were knocking down her house too. What Hitler couldn't finish, the council would.

When we first moved to Orchard Park, all the surrounding land was mostly mud. But later, after it was seeded, it eventually became a better place to live than Trinity Street. It was good to escape all the madness for a while and go and see a bit of nature, something we'd never done. All we had before was bombed-out houses and waste ground; now we were right next door to this stuff called grass and these things called trees.

It was an even better place to take girls. That was another kind of exploring that came on in leaps and bounds. I was probably in those fields more than the council gardener. I suppose we were just sowing different seeds.

2. Whatever You Do, Don't Win

If it breathes, moves or has hooves — bet on it

Eventually we left Orchard Park, which was a good move for my health – all that clean country air was making me cough. Or maybe it was the smoke coming off the roof of the school, I don't know. By that time I was fifteen and I'd already left school. I didn't sit any exams. And I didn't sit on the back of any more cart horses. But I had become more educated in girls, guitars, rock, maths and how to put out the flames on a teacher's head.

My mam and dad must have been homesick for our old place because we moved back down to the new houses at Stanley Street, and opposite where our old house on Trinity Street used to stand.

Something important happened after we moved, although I didn't realize how important it was at the time – I first started playing poker. At home, the five of us used to play games around the kitchen table. A real family affair. I suppose one way of finding out how ruthless you can be as a poker player is going heads-up with your own mother. I never showed any mercy.

I hadn't bothered with cards that much until then but I had always had what I learned was the gambler's need for the buzz. The adrenaline kick was something that I'd always looked for, and soon I'd learn to get it from gambling.

When my dad came back from William Hill's we could always tell whether he'd won or lost by his mood. If he'd lost I'd get a right thump and if he'd won I'd be all right. Unfortunately he didn't win very often.

One Saturday my mam sent me to fetch him from the betting shop. At fifteen I walked into my first bookies.

When I entered, the bookies was full of smoke and blokes, and a race commentary was blaring from the speakers. The whiteboard at the back with the written-on prices was the first thing you saw. It was like the screen in a cinema, or a stained-glass window behind the altar of a church. There was always a lot of praying going on in bookies. If the Church wants to find converts, just visit a bookies one minute before a race starts.

So this was where dads and uncles and older brothers disappeared to. Here and the pub. The windows were painted over, so no one could see who was inside. All the better to hide from the missus.

The only time women really ventured into these places was to drag some poor bugger out or to have a stand-up row if the poor bugger was too big to drag out. Over the years I'd get to hear a lot of these encounters, and I'd also be involved in a few. During these scenes, just before the woman stormed out, she'd always have the last word and that word was usually '*then!*' . . . shortly after '*off*' and '*fuck*' and '*just*' and '*Well*', in reverse order. Other popular pay-off lines included:

1) *'And don't think I'll be there when you get home!'*
   (always a lie . . .)
2) *'Well you should have married a bloody horse, then!'*
   (sometimes true, depending on the wife . . .)
3) *'Your dinner's going straight in the bin!'*
   (usually the best place for it, according to the
   bloke . . .)
   And, of course, the ever-popular . . .
4) *'You – selfish – BASTARD!'*
   (nearly always true . . .)

If a women's hairdressing salon was no-man's land for a bloke, then the betting shop was a no-go area for women. Which is why they were always full of men.

I saw that my dad was talking to Uncle Ernie. He saw me but he didn't seem surprised. He worked hard all week and this was his little escape, but I think he always knew I'd join him. Straight away I forgot why I'd been sent there and I started looking around at the board and asking my dad what he fancied and how he'd been doing. My dad was a recreational punter, not a hardcore gambler. He never had the money to gamble seriously.

Looking at the list of runners for the next race, for some reason I fancied a horse called Chatley Princess – I don't know why because it was 50–1. A jockey called Eddie Hide was on it and I knew from watching some racing on TV that he wasn't bad. I didn't know that he was actually a top northern jockey. To me, something felt right about him and the horse. I also saw that last time out Chatley Princess had come in fourth. What I didn't know was that it had been only a four-horse race. Anyway, I had a ten-bob note in my pocket and I put it on the horse. My dad thought I was mad backing a 50–1 shot.

It won by a mile.

My winnings were £25, or about two weeks' wages. It made me think three things: one – this betting lark isn't a bad game; two – working two weeks for that money is a mug's game; and three – if I'd had £10 on I'd have won £500. And if I'd had a hundred quid on it I'd have got five thousand. I was already thinking ahead, and this was only my first bet.

The first win is the worst. It's called beginner's luck.

From then on, I was a regular at the bookmaker's: inside, I'd meet mates; outside, I'd meet girls.

Already I wasn't betting for the fun, I was betting for the buzz. And, of course, for the winnings. But the money was just to fuel more betting . . . to try to win even more fuel. And that's what money is to a gambler – fuel. It's the stuff you throw in the furnace to get the engine working hard enough to take you where you want to go. But where you want to go isn't a destination – it's more like a feeling. And in my first six months I probably bet more money and lost more money and won more money than my dad had in ten years. And it felt great.

It was 1969 and the papers and TV were full of the news of men walking on the moon for the first time. In the betting shop I'd discovered my own little new world. It was one small step for a fifteen-year-old, but one giant leap for Dave Ulliott. (By the way, if Neil Armstrong was the first man on the moon, who was holding the camera?)

My old man had been a Para during World War II. I didn't know too much about his experiences because he didn't really do storytelling. I did know that he should have been killed once. He was supposed to be in a squad that went up in a glider so they could parachute in with the element of surprise. But he suffered from bad dermatitis that cracked the skin on his fingers, so he couldn't go. The plane was shot down. Everyone on board burned to death. From then on he felt like he was free-rolling. Old Stanley Ulliott was lucky in life, too. He certainly wasn't lucky on the horses, though: I can't remember him ever backing a winner, but the back of my head remembers every time he lost.

Later, my dad's brother Arthur told me that he joined the army a few years after my dad, and because Ulliott is an unusual name he was recognized as Dad's relation. He said that when they learned he was Stanley Ulliott's brother he was given a lot of respect because my old man had been such a hard case.

I now needed to get a job and my first one was at a gents' clothing shop. I was a hopeless nine-to-fiver because one thing I couldn't stand was people telling me what to do. So when the manager told me to stop trying to embarrass the customers, I knew my work there was over. I'd given them the best two whole weeks of my life ... and that's how they repaid me. Bloody cheek.

The next job I got was loading lorries at a supermarket called Fine Fare, which was ridiculous, because it wasn't fine and they weren't fair. It should have really been called Crap House, but I guess that wouldn't have looked so good on a carrier bag. The best thing about working there was that I met a couple of good kids who became my mates, Chris and Pete Jackson.

Just to show you what a one-track mind I'd developed regarding the opposite sex, there was a girl who worked in the food department called Eileen and she was going out with a guy called Graham. They invited me to their engagement do at Graham's house, which was full of their family and friends. Graham's sister had a German boyfriend who was a ship's captain and a big blond bastard to boot. Looking at him, you wondered how they'd ever lost the war.

At one point in the evening I had a slow dance with Eileen – and don't forget, I was in her fiancé's house with all her family – and for some reason I decided to kiss her. You can imagine how that went down. There was the sound of a needle scraping off a record, everyone stared at me as though I'd just shat in the trifle, and then bedlam broke out. Graham punched me on the chin, everybody else jumped in, and we all ended up fighting around the house for ten minutes. I'd never seen so much bric-a-brac smashed. And I'd never been punched by a German ship's captain before.

And it must have been a hell of a kiss because Eileen dumped Graham and we started having a wild time together. We'd shoot up to my aunt's caravan on my Suzuki 80 and not come out for two days.

My next attempt to lead a normal working life was at

G. K. Bueller, a trophy maker in Hull. I didn't expect a medal for working there, though there were plenty to choose from. I learned a lot at Bueller's, mostly about poker because I'd play the guys every lunchtime. Even without being taught I found I could quickly calculate the odds. But I still usually lost more than I won.

If I wasn't playing poker I was punching this big navy kitbag full of sawdust that was hanging up in the back. And if I wasn't punching that I was punching anyone daft enough to spar with me (usually a lad called Dave Brown). And I sometimes used to nip around to Stan Ashford's bookies to put a bet on for my workmates Ron and Pete.

The bookies was also a good place to meet other little villains. Not that I was one. But I'd always viewed the police as the enemy, so that was a start. Through the guys I was meeting I'd started playing poker even more. I was only sixteen but I was always older than my years and, at six-foot-one, I measured up to the older guys physically. A lot of these fellas were about twenty-five and were the top tough guys in the area. Guys like Terry Willis and Stuart Herring. They would turn up at our house to pick me up and my mam or dad would answer the door to these two blokes, suits and gold jewellery, looking like Hull's answer to the Krays.

My dad would just shake his head at who I was mixing with. On Saturday night five or six of these geezers would come to pick me up, them suited and booted and their piggy banks looted. They looked like a cross between the Great Train Robbers and the Dirty Half-Dozen.

Some of the wins I was already having on the horses

gave me the cash to finance a different life now. I wouldn't roll back home until Sunday morning, stinking of fags and booze, still half-cut, leaning in the doorway as everyone else was just sitting there munching toast and looking at me.

I lived at Stanley Street only until I was sixteen, when I had a big bust-up with my dad about my behaviour. It was one of those 'the trouble with you' arguments, and as Dad was walking up the stairs, I let go with a volley of abuse. I knew I'd gone too far when he paused halfway up. My brother Paul had run out of the living room when he'd heard the commotion, so we both saw the critical moment when my dad decided he was going to come back down. I might have been a cocky little fucker but I knew I was no match for my dad. Paul knew it too and he jumped for the front door, opened it and said, 'Quick!' I shot out like a firework and didn't look back. I'd never live at home again.

It took a while for things to heal and for me to be able to visit without the threat of World War III breaking out. I'd sneak back on a Sunday while Dad was in the bath and Mam would have a full Sunday dinner laid out for me on the table. Then I'd leave and Dad would come down and wonder why there was less roast beef and Yorkshire pudding than usual.

I got a flat of my own in Leicester Street. You know how estate agents always put on a positive spin, so a house near a busy road is 'close to amenities' and one next to a cemetery is 'in a very quiet area'? Well, this tiny, cold, damp shithole of a flat of mine would have been described by an estate agent as a tiny, cold, damp shithole of a flat.

(But it was near to local amenities, such as the sewers.) It was so small that if you lost your key you could put your hand down the chimney and open the front door from the inside.

The best thing I could do in this new place of mine was get some sleep. But even that was off the menu because of a constant *thud-thud-thud* coming through the ceiling from the flat above. Night and day, it drove me nuts. I thought, what is that guy doing, building the Ark? I mean, I knew it rained a lot in Hull but . . . Eventually I couldn't stand it and stormed upstairs. I knocked at his flat. And a guy with a wooden leg answered the door.

What could I do – ask him to put a wheel on it?

I was fully fit when I applied to join the Paras at seventeen, so it came as a shock when I was told I hadn't made it because I was one-third colour-blind. It was the first I'd heard of it. Apparently I was colour-blind between brown and red. Mind you, that did explain a few things: why HP sauce tasted of tomatoes, why I got such odd breaks at snooker, and the fact that Marilyn Ferriby had red eyes.

By now I'd started playing in this poker game in a joint down Lewis Street run by Abdul and his missus Janet. Two of us were waiting for the game to start and suddenly Abdul said the buy-in amount to join the game had gone up. It was originally two hundred quid to sit down and play, and I had that much and so did my mate. He said it was now changing to a £400 buy-in. I told him that he'd just priced us out of the game. He said that he'd waive the entry fee if I filled his new freezer. I said he had a deal.

So we left the game and found a nearby butcher's to break into, then started carrying full sides of beef and pork across the cemetery towards Abdul's. From a distance it must have looked like we were body snatching. If we'd found a body, we'd have probably taken it. We dumped the meat in Abdul's freezer and sat down to play poker. That was the first time my gambling stake was a steak.

Eventually, I beat everyone in the game, including Abdul, who was left skint. I could see him trying to figure out how he could get some more money to play. Then his eyes lit up and he said, 'Dave, you don't want to buy some meat, do you?'

Afterwards, when I was walking home, I saw Kenny Hocking sitting on a wall, looking as miserable as sin. Kenny and my sister Janet had gone out for a while. I asked him what was wrong and he said he'd had a big barney with his new bird and left their flat. By now I'd moved into a bigger flat on Spring Bank so I said he could kip at my place.

Kenny became a good gambling buddy. We'd gamble on anything – horses, dogs, pool, snooker. You name it, we bet on it. I was becoming a bit of a sick gambler. Any money I made in poker went straight on the horses, but because I wasn't yet betting smart on the horses, my money went straight to the bookies' pockets. I wasn't a controlled gambler. They say every gambler has a 'leak', the weakness that causes most of his money to go down the drain. Horses were mine. You know when you see a stallion pissing in a field and it's like a burst pipe that goes on for ever? Well, that was what I did to my money down the bookies.

Early on in gambling I was quick to learn that as well as being a game, gambling was also a war. A war against everyone else who wanted to take your money or stop you from taking theirs, whether that was other gamblers or casinos or bookies. Some people don't learn that lesson early on, if at all, and just end up being taken for a ride the rest of their lives. Casinos and bookies thrive off those kind of players. I hadn't completely learned it yet either. You have to go through the cycle of winning, losing, winning, losing, being flush, going broke, being flush, going broke. It was the juice I got from playing that was the reward.

But deep down I always hated being beaten, especially if there was something I knew I could have done to prevent it. And in the end, that was the thing that would save me.

I also was lucky enough to run into some older characters who had been round the block a few times. I was wise enough to know that I needed to wise up and that you can learn a lot from the right people.

I met an older gambler called Ray Golby. Ray was a wily character, and he taught me 3-Card Brag. Through Ray I met some other guys who showed me how to count cards, how to track cards through the deck. Card counting allowed you to keep score of what cards had been dealt and so narrow the odds of predicting what you might be dealt next; and card tracking was similar in that you tried to keep a bead on when the pictures and Aces might show their faces. Both of those tricks were just disciplines of memory, they were not illegal, but they'd still get you bounced out of a casino if you got caught using them. Which is pretty outrageous, because it means that a casino is effectively banning you from the premises for using your brain. Which just proves that they want their punters to be a bunch of idiots.

I started going to this casino in Hull called the Fifty-One Club. It was legal but it had the atmosphere of an old illegal gambling joint – the front looked normal but you got in through the back. It was small, with only a few rooms, but it could be full of action.

Another good player who became a friend was Les Houseman. When I first started playing Strip-Deck Stud, the first two guys I met were Les and Dennis Cook. Both were good poker players but they both had the classic weakness – a bad leak. Les loved the dogs and Dennis loved the horses *and* the dogs. Trouble was, the horses and the dogs didn't love them back. And it didn't matter who you were, if you went to enough greyhound meetings you'd end up skint. I'd never met a dog trainer with tax on his car, so if the trainers couldn't make money, what chance had the punters got?

Dennis would end up dealing a lot of the poker games. Les would end up playing in most of them. When I was learning poker in the beginning, I thought Les was the best player going at the time.

There was also a guy called Doc who played a lot locally.

Doc didn't like me much because he was a bit jealous of how well I got on with the female croupiers in the casino where he worked. Doc was as pale as Dracula's feet. He looked like he was running on one pint of blood. But the thing I noticed about playing against people who had taken a dislike to you is that they'd try to beat you with cards they shouldn't be playing. I saw that it wasn't always a disadvantage to be the bad guy at the table: you'd scare off some people and make others play loose.

There was a good Stud player called Murrat (or 'Chef' because he was a cook), who used to run a game at his house. Four of the guys who played there were called Shaun, Eli, Mal and Mustafa. Poker's always been international, even in Hull.

As soon as you start hanging around with gamblers, gambling comes easier. It's because you move from a circle of non-gamblers, who often disapprove of betting, into the circle of people who encourage you to gamble. Or at least who don't think it's abnormal to gamble. To me, it was completely normal, in the same way that whacking a small white ball with a bent stick and dressing like someone with a mental illness is normal to people who play golf. Or like wearing a silver leotard and little boots and sticking your head between men's legs is normal if you're an American wrestler. Or Elton John.

What I mean is, if you're surrounded by enough people who live the same way then it's easy to carry on living that way. We'd bet on the horses in the bookies, bet on the dogs down at the track, bet on games of pool at the Golden Nugget Pool Hall, bet on snooker at the Monica

Snooker Club, bet on fights in the gym and bet on which girl we could pull in the nightclubs.

When your dad's working hard six days a week for sixty quid, and you could win two hundred in a week – in a night, even – it's very difficult to motivate yourself to do a straight job. I already had a problem with authority and people telling me what to do. By now my answer-back muscle was too well developed, and soon my right hook would be too. That ain't an attractive combo in an employee, is it?

I was already handy when it came to a scrap, but I decided that if I ever got into another fight with a German ship's captain then I'd better improve my punching power. I started to go down to Hull Kingston Boxing Gym. I was lucky because this was a really good era for Kingston boxing: we had Chris Earlwood, Mally Heath, Arthur Heath and a kid called Steve Pollard. Some of the best boxers and toughest kids in the area. Steve was still a young lad, but Chris, Malcolm and Arthur were in their prime.

They were all older than me but because I was tall for my age I used to spar with them. Other good boxers that I became mates with were Alex Brantio and Paul Sali and Johnny Fallon.

Johnny was a great character. The two things he most liked were fighting and fucking. I was one of the few guys who would go out on the town with him. I think Johnny respected me after he saw me fight two sailors in Romeo and Juliet's nightclub. I broke one's nose and got my thumb in the other one's eye before you could say 'Popeye'.

For the first six months of my boxing career I got ten bells knocked out of me. Eventually, I started to get a lot better, and the better the guys you're boxing, the better you get. You have to improve or they mop you up in the ring with a sponge. So I went from being one of the unluckiest fuckers in the gym – the one being knocked about – to being one of the luckiest, because I'd been given the chance to learn from the best. I trained hard and never missed a session.

Then came the night that every boxer looks forward to and dreads – the first fight. I managed to win it. I also won my second bout. The third, though, was different. It was at the Apollo Club and all my mates turned up. I was supposed to be fighting some geezer from the boxing team of the Army and Navy (the forces, not the shop) but he didn't turn up. So my trainer decided to put me in against a guy who'd already had twelve fights and won them all, most by knockout. He was heavier, more experienced and unbeaten, but I was too stupid and too proud to say no, especially as a big crowd of my mates had come down to watch. One of them, Pete Jackson, said I was crazy to fight him.

For about 90 per cent of the first round I managed to just about keep him away from me with jabs, but then I decided to come over with a right cross and he ducked underneath it and cracked me on the chin. I suddenly saw a face in the back row of the crowd that I recognized . . . it was mine. I should have charged for advertising on the soles of my boots.

They slid me out between the ropes like an ironing

board. Now I realized why I'd been given boxing shorts with handles on them. I came round on the table in the dressing room without even knowing how I'd got there.

Afterwards, I went round to see my dad and my old man said that if my trainer was putting me in with fighters with twelve fights and KOs then I should think about not boxing there. He said I should try being a painter if I liked canvas so much. I decided he was right about the boxing. But I'd had a year of sparring with some of the best boxers in the North East, which would come in useful, considering the troubles waiting for me.

I always felt protective of my younger brother, Paul, and it fired me up if anything happened to him. One day, when he was about twelve, he came home shaken with his shirt ripped. Some skinheads had attacked him. I went out straight away and found all four of them and gave them loads of verbal. I didn't want to risk Paul being ambushed again, so I identified the ring leader and knocked him down. The rest stood there, not moving, like three coconuts on a shy. Typical bullies – cowards when confronted.

I'm glad my boxing career ended when it did: getting knocked into the rafters was a blessing in disguise. It didn't feel like it at the time, but not many boxers make it. Most fall by the wayside and a lot end up with long-term damage. I had a talent for boxing but it was a dangerous talent – meaning that I had enough talent to get me a career but not enough to get me through undamaged. That one crack on the chin saved me an awful lot more.

Sometimes the right thing happening at the right time

can send you down the right path. In the same way that that 50–1 shot on the horses got me into gambling, so that shot on my chin got me out of boxing. Which just proves that sometimes winning is worse than losing. Everybody always thinks it's the losses that cost you the most, but sometimes the victories can too.

All you can do is hope that you catch the right breaks when you need them, and that if you go too fast you can apply the brakes when you want to. Timing is everything. And sometimes timing can put you in a bad place. I'd find that out soon.

3. The Golden Nugget Pool Hall Massacre

If they can't beat you inside, they can't beat you at all

You definitely meet a better class of bastard in a betting shop. Lots of good people too. And lots of people in-between that are difficult to classify. Two people I met there were Fred Allison and Dave Barclough. Dave looked like a big gorilla and Fred like a fox. They were two Disney characters drawn by a madman.

They were local wide boys who specialized in a certain kind of villainy – safe-cracking and burgling commercial premises. Sometimes the targets were in on the jobs in order to claim more from the insurance, and sometimes even the police took what they could. They decided to take me on as part of their crew. I didn't realize that I was supposed to be the brains of the operation . . . for all three of us. I'll come back to them later.

One day I went to see Kenny Hocking and his girl-friend Maureen at their flat. I noticed the girl pass by who lived in the flat above, and I looked at her and she looked at me. She was called Sue and she had a boyfriend. But the only way a girl gets a new boyfriend is by getting rid of the old one. So, not long after, I had a girl called Sue and she had a new boyfriend. The two of us moved into a flat off Anlaby Road.

It was better than the place I'd been in but not exactly the Ritz. It had a communal toilet for the whole block, down one flight of stairs. One time I was laid up with flu and had been pissing in a bucket in the kitchen. Sue had just put the tea on, lighting a gas ring with a piece of paper which she then threw into the bucket. She came into the bedroom and sat next to me. A few seconds later I said, 'What's that noise?' There was a roaring. It sounded like an aeroplane landing on the roof. Sue opened the kitchen door and it was on fire, blazing. It was like opening the door to a furnace. We had to abandon ship, with me half-naked.

The fire brigade managed to put the fire out. One of the firemen was a cocky sod, and I watched him pick up the bucket and walk over to us. He said, 'So you threw a piece of lit paper in this bucket, did you?' He said that it certainly looked like the place where the fire had started. He had his hand right inside it, and he asked what was actually in the bucket.

I said, 'Oh, I've been pissing in it, mate.'

Instinctively he flung the bucket across the room. I had to give him ten out of ten for reflex action – but no handshake.

Sue flooded the next flat when she overran a bath. It was above a butcher's shop and the butcher collared us on the way out. He said, 'What am I going to do with *those*!' and pointed up. The ceiling of the shop had a dozen big globe light fittings. Every one of them was full of water. The only thing I could suggest was that he get some goldfish.

By now I was playing so much poker at Abdul's that

Sue would bring my Sunday lunch there. The other players were living off crisps and coffee but I had a roast beef and veg dinner. It was funny. The rumbling bellies almost drowned out the sound of me munching away. I think I won more big pots when the other players were drooling.

We decided to get married. Neither of us was religious – sex before marriage was OK as long as it didn't hold up the ceremony – so we tied the knot in a register office. Anyway, in my world only posh people had big weddings and everyone else got what they could afford. If I'd had a win at the bookies at the right time I could have financed a big do. (In fact we could have got married in the Bahamas on the money I'd already lost across the bookies' counters.)

There's one thing money can't buy, though, and that's a beautiful son, and almost twenty years to the day after I was born, on 10 April 1974, Sue gave birth to my first child, Paul. So now I had a wife and young son and we were living in our own place.

Yet card tables and bookies were my real home from home. I started to have my own 'the trouble with you' arguments with Sue about it. Not that I'd ever pretended to be any other way. They say that when you marry a girl, you should look at her mother to get a measure of the girl. Well, I must have been struck blind and deaf because Sue's mother was what in the old days we used to call a battle axe. She was the kind of mother-in-law that mother-in-law jokes were made for: a dead ringer for Les Dawson, in drag or out.

One day Sue's mother came round to our house, upset about something. Susan started to comfort her by stroking her mam's hair – which wasn't that easy because she always had so much lacquer sprayed on it that she was like a human Brillo pad. So she was stroking the hair, trying not to cut her hand open, and comforting her mam about . . . whatever the hell it was she was upset about: I think her favourite knickers had been drying on the line and they'd caught the wind and pulled down the side of the house, or something. I was sat there, miserable as sin because I'd done all my money on the horses – I'd missed a four-horse accumulator by *only a nose*. Suddenly I saw something rising off Sue's mam's hair. I settled back in the chair, thinking, yep, that is *definitely* smoke . . . *I* know smoke when I see it . . . it takes a good one to get past me and *that* is definitely smoke. Sue's cig had set her mam's hair on fire.

It cheered me up. I was flat broke but I was giggling like a schoolkid. After a bit of smouldering, a spark flew off the cig and a few flames burst into life. That stopped the crying.

Her mam did get her revenge, though, and she wasn't even there at the time. Me and Sue went round to her mam and dad's to babysit her younger sister, Alison, while they went out for the night. I hadn't had time to shave for the last few days because I'd been living between poker games and the bookmaker's. I went upstairs to the bathroom for a shave. My face was all lathered up and I was halfway through shaving when in the mirror I saw Sue behind me, leaning against the door. I carried on, tapping the razor on the side of the sink and rinsing it under the tap.

Finally I said, 'OK, what?'

She said, 'I was just thinking.'

I said, 'About what?'

She said, 'About that razor.'

I said, 'What about it?'

She said, 'It's my mother's.'

I said, 'What for, her beard?'

She said, 'No.'

I said, 'Her tongue, then?'

She said, 'No . . .' and she turned to go back downstairs. 'She uses it on her fanny.'

I had some kind of spasm: I screamed, threw the razor across the room, dunked my face under the hot-water tap, and then ran downstairs and baked my head in the oven for half an hour. Given the choice I'd have rather set my hair on fire.

Things didn't always go smoothly with Fred and Dave. The escapades with those two often led to my door getting the copper's knock.

Not all police are bastards. There are some nice ones who just spoil it for the rest. But it's interesting how your relationship with the police changes when they start becoming the enemy. Or you start becoming the enemy to them. Before that, you tend to be respectful or even frightened of them, but when you see them at work you realize they can be just as big a bunch of cunts as anyone else. Not all of them, of course. The ones that stop me for speeding and let me off are the absolute salt of the earth. But once you get known to them, *you're known to them*.

The Old Bill came to the flat one day in the middle of a snowstorm because they wanted to take me in on suspicion of robbing a firm. They'd found a shoeprint on the floor and wanted to get a match. With the cuts and scars you get in your shoe soles, they become like fingerprints. I hadn't done what they were accusing me of but I had to go with them. At the station, they took my shoes for forensics. I said I'd also like them spit and polished before I got them back. I knew I'd get the spit.

So they sent my shoes off to the lab. And then they said right, off you go then, Mr Ulliott. I thought this was a bit much, even for them, and that they must be joking. I pointed out that it was snowing, below freezing and I was only in my socks. They pointed out that they didn't give a flying fuck. I pointed out that I'd stay here all over Christmas and make so much noise they'd wish they were on Ramadan.

In the end, I caused such a commotion that they called a taxi to take me home, just to get rid of me. So I was home for Christmas. Barefoot.

Now that my life had turned into a round of gambling and villainy, I decided it might be best to keep my head down and lie low for a while. All I'd do over the next few days was go down to the Golden Nugget and shoot some pool with Kenny and the boys. I mean, what could go wrong? It's not like I was going to get beaten to a pulp by a mob . . .

Usually, getting beaten to a pulp by a mob would make you think you were unlucky to have been in the wrong place at the wrong time. But as I took what felt like the tenth kick to my face, I couldn't even bring myself to think that I shouldn't be there. Because if I hadn't been there, things would have been much worse.

It started when I left the Golden Nugget Pool Hall one Saturday night. I'd been playing pool with the boys. I don't know why I decided to go home early. I've always been a night bird.

Hull on a Saturday night was like any other seaport – full of locals getting rat-arsed and shit-faced. Cop cars, Black Marias, ambulances, taxis and night buses. There should have been a few hearses as well, but I think they found it easier to cruise the streets on Sunday morning with a boathook.

I was waiting for a bus on Spring Bank when I heard a commotion – shouts and threats and someone scream-ing blue murder. The usual. A couple of young lads crossed the road, backing away from a mob of half a dozen people, four men and two women, who were making all the noise. I looked more closely and saw that one of the lads was my brother Paul. I ran across the street and stood between Paul and the mob. Even by drunken-Saturday-night-in-Hull standards they were an ugly bunch.

I tried to calm things down: I said that he was just a kid and maybe they could give him a break . . . no one wanted any trouble . . . let's all just go home. Yeah, all that pre-fight *let's-not-fight* bullshit that only does one thing – it just delays the fight. I knew it wouldn't work. The idea was to give Paul time to escape. If one of us was going to get royally fucked up tonight, I didn't want it to be him.

I don't know what tipped it but it suddenly started. A big guy to the left came over the top and sucker-punched me and I felt a front tooth snap. I hooked him in the face and then headbutted the guy next to him. Then it was a blur of shouts and punches. They all jumped me. I ended up on the ground with this big fucker on top of me, pinning my arms. I looked up and said, 'You're a brave bastard, aren't you!' They were all getting in each other's way trying to get to me. The fact that they were all pissed didn't help. I managed to struggle up, kicking the bloke off me. I had that metal taste of blood on my tongue and I felt my front tooth dangling in my mouth. I got up right next to the big bastard that had sucker-punched me so I hit him full in the face as hard as I could. He dropped like a sack of shit and hit his head on a small black wall bordering a garden. I jumped on him, grabbed him by both his ears and started smashing his head on the wall. Then things got nasty.

My head was pulled back and I felt something cold draw down my face, and then something warm run down my neck. I turned round and there was a screaming woman holding a steel comb covered in my blood. The rest of the mob went for me again. I punched one in the face. I was overpowered and knocked down. I staggered back to my feet. Which surprised the shit out of the ugly lass stood over me with the steel comb, because I smacked her right in the mouth and then elbowed the guy behind me in the face. Another one hit me from behind. Then I got a knee in the face. I went down again and I got a kick in the face, and then another kick in the face. I could tell that the next kick was from one of the women – it was the pointy shoe that was the clue. And the ankle bracelet. Then the big bloke knelt down to punch me in the face a few times. Because I was on the ground, there was no 'give' behind my head, just paving stone, so every punch felt double. I blacked out.

I came round to the sound of a police siren. Everyone was gone. There was blood all over the pavement and a tooth. I didn't know whose, because mine was still hanging by a thread. I crawled over the little wall splashed with blood, got up and staggered away. I hadn't done anything wrong but the police were no friends of mine, they'd probably charge me with recklessly throwing my head against someone's boot or damaging the teeth of a steel comb with my face.

Later it said in the local paper that someone had witnessed the attack and called the police. They said: 'It was terrifying. I didn't think he'd come out of it alive.'

Neither did I.

As I staggered home I could feel the skin of my face tightening from the swelling. It felt like wax. My front tooth was still hanging loose. I was covered in blood, my shirt ripped open and I was limping. The people I passed in the streets gave me a wide berth. Kenny and his missus were at my house visiting and, luckily, it was Kenny who opened the door and not Susan. I'd never seen anyone so shocked. I suddenly realized that he didn't recognize me. I tried to speak but my swollen lips made me sound drunk.

Kenny helped me upstairs. We passed the hall mirror and out of the corner of my eye I saw the reflection of the Elephant Man limping by with a really bad nosebleed.

Kenny lowered me onto the bed, with me cursing all the way. There was no way I could get undressed. My clothes would have to be cut off me. From what I'd seen in the mirror, I knew my face was already going black. My eyes were tightening with the swelling and I couldn't see out of the left one because it had swollen shut. Now that the adrenaline had worn off, I was in agony from head to foot. Kenny went to get me a glass of water, and a straw. I suddenly got sick of the tooth hanging in my mouth so I tugged it out.

I guessed I looked as though I'd swapped heads with a Halloween pumpkin. One that had been dropped and smashed. But inside, I felt kind of elated. I hadn't been afraid. I'd defended my brother, and myself, even outnumbered. I could have run, but I never. Even though I'd been beaten down, I'd got back up. If the fuckers had lined up in a queue I might have had a fighting chance.

It made me realize that I couldn't be beaten inside. I could be beaten physically, anybody can – especially if you're outgunned – but inside I knew I couldn't be beaten. And that's where it matters. Whatever strength you have inside, that's what keeps you going and keeps you strong. That's what keeps you from being defeated, even when you're beaten – and they are two different things.

You can't have that big discovery without taking the

big risk. To find out what you're made of, you have to be in the wrong place at the right time. Luckily, I was. For me and for Paul.

Fighting the gang had been one of the biggest gambles of my life so far, more than any card game. I could have been in a coma or beaten to death. It happens to someone nearly every weekend. One single punch can do it, never mind twenty to the face, a knee to the mouth, ten kicks to the head and a steel comb slash. But I already had a strong hand and, for once, I got a lucky draw.

I'd learned something in life that I was learning in poker: you can only *win* big if you *risk* big. There's no way round that. No short cuts. No easy street. That's just the way it is. And, as odd as it might sound, I knew that tonight I'd won big. I knew that the great feeling that I had, and the discovery that I'd made – I'd earned it.

So that was a bit of a conversion moment, like my dad missing his appointment with death on that glider. In my own way, I'd parachuted in through a shitstorm, landed in a minefield, walked into an ambush, stormed a bunker and still come out alive. And all while colour-blind. So the Paras could take my red and shove it up their brown.

I went to sleep counting the thuds in my skull.

4. Safe: Not Safe

I knew it was a bad sign when he fell into an open grave . . .

One night I got a call from Fred and Dave saying that a job was on. We arrived at this commercial garage, got in and found the safe inside. I thought it looked a bit small for the size of the place. When we got the safe open, all that was inside was a set of keys. So we searched until we found a much bigger safe hidden in a back room. This looked more like it. This safe was ten times bigger than the little one. But now we had the problem of getting into it. Fred and Dave had a pow-wow about what to do.

Now at this time, safe-breaking methods were limited, but fortunately most safes were crap. Our favourite way was to get the safe on its back, get a chisel into the corner and then another chisel into the other side; then work a crowbar into the gap. Once you've got two crowbars in a safe door and two lunatics jumping up and down on them, something's got to give . . . usually it was the door. Or Fred.

On other occasions we'd chop the hinges off the safe or take the back off (what's known in America as 'skinning'). I know you see people on TV and in films blowing up safes, but believe me, Fred, Dave and dynamite were not a good mix. But it would have been a quick route to heaven. Or onto the roof of the nearest building.

I thought it was obvious that the keys from the small safe were for the big safe. They both looked at me like I was a nuisance. Maybe this should have tipped me off that working with these two wasn't going to be the smoothest operation. Five minutes later they gave in and tried the keys and we heard the loud metal clunks. The door opened.

This was where the money was but it was all separated into lots of brown envelopes with car part names written on them. We threw them into a bag. There were so many that we sat up all night at Fred's house, opening envelopes, taking out money, throwing envelopes on the open fire. Every now and then one of us would pick up and accidentally fling a full envelope on the fire. Then we'd all leap up and start trying to beat out the flames. Nobody likes burning money, even when they've got money to burn.

We returned to the same place to do it a couple more times, and the odd thing was they never made it any harder to get in. I figured they must be scamming the insurance company by claiming for much more money than we took. They were probably making more than us. We should've been on a percentage. Sometimes we'd see local newspaper reports saying that five times as much money had gone missing. Everyone was at it.

You've got to remember, most people who open safes rely on inside information from someone who works for the company. They might have a grudge against the firm or they might just want a piece of the action. But most are inside jobs.

Robbing the garage was getting to be something of a habit, and even though we left six months between visits

I felt we were pushing our luck. One night we scaled the usual wall and dropped down into the compound. Everything was deathly quiet. The only noise was the buzz from a broken street light. When we spoke, we whispered. And when everything's quiet at night, any noise sounds extra loud. Suddenly a woman started screaming blue murder from a nearby window – 'I'VE SEEN YOU! I'VE CALLED THE POLICE!'

We made a run for it and pelted to this fourteen-foot chain-link fence. It wasn't until we got halfway up it that we saw it had barbed wire on the top. But me and Dave still went over it like a shot. Funny how fear can turn you into an Olympic high-jumper.

We landed on the other side and started to run, until we heard screaming from behind us. We turned round and Fred was hanging there on the fence, caught on the barbed wire and wriggling. He was like that prisoner of war in *The Great Escape* – I kept expecting searchlights to sweep around the wall.

We just bent over double laughing. In these situations, anything funny that happened was always *super* funny. Every emotion was exaggerated by the quiet and the nerves and the fear. There's something really funny about trying to argue *and* whisper at the same time.

There's also something really funny about a guy hooked on a barbed-wire fence, wriggling like an electrocuted scarecrow, especially when he's shouting out, 'Get me down, yer pair of bastards! Don't you fucking-well dare leave me!'

Still laughing, we were just about to run back and pull

Fred down when we heard a loud noise. We froze. What the fuck was that? Even Fred stopped wriggling. We looked at Fred. Then the noise started again, but didn't stop. Fred dropped a little, the ripping sound got louder and suddenly Fred fell down to the ground. Amazingly, he landed flat on his feet. I thought, 'Nine-point-eight for the landing, son.' We looked up from Fred to the fence, and snagged on the barbed wire were both of his jacket sleeves, flapping like a couple of wind socks. For a second we thought his arms were still in them. But then we saw two white things hanging like rope by his sides. He looked like Hull's answer to Fred Flintstone.

By this time, Dave and I were nearly in tears, just killing ourselves laughing. The sound of a police siren snapped us out of it and we legged it.

I don't know if there was ever such an outfit as CSI: Hull, but I couldn't imagine anyone in white coats putting Fred's sleeves under a microscope. They could've got a bloody good DNA sample from all the sweat, though: 'Local police say they're looking for a small, nervous man with very cold arms.'

I've got to admit that, as criminal masterminds go, we weren't at the top of Britain's Most Wanted. More like Keystone Kops.

One night a few weeks later we went out on a job and on the way back we had more trouble – the van broke down. By now we must have held some kind of world record for the lousiest getaways in history. If an alarm went off in the police station and they thought it was anything to do with us, the coppers probably polished their boots and did their hair before they even set off.

So we had this knackered van full of contraband, but we were near to Fred's house. We'd have to carry all the stuff across Chanterland Cemetery to get to his place. If things had seemed dark and deathly quiet when we broke into the liquor store, imagine what it was like in the graveyard. Not even the hum of a street lamp. On the plus side, there was no barbed wire for Fred to get hung up on.

We'd have to go back and forth across the cemetery to Fred's place, carrying crates of spirits from the van. It was pitch black. The only light we had was from the full moon, and I didn't like that – I kept half expecting to see a swarm of bats flying across it. The quiet soon ended as we started traipsing across in formation like a *Crimewatch* version of the Three Kings. Anyone passing by Chanterland Cemetery at that time would have heard plenty of whispering, swearing, shushing, arguing, tripping up, smashing, *what the fuck*-ing, *shut the fuck up*-ing, and bottle clanking. It must have sounded like a gang of grumpy ghosts having a piss-up.

We were nearly finished when I heard a scream behind me, followed by a crash. When I turned round there was no one there, just a puff of dust. I retraced my steps and looked down. I could see a freshly dug grave, waiting for a coffin the next day. Except there was already something in it – *Fred*, on his arse, six feet down in the mud, with a crate of whisky on top of him. I bent down to look into the grave:

'Fred, for fuck's sake, you haven't broken anything, have you?'

He said, 'No, Dave. I think I'm all right.'

I said, 'I didn't mean you, you fucking idiot, I meant the whisky . . .'

One time we did a job at this big tool-manufacturing plant. The alarm went off, screaming like a banshee. We had to get out quick. Up on the roof, me and Dave legged it across and dropped down into the yard. Fred got onto the roof as well and followed our path across it. Maybe it was because we'd weakened it – or maybe it was just because he was an unlucky bastard – but the roof started to cave in underneath him. It was made from asbestos and it started to crack and powder every time he took a step. First Fred's right leg went through, then his left. Then he dragged out one leg, took a step and it disappeared again. He was gradually moving slower and both his legs were going deeper through the roof. It was like watching a man run in three feet of snow. On a roof. In moonlight. At least this time he still had arms on his jacket. We managed to get him home.

I went to see him the next day and he was laid up on the sofa like an Egyptian mummy with his legs bandaged from ankle to thigh. I told him that I thought his ballroom dancing days were over but he might have a new career as a mountain rescue dog.

Being known to the police means you often get pulled. If anything goes down that's within the field of what you're known for, then they come knocking. So one day I got taken down to the police cells by this detective who worked for the Regional Crime Squad. He was a big, evil-looking bastard with a beard. He asked me about some job that had been done on Beverley Road near the town centre. I said, 'Nothing to say.' He asked me again and I said I had nothing to say. He asked again and I answered the same.

He said, 'Look, I'm gonna ask you another question and if you say "nothing to say" one more time, I've got three guys outside this room and they're gonna verbal you up, you understand? They'll all say you were there. You're gonna be fucking done for this. So, I'm going to ask you a question that's got *nothing* to do with this job, so you've got no reason not to answer: have you ever been in the town centre?'

I said, 'Nothing to say.'

He glared at me, left the room and slammed the door so hard that I thought the lights would smash and the walls fold flat. Ten minutes later the door opened and he came in with two cups of tea.

'There you are, son,' he said. 'I've got to admit, I don't like those put-your-hand-up merchants either.'

Fred also used to do a bit of building work and he was working on a pub in Hull. The guy who owned it was obviously a top-notch judge of character because one day he decided to take Fred into his confidence and show him the hiding place for his safe. Showing that to Fred would be like telling Dracula that you suffered from heavy nosebleeds and you never locked your door at night – by midnight, the fucker would be sat on your bed with a couple of straws up your nostrils, draining you like a milkshake.

For some reason, it wasn't until a couple of months

later that Fred decided to tell us – his safe-cracking pals – about this safe and what an easy touch it was. Maybe he was saving it for Christmas and just couldn't wait. We asked Fred how we'd know when the coast was clear and he said the guy who owned the pub had a big white Jaguar and he always parked it outside in the same spot. Never went out without it. If the Jag was there, the guy was there.

We went along one night to case the joint. No Jag. So he was definitely out. Fred looked at me and nodded. Dave said right. We climbed onto the roof and got into the flat above the pub, which is where the guy lived. We decided to have a quick look round before we went up to the bedroom to get the safe. We crept into the living room. It was all dark apart from one low lamp, but we could hear some noises in the room.

Now I don't know if there was a full moon out, but there was definitely a full moon *in* – we looked down and saw this geezer's arse bobbing up and his girlfriend underneath him. I looked at Fred, he looked at me, we both looked at Dave, then we all looked down and saw the bloke was looking at us. He went berserk. None of us really fancied the prospect of wrestling a big naked geezer with a hard-on – I mean it could have gone off accidentally in the struggle. There was a lot to consider.

We ran and jumped out the window onto the roof, then slid down the drainpipe into the garden. Fred, as usual, was last out, and we turned round and saw him do a desperate Superman dive out the window, roll down the roof and land in the bushes below. We just doubled up laughing. Then we heard this commotion from inside the house and shot off down the street. I had a vision of the guy bursting out the front door, stark bollock-naked, with a twelve-bore shotgun. And I didn't fancy having to pick pellets out of my arse for the next two weeks.

When we got home, I asked Fred about the white Jag. It wasn't there but the guy was home. Fred had an odd look on his face.

I said to him, 'What?'

And he said, 'Nowt.'

I said, 'Fred. I know you. So what is it?'

He said, 'Well . . .'

I thought, here it comes.

He said, 'Well, I've just thought . . .'

I said, 'Yeah?'

'When I was doing that work at the pub . . .'

I said, 'Yeah?'

'What I was actually building for the guy . . .'

I said, 'Go on.'

' . . . was a garage.'

Me and Davey both shouted, 'YOU *WHAT!?*'

I said, 'A garage? Those things that cars go in? You idiot. No wonder his Jag wasn't outside! Why didn't you say so!'

Thank God we hadn't got caught. Another bad headline: 'Britain's Dumbest Safe-crackers Build Their Own Trap'.

I sometimes wondered how Fred ever managed to fasten his shirt without choking on a button. I didn't know then that Fred was going to become an even bigger wanker. Because he grassed me up to the police.

5. World 1, Ulliott 0

On the run . . . and doing time

There was a guy we used as a fence to sell on the gear, but Fred got caught trying to sell some stuff himself. The police nicked Fred and he grassed on me. The police came to nick me. That's how it works. The cops depended on informers and Hull was full of them.

I'd been well and truly dropped in it and the Old Bill came round to my house for a little social visit. They wanted to give me a guided tour of the local nick and offer me the chance to sample the best prison food that the system had to offer. Nice.

We were living in Kates Terrace, which is quite a posh-sounding name, but there was a fish warehouse nearby so you can imagine how it smelt on a hot summer night. When you live slap bang between a fish house and an abattoir you're happy when you catch a cold. Anyway, in their usual delicate fashion, the police came tramping into the house to search it. I'd hidden the cases of cigarettes and salmon in the empty house next door – I loved salmon. Unfortunately we got a Detective Inspector Love on the case. He was one of the old boys and knew all the tricks. He asked if the next-door house was empty, and then said search it. Sure enough, they found the salmon and cigs.

DI Love returned to the house to interview me. I shot straight out the front door, knocking over the copper who was blocking it. They weren't expecting that. Luckily, Kenny's house was across the road, so I jumped over his back-garden wall and ran inside. Kenny looked a bit surprised.

He said, 'What's up?'

I said, 'Nowt much. I'm on the run from the Old Bill. Put the kettle on, will you?'

He said, 'OK.'

We went upstairs with our cups of tea and from one of the windows we watched the cops running round looking for me. It wasn't good for them to lose someone they were apprehending and bringing into custody. They were running round like blue-uniform-arsed flies. Supping a cup of tea with a mate while watching the police fuck up . . . it doesn't get much better than that. Maybe if I had a biscuit . . .

Actually, I knew it was only going to get worse. I knew I couldn't stay on the run. Kenny would run out of tea, for one thing. I went to see another friend, Terry Willis, and stayed at his place. The police were searching all over for me and every night, when I climbed over the roofs, I could see a cop car parked at the end of our row. I'd sneak out at night and head home, climb over the fish-house roof to get to our back-bedroom window, and slip into bed with Sue. It's always nice to be wanted by someone other than the police. And if you're gonna get caught for anything then getting nicked for having a shag must rank as a good reason.

A few nights later I was asleep in bed with Sue when

there was a BOOM-BOOM-BOOM! on the door. It had to be Old Bill – they must go on some kind of Coppers' Heavy Knock course. They were shouting for Sue to open the door. When I looked out the back-bedroom window I could see more coppers coming that way. I quickly got dressed and started trying to think of a way out. We had a cot in the bedroom for our newly born – our second child and my first daughter – a beautiful girl we named Kerry. I told Sue to tell the police not to turn on the light if they searched the room because it would wake the baby. Then I did the only thing that was left to do . . . I hid under the bed.

The next BOOM-BOOM-BOOM! I heard was the sound of size-14 British police-issue boots banging up the stairs. That must be another exam that all coppers take – Very Loud Stomping Up Stairs. This lot had obviously passed with flying colours. Dust from under the bed was shaking down into my ear.

I was lying under the bed in the pitch black, listening to my own breathing. And even that stopped when the door swung open and I saw some shiny black boots. He stood in the door, then moved into the room. He didn't put the light on, though, so the baby-in-cot thing worked. So I was looking at this copper's feet . . . then the next thing I saw was his knees . . . then his head. Because my eyes had adjusted to the dark I could see him looking at me, squinting. But he couldn't see me. He stood up and paused. I thought, hang on, this might really work. The worst hiding place in the history of hiding places might just work. Un-fucking-believable.

Then I heard him take something out of his pocket and I knew it meant I was going to prison. He shook the box a couple of times, then struck a match. I couldn't do anything but wait. He knelt down again and his head reappeared, all lit up from the flame.

He said, 'Now then . . .'

I said, 'Now then . . .'

Bit of an embarrassing moment, actually, laid under your own bed covered in more dust than Tutankhamen's tomb, with a copper looking at you.

He said, 'Shall we go downstairs and have a cup of tea?'

I said, 'Good idea.' And he blew out the match. That was also the light going out on my freedom.

We went downstairs, had a cup of tea, and they marched me off to the station and threw me in a cell – on a seven-day remand. I was charged with doing three jobs – a tobacconist and two off-licences. They came to see me in the cells and showed me the statements Fred had given against me. This being my first arrest, I didn't realize that, because Fred had been charged too, he was my co-accused, so his statements didn't carry as much weight as the police were making out. But I thought they had me bang to rights, and I pleaded guilty.

The Old Bill wanted to know the name of the guy I'd sold the stuff on to. I made up a story that I'd sold it to a guy I'd met in a club called Cameo. I gave them some bullshit first name, let's say 'Frank'. So the police decided to take me out to Cameo every night and leave me in a parked car with a flask of tea, telling me to flash the lights when 'Frank' appeared. I couldn't believe they'd fallen for it. Sitting in a warm car with a radio and hot tea was better than being in a cell.

It's weird how different things look if you're just watching. Usually I'd be buzzing around at night, doing my own thing. But being in the unmarked cop car all night watching this club was like being one of those cameramen on the TV wildlife programmes. I'd never seen so many cat fights, screaming rows, girls crying, kids puking, bloody noses and bad language since the last time Sue had tried to drag me out of an all-night poker game. It was that bad.

From the outside looking in, a Friday night in Hull was like a dress rehearsal for World War III. It almost made you feel sorry for the police having to deal with it every week. Almost. Anyway, my observation of the local wildlife went on for a few more nights until the Old Bill decided I was wasting police time and threw me back in the cell.

Regarding all this nicking stuff. You've got to understand that everyone was at it. Well, not everyone – my family were as straight as a die, for instance – but an awful lot of people were at it. I realized just how many people were crooked when we were doing over a shop one night. We couldn't get all the stuff in the van so we went back for another load. In the meantime the police must have been passing by and noticed the shop had been broken into because there was a cop car parked down the side of the place. We stopped at the top of the street, saying how lucky we were that we hadn't come back quicker. We were just about to leave when we saw one of the coppers crawl out of the bottom part of the door where we'd removed a panel. He was carrying boxes of cigarettes and he put them in the boot of the police car.

It was a bit like one of these movies you see about the old days where everybody was at it. It was confirmed even more when in the newspaper a week later, the guy who owned the shop said he'd had three times as much stuff nicked as had been taken. So the only people really getting fucked were the insurers. And you can hear the world's second smallest violin being played when an insurance company gets screwed. (The smallest violin is reserved for a bookie going bankrupt.)

Everybody seemed to find their own little scam, dodge or con to try and keep their heads above water. Most people wouldn't think twice about buying something cheap that had fallen off the back of a lorry. But because I never did things by halves, I'd actually nick the lorry. Any mate of mine with a job would bring home from work something that had 'fallen' into his back pocket. Everybody was nicking something; that's the way life was.

Even the robbers weren't safe. A local well-known villain I knew parked his van full of nicked gear outside William Hill's on Eastbourne Street and came in to see if I could sell it for him. Ten minutes later he left and I heard shouting. When I looked out, I saw that his van had been broken into and there were twenty guys all running away with armfuls of stuff. He didn't know which one to chase first. Half the punters in the bookies jammed into the doorway, laughing their heads off.

That's another thing about gamblers – and especially

ones who live in the bookies – they can always find something funny about someone else losing. I guess it makes everyone feel better about their own losses.

So businesses got robbed, then the businesses robbed the insurance companies, and even the robbers got robbed of what they'd robbed. And if the people who robbed the robbers put the stuff in one place for too long then someone would rob *them*. Including the police. Who would then arrest you for having only half the stuff you'd robbed in the first place because they'd robbed the other half. So the Old Bill robbed you *and* nicked you. I think that's called a double-whammy.

With this local crime wave going on, I'm surprised that Hull hadn't been twinned with New York. (Actually, I think we already had a suicide pact with Chicago.)

Now, all this kind of skulduggery might not have been going on in nice middle-class areas in England, but that wasn't the kind of place I lived in. Anyway, different classes just do different crimes. Businessmen fiddle their taxes, which was probably worth a thousand times more than what we got selling dented tins of nicked salmon.

So, I got done for the three jobs. But I learned a lot from the experience, and I knew that in future there were only two things you should say to the police – fuck all or 'Nothing to say'. I also knew that I'd never put my hand up to anything ever again.

I was kept in the cells at Hull police station for three weeks on seven-day remand. Then I was taken to the nearest remand prison: Armley in Leeds, fifty frigging miles away. Prisoners were held on a wing and locked up twenty-three hours a day. Lovely.

One good thing: this is where I first met Pete Robinson and Steve Jonas. We went through Armley together. It was their first time as well. It's a disturbing event when you arrive at a prison for the first time and go through the big gates. You get out of the van and enter the building and the sky disappears. And that's that. Freedom gone in a blink. No more pubs, clubs, cuddles from the kids, shagging, drinking, betting, waking up in your own bed. The big door clangs shut tight on all that.

I was shoved onto the conveyor belt of new arrivals. The way they treat you is designed to break you. The last thing they want you thinking is that you are different or special. Or human. Because we weren't.

I was thrown into a room with loads of other new cons. Well, these geezers were new intakes, anyway, but a lot of them looked as if this was their second home. The screws ordered us to get undressed, fold up our clothes and put them in a cardboard box with whatever other personal effects we had. I knew I wouldn't be seeing that stuff again until I came out. Then we were thrown into the showers and pelted down with flea powder. We were given prison clothes (which didn't fit), told to get dressed, and then marched by the screws into the doctor's office where we had to get undressed again so he could look us up and down and body search us. All those years at medical school just to end up looking into the crack of doom of a lot of hairy-arsed convicts.

Finally, at about half-seven at night, physically and

mentally fucked, I stood in front of the metal door of the cell I'd be living in. It was all quiet. The other blokes were scattered around the prison on other landings. Like me, holding their folded bedding in front of a cell door. Then the screws started opening all the doors and the prison became just the noise of keys and locks and hinges. I knew I'd be walking into a tiny cell that had two blokes sharing it who might already be good mates. You don't know them, they don't know you, and you don't know what you're walking into. Behind the door there could be anything waiting. It could be a couple of all right blokes who just want to get their time done or it could be a pair of lunatics.

The cell was about six foot by twelve, and that had to accommodate three people. There was a bunk bed and one single bed, with a foot of space between them, and a couple of feet space either end. In other words, fuck all space. In one corner there was a fitted unit where your water jugs sat underneath and a plastic bowl sat on top. There was a bucket in case you wanted a piss or, if you were really unlucky, someone wanted a shit. There was a bell to ring to use the toilet outside but the screws rarely answered. Someone using the bucket would really make for a good night's sleep.

One of the two other guys in my cell was Reg, from Barnsley, inside for shoplifting. How dangerous can a shoplifter called Reg be? Well, quite dangerous, as it happens. Because I'll tell you something now that I didn't know then: Reg turned out to be the Barnsley Beast, a violent serial rapist. I didn't find out about it until I'd got out of prison and I was watching TV one Saturday night. An advert came on for next day's papers: 'Get the *News of the World* tomorrow for the full story of the Beast of Barnsley!' – and then it showed the same photo of Reg and his wife that he'd been showing me in the cell in Armley! I jumped off the bed faster than if someone had set fire to it. Part of the newspaper's report was that even Reg's own mother said she'd considered chopping his head off with a cleaver when she realized that her son was the Beast.

The twenty-three-hour-a-day isolation is the real killer in prison. Especially to someone like me who was used to doing what I wanted. If I'd been a nine-to-five guy it might have been a little easier. But you can't put a wolf in a cage and expect it to play Scrabble. Not without it biting a few opponents, eating the letters and chewing the board.

On your first days inside you can't help but think about what you'd be doing at the same time of day back home. So when I was woken up by the alarm at 6.30 every morning to slop out my piss bucket, I thought about how this wasn't exactly what I had in mind when I'd booked a B&B.

Prison was no walk in the park. Unless your local park was concrete, smelt of piss, and was full of uniforms who locked you inside all day.

The thing about being on remand was that they could only keep you on remand for seven days at a time. When those seven days were up they had to take you back to court, get the authority to keep you another seven days, and then take you back to the remand prison. Because my court was in my home town, they were driving me the fifty-odd miles from Leeds all the way back to Hull, getting me another seven-day remand, and then driving me all the way back to Leeds. And I knew I'd have to do this every week for as long as I was on remand.

The worst thing about this was the way they took me from Armley jail to the court in Hull. It was in a police dog van. It was disgusting, just a little row of cells each side of the van and a tiny six-inch window. It was so small that when you were inside your knees touched the door. Also, it stank of fuel. By the time we'd driven the fifty miles to Hull, I fell out of the back because I was half-crippled and half-gassed. I got no time to recover or get fresh air before they threw me into the cells under the court. And these cells were fucking medieval. It was like being in a torture chamber. I expected to see a skeleton shackled to the wall in a prison uniform.

I sat there, no daylight, just strip-lights, for hours, waiting for the judges to finish their lunch or their round of golf or dressing up in stockings and suspenders, or whatever they were doing while we were rotting in the basement. I knew the courts were near to Hedon Cemetery, so they wouldn't have far to drag my body and bury it in a shallow grave when I dropped dead from blood poisoning.

It was one of the weirdest feelings of my life to be in those underground cells, knowing that I was only a couple of miles away from Stanley Street, where I'd grown up, and where my mam and dad still lived, and only half a mile from my place at Westbourne with Sue and the kids. Not to mention the thought of my mates running round getting up to all the usual tricks.

Eventually someone remembered I was down in the dungeon and I got pushed upstairs. I was sentenced to another seven days remand and then I got thrown back in the van – the Poison Box. After fifty more miles of sniffing petrol, I got thrown back into a different cell in Armley.

Sue visited with our son Paul and daughter Kerry every month – it was good to see them but worse when they left. My mam and dad didn't visit because I guess they were embarrassed about it, especially my dad. He was a straight-down-the-line hard-working guy.

One thing I learned about Armley was that it was where Britain's most famous hangman, Albert Pierrepoint, had dispatched some poor bastards on the end of a rope. Apparently Pierrepoint's father and his uncle had been executioners too. I bet those three were a barrel of laughs during Happy Hour. The best bit was that when Pierrepoint retired, he bought a pub in Manchester called 'Help the Poor Struggler' (it should have said 'Strangler'). I'd liked to have seen the pub sign they had swinging outside. Maybe there was just a noose.

The hangings might have had something to do with what happened next.

I'd been put on gardening duty and one day I turned something over in the soil that made me stop. It was the top set of some old false teeth. They were black and covered in dirt. Maybe some poor sod had dropped through the hangman's trapdoor and when he hit the bottom of the rope, his teeth had popped out of his head. I knew what I was going to do with them. I put them in my pocket, soil and all.

In the cell next door there was the greediest guy you'd ever seen. He'd eat anything. And he'd always shout to ask whether there were any leftovers: 'You got any spares in there, Dave?'

I'd got a mate in the kitchens who would send food up to my cell, and one day I got sent up some chicken curry. That night, as usual, Fatty started his food-shout: 'Got any spares, Dave? Have you?' So I made him a lovely chicken curry sandwich, garnished with a nice set of dirt-covered false teeth pressed into the middle. A chicken toothy masala. Then I sneaked it next door to him. In the cell, the three of us sat waiting. A minute later we heard a scream and a shout – 'Yer dirty *bastards*! Yer fucking dirty *bastards*!'

Funnily enough, he didn't ask for leftovers after that.

After four months of all this coming and going between Armley and Hull courthouse – about twenty trips and over 2,000 miles in the Poison Box – my remand ended and my trial began. I was sentenced to twelve months. By that time I'd inhaled so much petrol that, like a wine expert, I could tell by the smell which garage in Leeds they'd used to refuel – 'Ah, that's a full-bodied four-star, they must have used the Shell station behind the abattoir.'

I actually celebrated my twenty-first birthday in the nick. Although it wasn't exactly a celebration. I did get a card from my mam and Janet and one from Sue. Prison is not exactly where you'd want to be for your twenty-first, but that's where I was. Prison ain't no party. Not unless it's a really shit party with crap food, ugly guests, no birds and a strange door policy where you can get in, but not out.

Following another two months in sunny Leeds I was

moved. And I got a bit of a lucky touch because they moved me to Rudgate Open Prison near Wetherby, which was category D. Compared with Armley, Rudgate was like being in Butlins. Which doesn't reflect too well on holiday camps but it might give you a picture of how tough our holidays were as kids.

I was in a dormitory with twenty-six other blokes. Situations like that never fazed me because I got along with most people if they got along with me. It wasn't long before I became one of the lads and, like everyone else, tried to earn some money. I'd buy and sell tobacco. Or I'd 'change money up' for people. Wages in prison were never in pound notes, you only got coins, so if people smuggled notes in they were useless until they were 'changed up' into coins. So if a con got a £10 note smuggled in, you'd give them nine quid in coins and make 10 per cent profit. People could smuggle a rolled-up tenner in their arse but they couldn't do the same with twenty 50p pieces. If they could they'd be working in a circus. Or porn.

You would save the notes and then get someone you trusted in reception to sew them into the lining of your jacket – and hopefully you'd walk out looking like Arnold Schwarzenegger.

There was a blond-haired screw with glasses in Rudgate we called the Milky Bar Kid, for obvious reasons. One day he nicked me for having twenty-seven quids' worth of 10p pieces. I was in the process of changing it up for thirty quid in notes. So he wanted to know where I'd got all the 'smash', which is what we called coins. The only thing I could think to say was that I'd collected the money off everyone for tea bags, milk and sugar from the canteen.

The Milky Bar Kid looked at me. I looked at him. You couldn't flinch in the face of lying to these fuckers. He asked me to wait outside the room.

I knew he was calculating the best way to play this to his advantage. I got called back in and he told me that he was going to give me the benefit of the doubt. I thought, result, and walked out. Then I turned round.

'If you're giving me the benefit of the doubt, can I have the boys' money back for the milk and tea bags?'

He said, 'You'd better fuck off quick, son!'

Which was the last anyone saw of the twenty-seven quid. If he'd nicked me he knew he'd have to put me on report and he couldn't pocket the cash himself. Everyone was still at it, even inside.

They put me in the kitchens for some unknown reason – I couldn't cook a tin of soup. In fact, I couldn't even open one. Mind you, that was probably why they put me in there – to keep down the low standards. I'd been in the kitchens for about a week when I asked a guy there called Teal why he kept disappearing during lunch break. He said that he went to lie on the kitchen roof and sunbathe. We were in the middle of one of the hottest summers on record.

It was against the rules, but he didn't give a fuck, and neither did I. So next break we both went topside onto the roof. Laid down together we must have looked like a couple of piano keys because I was as white as he was dark. I was like an anaemic vampire. He said that he put butter on himself. I thought he was winding me up, but then he got some out that he'd nicked from the kitchen. I thought, I'll have some of that.

I dozed off in the heat and had a nice little sleep. Teal woke me up and said we'd better go back down, and by then I was pretty well cooked. I didn't feel bad, but you never do when you first get burned – it hits you later. And fuck *me* did it hit me. I started burning so much that I went to look at the menu to see if I was on it. Soon I couldn't move a muscle. I was bright red. I hurt so much that I couldn't even stand a bed sheet on me. My lips and eyelids scabbed over. I looked like a circus fire-eater who had sneezed in the middle of his act. But the bad news was that I couldn't go on medical report for sunburn because it was classed as a self-inflicted wound! Talk about adding insult to injury. So I had to grin and bear it. Actually I didn't do any grinning at all because I didn't want my face to split in two.

Next day I was kicked out the kitchen when I was asked to scrub the floor and told the screw to go fuck himself. I got put on a job called the Chief's Party. I'd have volunteered if I'd known about it before, because it was just walking round picking up rubbish, which sounds crap but was actually pretty cushy. I knew there was a quiet patch of grass hidden behind some bushes, and I'd get my head down there for a kip. Then I'd fill the bags with rubbish from the bins and act like I'd been working hard all day. Which I had – I'd been hard asleep.

Another part of the Chief's Party was tidying up the tip, but all we did was sit round a fire and smoke weed.

We also used to burn canned food from the kitchen whose labels had come off, so you didn't know what was inside – could've been beans, could've been custard. We soon found out. There was this Irish screw called Sharkey who was desperate to nick me. He'd try and sneak up on the tip to catch us out but we'd always see his big head and we'd all get our shovels out, whistling while we worked. One time we saw him coming so I made everybody grab all the cans of food and throw them on the fire. I knew what would happen when they got hot.

Sharkey appeared and stood with his back to the fire, warming his Irish arse, looking out from under his hat. We were about ten yards away, shovelling, whistling and slowly moving away. I never realized how difficult it was to whistle while trying not to smile at the same time. Our whistling started to get more and more wobbly the longer he stood there warming himself. Especially when we heard the first popping sounds from the cans. Then, suddenly, they all exploded in the fire and Sharkey disappeared in a big food cloud. He screamed and turned to the fire. From the back he looked like the Swamp Thing – he was plastered from head to foot in beans, peas, carrots, rice pudding, custard and bits of spam. If we hadn't just had dinner, we'd have eaten him.

Another favourite screw was named 'Killer' because he used to love nicking people. He wanted to nick me more than anyone else because he knew I was up to loads of skulduggery. But he could never catch me. He couldn't even catch his breath.

I'd walk around to see an old friend of mine called

Bobby Sanderson from Newcastle who worked on the kiln. He was a good old boy, Bobby, and though he was older he was lean like a greyhound. I used to run a scheme where I'd give guys so many yards' start down the football field and take bets that I could catch them. I was quick – I could really move. I was so used to running with crates of whisky or cash boxes under my arms that when I ran without I was like the wind. Like a racehorse running with no lead in the saddle.

One day Bobby asked me if I'd give him a yard start for every year he was older than me. I said OK, without knowing how old he was, thinking he was about fifty. It turned out that the wily old fox was sixty-six, so I was giving him forty-five yards' start over a hundred-yard race. And he was still pretty fit. But he had a weakness. So I said there was one condition – we'd have the race first thing in the morning, before breakfast.

Bobby smoked, and every morning he'd cough his guts out. Rest of the day he was fine, but in the morning he was like an old car trying to start on a cold day. I figured that was my only shot. Bobby had pulled a fast one on me, and I'd pulled one back.

Next morning, Bobby went to his starting position, practically halfway up the pitch. All the boys had come out of the dorm to cheer. We started, I shot off, and so did Bobby. I was gaining fast but the ground was running out. I thought I wasn't going to catch him. But then the old smoker's wheeze kicked in and he started to slow, and only a yard to the finish I passed him. We both lay on the floor, knackered. Bobby looked over at me and winked.

That race was legit. But one game I rigged was snooker. I arranged a match between Mick, the best in the nick, and a new guy who'd just come in. I started taking bets all round. Because this new kid was an unknown quantity, everyone wanted to bet on Mick. Which was the idea. As soon as all the bets were in I told Mick that he had to throw the match. He didn't want to do it because he was scared of what might happen if it was found out. I told him not to worry and that I'd look after him.

Trouble was, Mick wasn't very good at missing. He was so scared of the consequences that he kept potting balls he shouldn't. He managed to fluff enough shots for the other guy to get level but he didn't miss enough, and it ended up being a black-ball game. Now anything could happen. Mick might miss the shot but fluke it in another pocket. He realized I was looking at him. He went back to the table, bent down, cued up, and missed the black altogether. It wasn't even close. It was a suspiciously bad shot. Before I could get to him, one of his investors ran out of the crowd and headbutted him. Another one picked up the black ball and threw it through the window, someone jumped on the table, and then a riot kicked off.

I think it was the only snooker match in history to have had a pitch invasion. I never realized so many blokes could stand on a snooker table at one time before the legs broke.

See, I was still having to get my gambling buzz from somewhere. Being locked up wasn't enough because you took your need for the buzz with you.

I missed being in the bookies so I started a book inside. I took bets with a guy related to the jockey Brian Fletcher, who twice rode Red Rum to victory in the Grand National, so he knew the form and was a good source of information. That year the French jockey Yves Saint-Martin was riding Crow in the St Leger, and it was 6–1 before the race. We opened a book and everybody wanted to bet on Crow. French jockeys had a bad record in England so we took all bets. Now, the idea of a bookies is whatever wins, you win money; but we had such a one-sided book on this horse that we had to hope it dropped dead. It didn't. It duly won by a couple of lengths.

With it being 6–1, we owed out a lot more money than we could afford to pay. If a riot broke out over snooker, then this was going to lead to burning buildings. I'd need more than a couple of coshes made from battery-filled socks to get out of this one. Luckily, my bookmaker partner bottled it and decided to go over the fence rather than face the mob. Typical bookmaker. I told everyone that he'd gone over the fence with all the money. It's amazing what you can get away with if you hold your nerve.

All that money had already disappeared into a hiding place of mine. And by the end of my sentence I'd sold enough tobacco, run enough cons, won enough bets and fixed enough games to have a decent stash of £10 and £20 notes. As planned, they were all sewn into the lining of the jacket I'd be wearing on my release.

As I walked through the prison gates in my retailored jacket, my arms could hardly touch my sides. I looked as if I'd been bodybuilding for twelve months. The worst thing was that I could barely raise my arm to give the screws the V-sign.

Walking into fresh air and freedom was the best feeling in the world. All the things you take for granted are taken away from you when you get locked up, and it feels like they've all been given back to you when you walk out.

The first thing I did was head for the train station, which had a bar. They say the best things in life are free but I couldn't convince the landlord of that so I had to pay for the beer. With the change, I put a tune on the jukebox. And doing something simple like that – sipping a beer and playing a record I'd chosen – seemed like a big deal. It was the best beer in the world and the best rock'n'roll song ever written: 'Great Balls of Fire'.

Speaking of 'something simple', I thought it might be about time I caught up with Fred. But I soon learned that Fred had skipped town, and I never saw him again.

After I got out things felt different between Sue and me. It wasn't really the same but we tried to make it work. It had only taken me two hours after I got out of nick to find a safe place for all the money that I'd earned inside. Unfortunately, that safe place was a William Hill's betting shop. In an effort to show her what I could do, I decided to try to go straight and get a job. I chose a local timber yard to start my new working life. I knew this place didn't have a good reputation, but I'd just come out of nick so how bad could it be? I realized right away how bad.

The place was inches deep in thick mud and water and I had to wade through foot-deep puddles just to get to the wood-cutting machines. Some of the puddles had put in planning applications to become lakes. Everything leaked and dripped. The timbers were heavy already but after they got wet they were even heavier: big, wet, black pieces of wood had to be lifted onto the cutting machines. Because I was fit from the prison gym, I was one of the few who could hump around these heavy pieces of wood. We worked in the wet and cold and on twelve-hour shifts, from seven in the morning to seven at night. They gave us only two ten-minute breaks and a thirty-minute dinner. It was like being beaten up all over again outside the Golden Nugget.

The second day was the same but worse. The third day was like hell. I hadn't even thawed out or dried from the day before. It felt like ice had been injected into my bones. The tea break was a massive relief for every poor bastard that worked there and the only chance to get a hot drink. When the siren went off to order us back to work, I hadn't had my tea because one of the lads had gone for some milk. The foreman, a proper little Hitler, marched over and said I had ten seconds to get back to work or I was sacked. Which gave me nine seconds spare after I told him to go fuck himself. I launched my cup at his head as he ran like a rabbit.

Anyway, I knew if I'd worked there for a year I'd have ended up with webbed feet. So my attempt at going straight was a disaster. I'd gone for the worst job in Hull.

Sue and me split up when I met a lovely girl called Dawn. Sue went off to Liverpool and took the kids. She met a new guy who was a copper. I knew that wouldn't help with me trying to get to see Paul and Kerry. He'd obviously be no fan of mine.

I guess it did at least prove that Sue's taste in men had gone right off the boil. I mean, come on: from *me* to a *copper* – that's like losing a diamond and finding a button.

6. The Good, the Paddy and the Ugly

I'll raise you a Mini

However bad things got – split marriage, broken home, absent kids, bad bets, bad beats, bad cards – I could never get too down because I always was lucky enough to have the funniest mates. Half the time they didn't know they were being funny and the other half they didn't mean to be.

For instance, Paddy Burns. Funny name for an Indian. No, he was obviously a Scottish/Irish cross-breed by blood, but he was all-English by upbringing. He was actually quite a posh type.

I'd just split up with a girl and Paddy said I could live with him and his pals in a big house. They were all quite posh too – they had ashtrays with no adverts on them, and fruit in the house when no one was ill. That kind of thing. They were mostly professionals – teachers and college lecturers.

We shouldn't have got on, Paddy and me, but we just did. Paddy seemed to think I was the toughest nut on the block because he'd seen me knock over a few guys. I *was* a bit of a tough nut but I didn't want Paddy to be scared of me because I genuinely liked him. And not just because he had a betting shop. That was just a bonus.

Somehow Paddy had got hold of this driving instructor's car, with the dual pedals on the passenger side, which he used to hire out. To driving instructors, obviously. Or to guys with four legs. It was a Datsun Cherry. It was awful – it looked like a boiled sweet on wheels. One that had been sucked and spat out. Then one day I persuaded him to lend it to me.

'Now, Dave,' he said, 'the good news is that you can borrow the car; the bad news is that it's on hire purchase and I've stopped paying for it. So you can have it until they repossess it.'

I said, 'Paddy, that's fine, mate. They'll have to catch me first.'

I thought, hang on a minute, Dave, you don't have to be a guy who has just *borrowed* a driving instructor's car . . . from now on, you actually *are* a driving instructor. I already knew who most of the passengers would be. All girls like driving instructors because they want free lessons. So anytime I was out in the pubs and clubs and a girl would ask me what I did, I'd say driving instructor. Which was an even more outrageous lie because I didn't even have a driving licence. I'd been driving for years but never had any lessons and had never taken a test. I was the only 'driving instructor' in the country without a licence. I didn't even have a TV licence.

I ended up taking all these gorgeous girls out for driving lessons. It was a good way to pull if you offered five free lessons. They didn't know that I didn't know what I was doing. And how hard could it be to teach? I soon found out when some of these learners started crunching through the gears like they were stirring broken glass with a broom handle. Thank Christ for the dual pedals – those things are life savers, I can tell you. I did more emergency stops in one hour than I'd done in ten years. Still, it worked, because I gave out more lessons on the back seat than I did in the front. And a polished bonnet has other good uses.

One day I took a girl from her driving lesson straight back to the house. We walked out the door the next morning only to find that I'd lost my Cherry – the Datsun had been repossessed and been replaced by a big block of fresh air. I pretended that it had been nicked. I didn't want to lose the girl. I was getting away with it until the old lady who lived next door suddenly walked towards us, waving a letter in the air.

'They REPOSSESSED it, dear!' she shouted to me.

I said, 'Er, thanks.'

'They came this MORNING and towed it AWAY!'

'Yep, thanks.'

'They TOLD me!'

'OK.'

'They left you this PAPER!'

'Cheers.'

'Then they towed it AWAY, dear!'

'*Thank you.*'

'They said to give you THIS! About the REPOSSES-SION!'

'Jesus . . .'

So that was the end of that. I lost the car and the girl. I didn't know if it was illegal to pass yourself off as a driving instructor . . . and I didn't give a fuck.

Paddy, God love him, must've been some kind of a nutter, because of the number of vehicles he used to lend me and never get back. He loaned me this little bright red van that looked like Postman Pat's. There was zero chance of pulling a girl in it, unless I cruised past the local blind home . . . with a damp rag soaked in chloroform. Its horn sounded like a dying duck's fart. Paddy said that the van used a lot of oil so I had to make sure to put plenty in. I assured him that I'd do it, and told him to stop worrying.

Anyway, I blew it up.

It actually looked better when it was on fire. It was improved by being covered in flames and smoke.

I decided to use Paddy's next van as the main transport to my brother Paul's wedding. It might not sound like ideal transport for a wedding, but it was handy because I managed to get half my family in the back.

We all arrived at the church and everyone piled out of the back. It must have looked like an away-day from the local prison. But the real fun started when we left the wedding to go home, and the van started billowing black smoke. I pulled up at a red light. Flames started to flicker out from under the bonnet.

'Everybody out!'

Not that I needed to say that: it was men first, followed by women, then trampled-on kids. We joined the bus queue and stood and watched the van burning. People at the bus stop were staring at us, open mouthed. I suppose it wasn't every day you saw a burning van pull up and a wedding party climb out the back – the men in suits with buttonhole flowers and the women in their best frocks, all standing chatting and laughing as if it happened every day.

*

When I bet the horses, I was crazy. I'd bet everything until I had nothing or until I had ten times as much. Then I'd want to make twenty times as much. I'd put all my money on the last race and walk out of the bookies without a bean to my name. And money wasn't the only thing I bet with.

In a private cash game one night I was playing against an antique dealer. I was better than him and I knew it, and he knew it, but none of that made any difference because the trouble with bad players – as any good player will tell you – is that they make moves they shouldn't make. They make moves which are difficult to predict and if they get lucky . . . Of course I got a bad beat and the antique dealer won a long shot. It was such a long shot that even Lee Harvey Oswald couldn't have made it.

I said to my mate that we should leave. He thought we were going home. I had other ideas. I didn't have a penny to my name but I'd seen a grandfather clock in the window of an auction place near by. So we put the window in, got the clock, and carried it on our shoulders like a noisy coffin. We returned to the game and carried it upstairs to the card table. You can imagine the noise this thing made, laid on its side, chiming on every step. It sounded like we were shagging Big Ben.

We lowered the clock to the floor and stood it upright next to the table. I stood with my arm round it. Play stopped. I looked at the antique dealer.

I said, 'Deal me in, baby!' and everyone burst out laughing.

One day I was helping out in Paddy's betting shop. I

was helping out in more ways than one because when Pad wasn't looking I'd take some cash out the drawer, bet a race, and if it won I'd put it back. If it didn't win I'd try again on the next race. And then on another. My brother Paul, who was marking odds on the board, would catch my eye and then piss himself laughing. I justified it by thinking that Paddy was a wise guy, and if he could pull one on me he would.

As well as being the busiest day of the week, this Saturday was also the day that Hull's two rugby league teams, Hull FC and Hull Kingston Rovers, were playing each other in the final of the Challenge Cup at Wembley. It was the first time they'd met in the final so the whole town had gone mad and upped sticks for London. The main road out of Hull had a sign hung on it saying, 'Will the last one out please turn off the lights.'

Paddy was a dyed-in-the-wool Hull FC supporter so when the final whistle blew and FC had lost the final 5–10, he was so pissed off he decided to shut up shop. I'd never seen him so agitated, even when I blew up his cars. Punters in the shop were thrown out and punters who were outside were locked out – even those coming back for their winnings. They all ended up banging on the door for half an hour, demanding their money. Paddy just shouted, 'Fuck off! Fuck off!'

So now the takings were in the safe. But that didn't mean they *were* safe. At least not from me. So a little plan started to hatch. Go on, take a wild guess.

Earlier in the day I'd had a copy cut of the door and safe keys and I came back at night and emptied the safe.

I went straight down the Craven Park dog track. Dog racing was much more crooked than horse racing, but they ran at night and horses didn't, so where was I to go? You might say I didn't have to go anywhere. But the fact is that I did. You start gambling because you want to but you carry on gambling because you have to. It's when a liking for something becomes an addiction.

The dog track bookies used to love me; I was the only mug punter with no inside information – and winning at the dogs without inside info is so unlikely you might as well make a bonfire of your money in the car park.

The idea was that I'd bet with the £5,000 takings, and if I won I'd go back and put the five grand back in the drawer and keep the profit. And, of course, I knew I wouldn't lose.

I lost the lot.

In came Plan B. There was no Plan B. So I went to Plan C. That was crap too, so I went back to the shop and faked a break-in. That meant I had to lock the door then jemmy it open, and lock the safe and then force it open – all the time knowing there was fuck all in it because some idiot had lost all the takings. Anyway, at least Paddy could get a healthy insurance payout.

Paddy was no angel: like most of us, he got away with whatever he could. It was all part of the constant game between people, even mates. Everyone tried to get one up on everyone else. Not in a nasty way. It was like a constant, friendly war. When people fell on hard times or had their back against the wall, we'd rally round to make sure they escaped death row.

There was always money to be made somewhere to replace the money that had been lost somewhere else. Money was just something to have fun with and to keep the wheels spinning.

Anyway, Paddy probably got a good laugh out of what I got up to, otherwise why would he put up with me?

One time Paddy had to go into hospital with appendicitis. He got one of his best mates, Graham Beasley, to look after the shop. Graham was a mate of mine too, and a dead straight kid, which meant that it was a lamb-to-the-slaughter situation. Even with Graham keeping an eye on things, putting me in the bookies was like letting Lester Piggott do your tax returns.

Anyway, we had a really busy Saturday, and I kept taking money from the payout drawer, popping over the road to another betting shop and betting there. By the end of the day, things weren't looking too good. At 5 o'clock Paddy phoned from the hospital. Graham answered. I could hear Paddy's voice rattling out of the receiver.

'How's it going, Graham?'

Graham said, 'Err . . . yeah not bad, Paddy. Not bad . . .' Then he held his hand over the mouthpiece and said, 'It's Paddy. He wants to know how we're doing.' I took the phone from him.

I said, 'All right, Pad?' I could hear his heart drop when I answered the phone.

'How much we took, Dave?'

I opened the drawer and rattled it about, there wasn't much there. A few sad-looking coins.

I said, 'Yeah . . . we've done pretty good, actually.'

'How much?'

'I wouldn't like to say.'

'I'd like you to say.'

I said, 'About twenty quid.'

He said, 'Dave. Could you pick me up from the hospital asap!'

Paddy made his money back off me in other ways: on jobs that I put his way and on stuff that I got for him. And also on all the cash that I lost in his betting shop. Some of it was mine.

The car that I used to pick up Paddy from the hospital was his beautiful red 1275 cc Mini GT. He loved this car, so why he loaned it to me I'll never know. Especially with my history of vehicle GBH.

I drove around to The Omelette to play in the game that Johnny Dunn ran upstairs above his restaurant. It was Strip-Deck Stud, my best game. Famous last words. Actually, Strip-Deck was just about the *only* game in town – Strip-Deck and 7-Card. And Strip-Deck is a great game because the best player will beat the bad players, most of the time. That's the theory, anyway. I was in this hand with Johnny and he had only one card to catch with only one card to come. By this time we'd had three streets of betting and all my money was in the pot. He looked across the table at me.

'Have have you got any money left?'

I said, 'No.'

'Pity.'

See, no friends in poker. They want to win the money you've got, but that's not enough – they also want to win money you *haven't* got.

Are you thinking what I'm thinking?

I said, 'I've got this Mini.'

Johnny asked me what it was worth. I said about three grand. Johnny was a great guy but bad at poker. There were eight cards left, so he had a 7–1 chance.

He said, 'Well, let's put it in the pot.'

I threw the keys in.

The last card was dealt.

Johnny hit his long shot.

I was walking home.

Paddy was walking everywhere.

I had to ring Paddy and give him the good news. I suppose it wouldn't have been so bad if I hadn't already had his Datsun repossessed, blown up two vans and burned out a third. So I thought I'd try to break it gently. I rang him at the bookies.

I said, 'Paddy, how much will you sell me your Mini for?'

He said, 'I don't want to sell it.'

I said, 'I wanna buy it.'

He paused. 'But I don't want to sell it.'

I said, 'What's the rock-bottom you'd take for it?'

'Three grand.'

'OK, I owe you three grand 'cos I've just lost your car in a poker game.'

But Paddy being Paddy, he knew that I'd get the money to him somehow. Well, as soon as I'd won it off someone or emptied his safe again.

7. Riding the Luck

The trouble with you is . . .

You'd think the only disadvantage of having two women in bed with you would be that you'd be spoilt for choice. You wouldn't think it could lead to you being made homeless.

By now I'd got a little flat on the corner of Spring Bank. Things were pretty grim. I wasn't long out of prison, I'd split up with Sue, I didn't see the kids as much as I wanted to, I was living in this tiny flat and I didn't have a pot to piss in. You can hardly blame me for trying to cheer myself up by pulling a girl and her best friend. Now a good three-way bet in the bookies can get you a lot of cash. But a three-way with two women pays off even better. That's another kind of jackpot. Waking up in the morning should be a real pleasure, and it was, until the landlady burst into my room with her vacuum cleaner on full throttle.

She switched it off, crossed her arms, looked at us in disgust, and told me to get out. I was evicted. I wouldn't have minded if the place was decent but when I first moved in I'd had to have a conversation with the landlady about fixing a few things.

I said, 'It's the ceiling . . .'

She said, 'What's wrong with it?'

I said, 'I'd like one.' I said it didn't bother me, it was the guy upstairs that was complaining.

I thought the row would blow over so I went down the bookies to see if I could make some money. I lost, for a change. When I got back to Spring Bank, the landlady and her husband had thrown all my stuff in the garden. The husband was standing on the step with his arms crossed.

'You've got to go,' he said, 'you're lowering the tone.'

'You're kidding me,' I said. 'Jack the Ripper couldn't lower the tone of this place.'

I walked up the path and the husband ran back inside and slammed the door. Mine was a ground-floor flat so I broke the window and threw all my stuff back inside. Then I climbed in and settled down for the night.

They offered me cash to leave, so I left. I could hardly stand in a street holding a sign that said 'HOMELESS DUE TO A THREESOME, GIVE GENEROUSLY'. So there I was with my suitcase, headed straight for the only place you can go in a time of need. The bookies.

In the bookies I found a mate of mine called Phil Rea with his brother John. Both good kids. Phil was living with his girlfriend, Diana, in a flat round the corner and he said I could kip on the couch. Like a falling cat, I always seemed to land on my feet.

Doubly lucky, actually, because when I walked into the flat I got a glimpse of Diana and I could see that she was a good-looking woman. But that thought didn't get much further because when she turned to face me, I saw that she was about eight months pregnant.

It turned out that the flat where I was kipping on the couch was actually Diana's, not Phil's. It also turned out I got on really well with her. We made each other laugh.

Soon she had the baby. I knew that Phil had another girl on the go and was only coming to see Diana when he felt like it. I didn't say anything, of course, because you don't. Well, men don't. But it did mean that I felt less bad about it when I realized that Diana and me were falling for each other. Phil came around less and I knew he was spending more time with his other girl, so it felt inevitable that me and Diana ended up together.

One day when we were still in bed, the front door smashed open and Phil burst in. Phil was a hard case. But when he saw me and Diana together, he actually wasn't that bothered. And he knew I could fight. I pulled my pants on and we went downstairs for a cup of tea.

So now me and Diana were together. She was a real tough cookie. She'd fight in the street if she had to. We were a good match. We were like Bonnie and Clyde on a budget.

After one night out safe-robbing, I came home with three grand. I didn't want to walk upstairs with that cash and start explaining it to Diana, so I spread the money out underneath a corner of the living-room carpet.

The next morning I woke up and I could hear Diana downstairs doing the vacuuming and, as usual, singing. She was belting out a Sandy Posey song – 'A Single Girl' – which soon she would be. It got a bit softer, then quieter, and then it suddenly cut off altogether. The vacuuming also stopped. I thought, thank Christ for that, now maybe I could get back to sleep – I sat bolt upright in bed. I realized she'd found the money. The next second, I heard the front door click.

I looked out the window and, sure enough, she was running like fuck for a bus with a holdall leaking £20 notes. I squinted and thought she looked like the fucking Road Runner. Her singing had turned into a 'Beep, Beep' sound as she dived on the bus.

Diana eventually came back in a taxi with a carload of shopping bags – clothes, food, things for the house and gifts for the kids. I couldn't really argue with that. I wouldn't have got a word in edgeways anyway. Whatever problem Diana had had with me that day, it was guaranteed to be one of the 262 problems that women who live with gamblers have with gamblers. I've counted every time one has been thrown at me. Usually in the middle of one of those 'the trouble with you' arguments:

The trouble with you is, you don't listen . . .

The trouble with you is, you're just selfish . . .

The trouble with you is, you're not part of the family . . .

The trouble with you is, you might as well live with your gambling pals . . .

Which, to be fair, was all true. And is true of all gamblers (and most men, come to that). Especially the first bit about not listening. And he only hears the bit about the listening because it came *first* – if it had been second he'd have already tuned out. He wouldn't have been listening.

To all women, I'm offering this as a tip for the next time you have one of those 'the trouble with you' speeches for your fella: *put the most important problem with him first on the list.* It's the only one he'll hear.

If it was a roller-coaster life then most gamblers' women clung on for as long as they could, until they got off, got thrown off, or the whole thing derailed.

Like I said, Diana was a tough cookie. But the gambling life is tougher. More so when you've got a family. The biggest 'win' I had around this time was when Diana gave birth to our beautiful son David on 4 June 1980. Whatever your troubles, when a new baby comes along it makes everything seem fine. She already had a boy called Phil and was eight months pregnant with Johnny when I met her. They're lovely lads and I always looked on them as mine, so now we had three sons.

Don't ever let anyone tell you that gambling can't be as strong an addiction as any drug, because it can. Poker and horses were my poisons. And I started to travel further afield to play, tracking down bigger poker games, although my time was split about 30 per cent poker, 70 per cent horses.

Fortunately, Paddy's betting shop had burned down. I say 'fortunately' because it led to a good insurance payout. I also had a good alibi by the time the flames took hold. I'd been visiting Diana in hospital when she was having the baby, so at least I couldn't get the blame. I mean blame for the shop burning down, not the baby. I had to hold my hand up to the baby.

As I said earlier, being known to the Old Bill means you get picked up even for things you didn't do. Once you've been inside, it gets worse. Like the day we were at home celebrating Diana's birthday and the front door got smashed off its hinges and went flying down the hall like a surfboard with two armed coppers on it. The rest of the squad ran in, screaming at everybody to get on the floor and pointing guns at me. I thought, *Well that narrows it down then – it's definitely* me *they want*. For a second I thought that Diana might have missed a catalogue payment.

Apparently there had been an armed robbery down the road at Jacksons. The number plates on the getaway car belonged to Paddy and I'd been the last one at his flat where he'd kept them. I was innocent of the charge but try telling that to half a dozen armed cops in bulletproof vests while they're tramping through your missus's birthday cake.

After three days in the cells they set me free. They never did pay for the door. They never do. I think they're sponsored by B&Q.

We moved to Home Thorpe flats on the thirteenth floor – unlucky for some. And it was for me on one New Year's Eve when the police came calling. We were in the middle of a blizzard, snow blowing everywhere, and it was fucking freezing. I knew the Old Bill were only calling for maximum inconvenience, probably so they could throw me in the cells over New Year. So, while the cops were still at the door, I went out on the window balcony and, with the snow blowing around me, I balanced on the wall and somehow got hold of the metal bar of the balcony above. The metal was so cold it went right through my fingers. I started to pull myself up. Diana couldn't look. She told Phil to tell her if I went past the window at high speed! I couldn't look down. I managed to pull myself up onto the balcony above.

Unfortunately, the old guy in that flat was stood at his window with his pipe and saw me suddenly appear, fourteen storeys up, coming over his balcony rail like the abominable snowman. He locked me out and called the police. I spent five minutes freezing my nuts off before the Old Bill came. The copper that nicked me said I would've been taken away in a plastic bag if I'd fallen. And he said now that he knew that I was such a good climber, it put me in the picture for a few other jobs!

I spent New Year's Eve in the cells. What an idiot to risk falling fourteen storeys just so I could go out drinking with my mates.

To be honest, most of the time Diana was with the kids while I was out gambling with the boys. In the end she couldn't stand it any longer, and I couldn't blame her. She got her own flat for her and her boys. I missed Phil and John too because they were great boys. I was left in the flat with my two, and although I loved them to bits, when you've got a deaf son, as Paul was, who needs special help and there isn't any of that kind of help, or at least I didn't have any, then it's hard. I couldn't cope, to be honest. I wasn't even that good at looking after myself, let alone a family. But I tried my best because I wasn't going to put them back in a home.

We all fuck up at some point. I just hoped there was no one up there keeping score. I thought if there was, I'd be more likely to go down than up. I didn't mind the thought of going to hell as long as I didn't have to pay the gas bill. At least I'd get to play poker with most of my friends. There's no way those boys were going upstairs.

Eventually Sue returned, but only to tell me she was getting married to this copper and if I wanted to see my kids I'd have to travel all the way to Liveerpool.

It's over a hundred miles from Hull to Liverpool, so I had a 220-mile round trip across the Pennine moors, most of it down the M62, which is one of the worst motorways for traffic snarl-ups. Because Sue was with this copper, I had to meet Paul and Kerry in the park. Which is sick, when you think about it – four hours' driving for half an hour in the park with your own kids.

Wanting to be a well-dressed dad, I helped myself to Paddy's new shirt and shoes, and of course borrowed his car. The drive there and back was never pleasant so I took two mates, Dave Snow and Keith Mellors. After stopping off in Leeds, the three of us ended up fighting three skinheads outside a club. The first punch thrown knocked Dave out. I hit the guy with a right hook and he landed in the road with his teeth on the pavement. Then I smashed the granny out of his mate while Mel chased the other one down the street with a steel comb (Mel always wanted to be a hairdresser). We dragged Snowy to the car and sped away. I wondered why Mel was screaming until I saw the headlights – we were going the wrong way down a one-way street.

When I calmed down, I noticed I had a sleeve missing and Dave had lost a shoe. We all fell around laughing, even Snowy with his black eye. The shoe that was missing was the left one, we could replace it.

To try to get some regular cash – and a bit of normality – I started a job at a place called Bullimore's. I'd always had the habit of slogging away at ordinary jobs in between gambling when I needed to keep money coming in the front door. Even when it was going straight out the back, down the alley and into the bookies' till.

I still didn't have a driving licence but because I turned up to work at Bullimore's in a car they thought I did. One day the boss asked me if I wanted to drive a lorry. I thought, why not? I had a fake licence and I knew how to use it. They put me in a big four-ton Ford.

I knew I could do untold damage in this big truck, so I actually took it pretty carefully when I was driving around. Apart from when I knocked a bloke off his bike – I saw him do a triple lux through my mirror. It was his own fault as he was sneaking through a red light and his handlebars got caught on the side of the truck. The idiot was all right, though.

I also didn't want to get pulled by the fuzz (which is always painful) and risk losing this money-making job.

I didn't have to worry about that, though, because something much worse was about to pop up and bite me on the arse.

8. On the Run, Disco Violence and the Photo-Finish Kid

In danger money, I'm a millionaire!

Just when things seem to be going OK, you find yourself on the run from the police in the middle of the night. I hated it when that happened. It always seemed to be at the end of the week when they came for me, which just fucks up the whole weekend.

I'd got offered some old pieces of silver at a good price. I didn't know where they'd come from and I didn't ask. I took the silver bits around to a mate of mine, John, and we decided it would be easier and safer to scrap it. But John sold some of the items and got nicked. Should've seen that one coming. John was a sound guy and he didn't say a word to the police, but John's girl, Pat, wasn't the sharpest knife in the drawer and she told them that I had taken the silver round to the house.

The Old Bill picked up me and John and did the usual trick of trying to play one off against the other. After questioning, they accidentally put us together in the same cell. Modern policing at its finest.

I was charged with handling and finally bailed. John's girlfriend, being a bit naïve, had made a statement about what she'd seen at the house. John said he'd sort it out.

In the meantime, the boss at Bullimore's had found

out about the charge. He also used to dabble in antiques, so it made it seem worse that I was up in Beverley Crown Court charged with handling. He called me into the office and said he was going to have to fire me. Now, I needed to hang on to the job to show the court that I was on the straight and narrow. I pointed out that it would be unfair dismissal because if I was found not guilty I should be allowed to stay. He thought about it and then said that was fine, I could keep my job if I got a not guilty.

I went to Beverley Crown Court for a pre-trial section 7 committal to see if the case should go to trial. All the truck drivers from Bullimore's came along to support me.

During the trial hearing, when Pat appeared she was wearing a duffle coat . . . with the hood up. If this was part of a ploy to make her look like a mental case, then it was working. She looked like Paddington Bear. It got better. She was asked by the prosecution if there was anyone in the court that she recognized as having handled the silver. She turned, looked directly at me, turned back, and said . . . 'No.' Which was the opposite of what she'd first told the prosecution. Even my defence barrister looked puzzled.

The prosecutor asked her if she was sure. She said she was. And because it was decided that Pat was now a hostile witness, they decided not to take the case to trial.

I came out onto the steps of the court a happy man, but the celebrations didn't last long because a Detective Sutton appeared and immediately rearrested me for non-payment of parking fines. It was obviously some charge they'd cobbled together – a little get-me-back for the abandoned trial.

I was pulled away from the lads, thrown in a car and taken to Leeds nick. To make things even better, because it was Easter and there was a lock-down, I had no way of letting anybody know where I was or what had happened.

I stayed in Leeds nick for three days. Ironic, really – Easter was the time when Christ was resurrected, but for me, the Devil, it was the time to be buried. I was banged up and there was nothing I could do.

I asked to see the priest. I'd never been to church in my life, I wasn't even Catholic, but I knew a priest was one of the few people they'd let me see. They might have even thought I was going to confess to something that they could use against me. Although, I wasn't sure if priests had to inform the police about any crime they heard during confession. Which was a shame because I was planning on confessing that I'd killed Bambi, pushed Humpty Dumpty off the wall and that I was the northern connection to the Great Train Robbery. Even though I'd only been nine years old at the time (but I was always mature for my age).

They brought the priest to see me.

He said, 'Would you like to confess your sins, my son?'

I said, 'No . . . I'd like to use a phone . . .'

He said, 'Sorry?'

I said, 'A phone?'

I got marched back to the cell double-time. I don't think I'd ever heard a priest say 'fuck off' before. But I know the Irish are big on swearing.

I finally got shipped out to Rudgate again. Prison Officer Sharkey – the victim of our campfire cookout

– *could not believe* that I was back on the premises. He saw me on the tally. He screamed at the top of his voice, '*ULLIOTT!*' He had a chance to get his own back.

I'd been given twenty-one days for a fine non-payment, which was ridiculous. And they still hadn't let me phone anyone, but one of the good (and bad) things about being a gambler was that if you disappeared for days, no one worried too much, they just thought you were involved in a game. So I decided to do a Steve McQueen-type great escape – minus the bike and machine guns – and go over the prison fence one night to make a phone call. If I got through to Diana or Paddy, they could get the cash together to pay the fine and get me out.

I scooted up and over the fence pretty easily – Rudgate was an open prison, so the security wasn't exactly German prison camp standard. I knew there was an hour between the checks they did on the dorms.

When I hit the road, I could go left or right. Unfortunately I went right and found the phone box had been vandalized. I hate vandals. I didn't have time to find another phone so I ran back to climb the fence, get back in bed, get counted and then go back out again. But I was knackered and as I was hauling myself over the fence, a bright torch beam hit me full in the face. I was spotted. That meant they'd send me back to Leeds and put me in the block, so I dropped down onto the road and legged it.

It's a weird thing being on the run, especially at night out in the country. Because country dark isn't like city dark. This was proper *dark* dark; real can't-see-a-fucking-thing and where-the-*fuck*-are-we kind of dark.

It was also deathly quiet. I might as well have been on the run in outer space.

You wouldn't believe how many police they sent out searching for an escaped parking-fine dodger. You'd have thought I'd parked a JCB on the Queen's head. Every time I heard a car come up the road I'd dive into a hedge. I ended up inhaling more grass than Bob Marley. The police cars had spotlights which rotated so they could see in the hedges.

I didn't want to be around when they brought the police dogs out. Those twitchy-nosed beasts could sniff out a chocolate drop in a lake of shit. And that was just the handlers.

I finally managed to get to Tadcaster and walked into the town centre (well, four shops and a pub). I saw a young couple at a taxi rank waiting for a cab. I tried to smarten myself up so I didn't look too much like a scarecrow that had been out dogging. I was still in my prison gear, brown suit and stripy shirt. But these were the sort of nice kids that wouldn't know that, or thought prison gear was covered in big arrows. As I got nearer, I overheard them say that they were going to York, so in my politest manner I asked if they'd let me share their taxi, offering to pay the fare. They agreed. I didn't have a penny on me.

You've got to give me points for cheek, though, right? I was thinking on my feet. And my feet were caked in mud and cow shit, so that wasn't easy.

We took the taxi to York and they got out. I told the

driver I wanted to go on to Hull. That went down well.

He said, 'I'm from Tadcaster . . .'

I said, 'I'm from Hull.'

'But I'm not going to Hull.'

'But I *live* in Hull.'

'But *I* live in Tadcaster.'

'But I live in Hull, son, and if you want paying we'll have to go to Hull because I've not got a cent on me.'

We went to Hull.

By the time we got there it was 3 o'clock in the morning. The only person I could think of who might be still up was my Auntie Sheila.

Now my Auntie Sheila wasn't like any auntie I've ever known. In fact, she wasn't like any other woman I've known. She could fight for England, she liked a good old drink, she smoked a bit of weed, she liked a song and a dance. She was tougher and smarter and a bigger laugh than most blokes I knew.

She was married to a geezer called Nev. She used to go out on jobs with him and loved cracking a safe herself. It must have been in the blood.

One time there was a guy banging on her front door, looking for one of Sheila's nephews, Charlie. This guy who was shouting the odds on the doorstep drove ex-army vehicles and always wore combat gear – I think he fancied himself as a bit of a survivalist. Well, he didn't survive too long with Sheila because he banged on that door one too many times and without a word or a warning Sheila threw an axe straight through the glass door. It missed his head by about an inch.

Put it this way, they didn't get many door-to-door sales-men at Sheila's.

The taxi pulled up outside Sheila's gaff and, sure enough, she was awake. I think she was up sharpening the axe. I asked her for the fare but she said she only had a fiver in the house. The taxi driver said it was fifteen quid. I gave him the five.

He said, 'That's no good to me.'

I said, 'It's no fucking good to me either. I've just escaped from prison so you can take it or leave it. Give me your address and I'll send you the rest.'

He said he'd take it and shot off. I felt sorry for him. So later on I posted him twenty quid. That story will have earned him his fare share of pints in pubs, I'll bet. Not that I made a habit of betting. I made more of a life of it.

So, again, I was on the run from the law. I knew I had to get the fine money before I got picked up because if I didn't they'd just ship me off to the block in Leeds again. There'd be no escaping from there.

I must have had a natural talent for being on the run from the Old Bill because I managed to leave every house I was hiding in just before they got there (the noise from the sirens helped). Trouble is, it's a talent you can't really make any money from. And it ain't exactly gonna impress anyone at a job interview. Question: 'What are your skills?' Answer: 'I'm pretty good at evading the law.'

To give you some idea of how sick a gambler I was, a few times when I was on the run I actually managed to get money in my pocket from Diana and Paddy – more than enough to pay the fine – but then I just *could not bring myself* to hand myself in. I thought, fuck it, I can bet with this money, use it as a stake, and double it up – then pay the fine and have money in my pocket. But, of course, I lost it. Then I went in a bookies and won it back. Then I lost it again. Remember when I said money is fuel? Maybe that's why I found it so easy to burn.

In order to get to me, the police arrested our kid, Paul. Which is a pretty dirty trick, if you ask me. But they didn't ask me, and they wouldn't have given a donkey's dick about what I thought.

My mam and dad were mad about this happening to my brother. Not only was I the black sheep, I was dirtying one of the lambs. I went round to my mother's and said I was going to hand myself in. She insisted on coming with me to Priory Road police station, which was a bit embarrassing because, even though I knew she was coming along to see Paul, it looked a bit like my mam was handing me in. She might as well have held me by the bloody ear as we went through the door. I'd come on a bit since my early days of nicking soap, but not much.

I told the copper on duty that half the force was out looking for me so he better get his arse in gear before I fucked off. He ran round the counter with a pair of handcuffs. I said, 'I'm actually handing myself in, you dick.'

As I was being taken in, Paul came out and got a big hug from my mam. And I got dragged down into the cells. And shipped off back to Rudgate. This time, though, I wouldn't be staying. The Assistant Governor started giving me some bullshit about what had happened but I told him that I'd rung my solicitor and I knew that as long as I brought the prison clothes back, which I had, and paid the fine, which I had, they could do fuck-all. I remember his reply clearly.

'You're right, we can't do anything. But you'll be back, Ulliott. And we'll make sure you get sorted out.'

I yawned and said, 'Yeah, whatever . . .' And that was that.

My job at Bullimore's was long gone, but there was no way I was going back to work and having some mug of a foreman telling me what to do, anyway. From now on work would have to fit in around me.

I bumped into a mate, Lenny Norris. He gave me his job as bouncer at a place called the Grange Park Hotel. It was like being made head thong attendant in a lap-dancing club – you could see the attraction, but also the potential for problems.

From the name you might have thought that the Grange Park Hotel was a classy joint, but on Sundays it became Grange Park Disco. It was like a tour of Vietnam with disco lights and a DJ. There were hooligans, nutters, cheap booze, lots of glass, and girls in boob tubes. What could go wrong?

I worked out quickly why Lenny didn't want the job. If a fight started, the other punters would throw their glasses and bottles *into* the middle from the outside. I'd watch from a safe distance and then drag out whichever idiot had started the trouble, or whoever was the smallest.

It was ticket-only parties but I earned extra by letting people in for cash. The place would sell about 250 tickets but it was so popular that I could sell another 250 on the door at two quid each. And I'd have £500 in my pocket – I mean who'd do this job for a tenner?

Sometimes people were so desperate to get in that they'd climb in through the toilet windows. I'd hear shouting because someone had got stuck halfway. I put a kid on guard in the toilets and he'd fetch me so that I could charge them their two quid while they were hanging half in and half out. It's difficult to refuse to pay in that position. It's even harder to get money out of your pocket.

The girls' toilets were just as bad, but of course I didn't go in there, so I only saw the backside view of any bird that got stuck. No matter how cloudy the sky was on a Sunday night, at the Grange there was always a full moon.

Not many doormen would have stood on this door by themselves. I must have been mad. After a couple of weeks I met this beautiful girl that I'd already half-fallen in love with, even though she'd only said three words to me.

The management had started to count the people leaving and soon discovered the numbers had doubled. They decided to get another doorman to help out. Safety-wise, that should have made things better, but it made things worse. He was a real mouthy bastard, and a bully. Bad doormen actually create aggro, and cause knocked-back punters to come back later looking for trouble.

They also like to be top dog. Sure enough, he eventually took a swing at me; I blocked it and caught him with a right and knocked him over the desk in the foyer. He stayed on the floor, so I decided to fuck off sharpish. I walked out and decided to keep a low profile for the time being.

I was still trying to keep a low profile because of the Grange Park doorman incident, but I had to go into the town centre a week later to see someone. Five minutes later, three detectives jumped out of an unmarked police car, grabbed me and threw me in the back. I was sandwiched between two of them.

I said, 'This is all a bit over the top, isn't it, boys?'

One of them said, 'We saw what a fucking mess you made of that doorman.' Apparently when I smashed his cheekbone I'd also blacked his left eye, so he looked like a panda that had been hit by a truck. I got charged and bailed. When it came to court I was given a suspended sentence and 140 hours' community service.

Community service got you outside but wasn't necessarily good for your health. I'd never smoked, which was a miracle considering half of Hull grew up puffing like chimneys. The only time I did smoke was a bit of weed in prison, for the same reason that everyone did – the sheer boredom. Community service was just as bad, so most days one of the lads would roll a joint to pass round. It was heavy-duty stuff. Dogs would walk into the smoke and stroll out the other side whistling reggae. It also explained why we were painting everything in spots, stripes and checks.

I was also organizing some gardening work, on the side, to be done at this old lady's house. She was a lovely old girl. One day she asked me if I had a wife and kids. I said I had. She asked me if I had a car. I said I hadn't (not one I owned, anyway). She took me out to the garage and inside there was this little bright yellow Fiat. She said her husband had gone off and she wanted the garage to do her pottery work in. So she gave me the keys. I said thanks a lot. It wasn't a big car – a rat could've pulled it down a sink – and it was a horrible colour, but a free car's a free car, right? And it still had some tax on it. My first taxed car.

I hadn't had the thing a week when some idiot backed into it and smashed the wing off. How you couldn't notice this bright yellow fucker, I don't know. Maybe the driver had been smoking the same weed as us. I stuck the knocked-off wing back on with a load of filler. It was a bodge job but it worked.

While I was doing community service I met a mate of mine, Dave Pride. When we went on our lunch break, we'd jump in this little yellow Fiat. It must've looked hilarious – six-foot-one of me squeezed behind the wheel and even bigger Dave Pride wedged into the passenger seat. Every bit of us was touching every bit of the inside of the Fiat. We looked like two escaped lunatics joyriding in Noddy's car.

Being a horse junkie, I drove us straight to the bookies. On the way there we got pulled over by a traffic cop. I still didn't have a licence or insurance and the car had no MOT, and only had some tax on the windscreen because it had been left by the old lady. Luckily, before the copper asked me if I had all the documents, he got hold of the front wing that I'd reattached.

He said, 'That doesn't look too safe, sir.' Right on cue, it came away in his hand.

I said, 'I'm not being funny, but that wing was on nice and solid and you've just pulled it off.'

Pridey stuck his head out the little window: 'Yeah, I

saw that. You fucking well pulled it off! That's vandalism, that is! I'm a witness to it.'

The copper took one look at us and could tell we were going to be far, far too much like hard work. He waved us on. We drove off like a bat out of Hull, with the broken wing on the back seat (and Pridey struggling to get his head back in the window).

One day I was sent to Cottingham and I left the site to go on my dinner hour. Somehow, must be gambler's instinct, I found myself in a little bookies I'd never seen before. And there weren't many of those. It was one of those bookies that was full of old guys who would just fun-bet a few quid. Bit like my old man. These kind of guys were a bookie's bread and butter. While the sick gamblers came and went according to how flush or how broke they were, these older pound-betters would turn up day after day without fail. I think half of the attraction was because they turned it into a sort of social club. I had a soft spot for these old boys because they always had a story to tell, and loved to see you win big.

I listened to the race commentary while reading my paper. The race finished and they announced it was a photo-finish between horses 20 and 3.

There were no TVs in bookies back then, so nobody had seen the race, including the bookie. He shouted out, 'Does anyone want to bet on the winner of the photo-finish? Four-to-five the pair.' I could tell straight away that he was only offering it as a bet because he knew the old guys wouldn't take it, or they'd only have a quid on.

When none of them took him up on it, he really started taking the mickey out of them.

'Come on! You daren't have a bet? What's matter with you all?'

Not one of them said anything. I thought, right, I'm not having that. I knew that nine times out of ten, the first horse announced in a photo finish would eventually be called as the winner. I walked up to the counter, grabbed everything I had in my pocket, about £450, and put it down. He looked at it as if it was Monopoly money.

He said, 'What's this?'

I said, 'It's four hundred and fifty quid, son. I'll take your bet. Number 20.'

He said, 'No, you won't.'

I turned around to the old blokes, who by this time were all looking over. This was obviously the most exciting thing to happen here in years.

I said, 'Did you hear that, fellas? He's taking the piss out of you 'cos you won't bet and now he daren't take mine. What do you think about that?'

From the way they jumped in and started having a go at him, you could tell that he must have been making fun of them for years and this was their chance to get their own back. Eventually, he gave in and took the bet. I stood to win a quick £360. And, of course, defying the odds, number fucking 3 was called out as the winner. Every bloke in the place groaned. I hadn't heard a groan like that since the last time I'd borrowed one of Paddy's cars.

I lost the £450 but, to be honest, I didn't really give a toss about the money. I was much more pissed off about not sticking one in the bookie on behalf of the punters. If he was a smug bastard before, you should've seen his face when the result was called.

That's how bad my luck used to run sometimes in the gambling stakes – I couldn't have even picked a winner in a one-horse race, let alone one with two.

But even though I was in the right place at the wrong time in that bookies, all it cost me was four hundred and fifty quid. Being in the right place at the wrong time can cost you a lot more than that. Ask anyone who's ever been struck by lightning.

9. Only Trust the Face You Shave

From the straight and narrow to the bent and wide

Sometimes the wheels just fall off without warning. Usually when you're least expecting them to. All four wheels came off my trolley soon enough. I'd been going straight, or trying to, and doing well. Then I ran into Dave Barclough again. After grassing me up, our old partner Fred had gone AWOL after getting out of prison, so I hooked up with Dave to do a few more jobs. Bad move.

Cracking safes was like gambling: I was addicted to the buzz more than the money. Which is why the quicker I could get rid of the cash the better. I threw it around on gambling, drinking, gambling, wining and dining, gambling. But mainly on poker and horses. However much I took out of bookies' safes, I put ten times more back over the counter.

People talk about money burning a hole in their pocket: I needed a fire extinguisher hung from my belt.

I could also be a bit of a loner. I got on with the lads and always had lots of girls, but when it came to trusting people, I was wary. I didn't really trust anybody because I'd been let down too often.

Speaking of which. Bad history repeated itself when Dave got caught and the fucker grassed me up. As well as that, I was also being followed by the Regional Crime

Squad. You'd think you'd know if you were being followed, wouldn't you? Well don't count on it because the police use four cars when you've only got one. So it's weird to find out it's been happening.

It came to an end when I spotted them and then one of their cars cut me up. So I crashed into it. Truth is, I knew I'd be going back inside so I made the most of smashing into the coppers' car – it's not everyday you get a chance to do that.

They nicked me with safe-cracking tools in the boot. So all the running around and the gambling and late-night poker and just about everything else came to a grinding halt.

Being inside is never pleasant, but it's easier to deal with second time round. And in prison as in life, it depends on how you deal with it. Some people in prison spend their time mourning and looking at the calendar, but I've always tried to make the best of any situation. Plus, I couldn't afford a calendar. And, actually, the time I spent in prison and the time I spent in the Monica Snooker Club in Hull wasn't that much different. The Monica wasn't much more than an old wooden shed with crap toilets, no women, bouts of violence (mainly when I lost) and a strange smell you couldn't escape (mainly when they lost). A good training ground for being sent down.

The amount of trouble and shit that went down in the Monica was unbelievable. But as long as you had mates around you, it was survivable. Kev Allanby, Paul Davey, Pat Hughes, Sandy, Vinnie, Ernie, Pete, Eddie, Ziggy and Bootsy were all wide boys who played in the Monica.

Funnily enough, the guy in charge of the place, Arthur Greenwood, was a real gentleman. He used to tell me that he thought I had the heart of a lion because I'd stand up to anyone. I was probably more lunatic than lion.

I needed that heart when one of the club's worst bullies attacked me and smashed me into a coat hook on the wall. It sank into the back of my neck. I went dizzy and felt sick but I managed to grab him so he couldn't easily punch me – a bit of boxing training coming through: hold on till you clear your head or the towel gets thrown in. I bit down hard on his ear, pushed him off and shook my head clear. Then I punched him out and smashed a cup in his face several times – I wasn't sure how many lumps he wanted. Much to the pleasure of the whole club.

Pat Hughes took him to Hull Royal Infirmary. The guy didn't give up my name – he said a load of bricks fell on him – which is why I won't mention his.

What I didn't know was that I'd run into this guy again sooner than I thought, and in a place I didn't expect.

I was still on remand, but I knew what was coming. This stretch was going to be tougher than the last: it would be longer, and I knew I wasn't going to see Diana or our son David. Because when the Regional Crime Squad were following me around they'd seen me with other women and told Diana about it to try to persuade her to give evidence against me. She was angry at me but she still wouldn't let the police use her. But not everyone is that strong. That's why I told very few people about my outside work. You never knew when they might use it against you. Only trust the face you shave.

It definitely toughens you up when you're left alone. Sometimes it's just straight survival. There are people inside who will test you and then take advantage of you if you fail. This was about to happen to me when I got sent back on remand to my favourite place, Armley prison in Leeds.

Things got off to a bright start when I got myself thrown into solitary confinement – 'the block'. I'd been sharing a cell with a geezer I knew called Barry who used to live in Hull. I hadn't seen him in years, so it brought a whole new meaning to the question 'What are you doing here?'

Outside each cell you'd have your worksheet and it would tell the screw where you were working – in the kitchen, gardens or mailbags. There's nothing worse than sewing mailbags all day, so I changed the worksheet and put Barry and myself down as non-workers. We didn't get the screws' early-morning knock and we had a nice sleep-in. But only until the screw looked closer at the worksheet and then bashed on the door and sent it flying open and demanded to know which one of us had altered it. I said that somebody else must have done it, and we had wondered why we hadn't had our early-morning alarm for breakfast in bed.

I got put straight in the block for that. For a week. It was down in the basement but you felt like you were deeper underground. When you looked out you couldn't see anything but the concrete wall of the moat. Armley must have been built on the site of an old castle. To make things worse, the small windows of the cells were covered in blue plastic, so you didn't even get sunshine, just this depressing blue light that barely made it through the glass. You really did feel like you'd been buried underground.

I sat on the floor and leaned back against the wall. I'd gone from the bit in *The Great Escape* where Steve McQueen jumps the fence to the bit where they throw him in the cooler. And I didn't even have a baseball to chuck against the wall. I thought at least things couldn't get much worse. Right on cue, a loud engine noise started up in the room next door and I realized I was right next to the generator. On full power it sounded like ten guys were hitting the cell door with sledgehammers. After a few days I felt like I didn't hear it any more. It's funny what you can get used to if you put up with it long enough. Ask anyone who's married.

We had to fold our bedding up super neatly, squared off like they do in the army. Take a wild guess how neat mine was. I reached new levels of bad folding. I'd never made a bed in my life.

I'd fold my blanket and then I'd hear a screw's voice screaming down the corridor.

'ULLIOTT! Have you been doing fucking ORIGAMI with your bedding again! You are NOT Japanese, man! Fucking sort it out!'

I surprised him when I shouted back in Chinese – 'Fuk yu tu!'

One morning I folded it into a triangle just to piss them off.

You'd think the punishment of living in isolation in a concrete hole in the ground might be enough. You'd think they might at least let you sleep. No way. Every morning at seven o'clock the boys in the block had to hang their beds outside the cells. Just in case you had any ideas about lying down on it during the day. How spiteful is that? All they left in the cell was a chair, like an old school chair with metal legs and a wooden back. That's all you had to try and sleep on until they gave your bed back at night. Unless you wanted to curl up on the freezing cold floor.

The block was grim – a pretty shitty experience. You got half an hour's exercise in the morning and had an hour in the afternoon, unless it was pissing it down with rain, which it usually was.

If you were lucky someone might smuggle you in a book. But it was usually the Bible. You'll find that a lot of ex-cons have read the Bible. (And I don't want to spoil it for anyone who hasn't read it yet, but in the end he dies.)

In the block you'd pace around the cell like an animal in the zoo. But at least a lion could lick its own balls. I wish I could.

Even though the block cells were so blank, there were small signs of life about the place if you looked out for them. If you put your hand into the peeling plaster, you could find another piece of plaster jammed behind; and that would have scratched on it the name of the last guy who'd been there, or the one before, or maybe it was from years ago. That's pretty sad – to be so bored out of your mind that you'd think of doing that. And then go ahead and actually do it. Like I did. And when I read what others had left there, it turned out the Count of Monte Cristo had been in my cell.

You might think the block experience is much worse

than sewing mailbags, and in a way it is. But the kick that I'd get from changing the worksheets or telling the Guv'nor to fuck off was worth the punishment because the buzz came first. It was all that mattered. It wasn't even spoilt by the thought of the punishment afterwards. It was the same feeling I got from gambling.

I certainly had plenty of time to do nothing but think. And listen to that old generator. I know they say, *That which does not kill me makes me stronger*, but try telling that to someone who's got to fold perfectly square bedding at seven o'clock in the morning. So in my mind I changed it to *That which does not kill me makes me stronger – or really, really pisses me off.*

I knew that there was a cost to other people, mostly wives and family. So I started to think that the best thing would be to get enough money so that I could play poker well enough to do nothing else. I was playing more games in Hull than before but it involved a lot of time for not great returns (which is why I kept returning to the nags – the possibility of the big win). I was already better than most people I played against but I wanted to turn that into cash. I needed bigger games.

So, it was decided: that's what I'd do when I got out.

My spell in the block completed, one day I was on my way to the gym and I saw the guy who had impaled me on a coat hook in the fight in the Monica. I knew we had to get our next clash out of the way straight away, so I went and asked him if he wanted to finish what we'd started. He said as far as he was concerned it was all over.

I later heard that he was in for stabbing someone, so maybe I had been lucky again.

In the gym I was put on a bar with a con who'd got five years for GBH. He'd shaved his head down to the skull and was known as a nutter. I just got on with the weights, but pretty soon he was threatening me.

I smashed him to the floor. I jumped on top of him, picked up a ten-kilo weight and gave him a slap round the head with it. What happened next probably saved his life.

I had such a temper that if someone picked on me I'd go at them until it was all over. After giving him the first slap with the weight, I drew my arms back to smash it down on his head again. But one of the gym screws grabbed me round the neck and threw me in the showers. I was nicked. And he was fucked.

Three mates of mine from Hull were sat there watching – Ray Jessop, Paul Lucas and Carl Simcox. They all gave me the thumbs up.

The screws jumping in was a lucky move for both me and the skinhead. Lucky for him because I could have killed him with that blow, and lucky for me because I would've been done for it. I'd probably still be in there now. Prison is exactly what you might have seen in the Charlie Bronson story: if you're in there and you're proud then you can end up there indefinitely. It's a jungle inside and there are always trouble causers.

I was one of those kids with something to prove – I was proving that I wasn't gonna let any bastard grind me down. That's OK if you're going against one guy, or a gang. But what you can't beat is the system. The system will bury you.

During this second term inside, when I was a bit older, more savvy and stronger physically and mentally – I was at my best. Or at my worst. I wasn't going to take shit from anyone.

So I was nicked and thrown back in the block. Another two weeks of concrete floors, darkness, noisy generators and really bad bed folding. They moved the guy I'd had the fight with to Durham prison, but his two cellmates were after revenge. They'd marked my card. There was nothing I could do about that but wait.

One day I was going to get my water jugs filled up to have a wash and a shave, one jug with boiling water and one with cold. That's when they made their move. I saw that they were marching over the bridge between the landings, looking directly at me. I filled up both jugs with boiling water and I had them in my hands as they crossed the bridge and came to the recess. They stopped dead. They could see the steam coming off the tops of the jugs. So they took off back across the bridge as quickly as they could. They didn't want to become human lobsters. They didn't bother me again.

Prison wasn't all fights and death threats. You can also make good friends inside. Like Pete Robinson. I first met Robbo in the cells in Hull, along with Steve Jonas. We got sent to Armley together and I gave them some legal advice. Some of these lads had admitted to things they hadn't needed to. I used to help them with their depositions. Pete brought his deposition to my cell, and became one of my best pals. He was a great kid with the heart of a lion.

It was at this time in Armley that I ran into one of the most interesting guys I'd ever met. John, my new cellmate, was one of the most aggressive hard men I'd ever come across.

This was another point where I was grateful to be luckier in life than at poker. One day I came back to the cell and found that the photo of my kids on the sideboard had been knocked to the ground, and a chess set which John's wife had brought in for him was there instead. Seeing a picture of your kids thrown to the floor isn't nice and I went mad and smashed the chess set all over the cell. Fortunately for me, John understood why I was so upset about the photo and said it had been an accident and that he hadn't noticed it was there. He'd seen me do the guy with the weight in the gym, he knew I was just out of the block, and he knew the psychological effect that can have on you. He'd also read my deposition, which showed what I'd been charged with and that I'd said nothing to the police other than 'Nothing to say'.

One day the cell door opened and a new cellmate stood there, a big rum-looking fucker with unruly hair. He told us he was in for some minor charge which didn't sound right to either of us, so when he left the cell I decided to look through his stuff for his deposition. Now the reason you looked at the dep was because if someone was straight-up, they wouldn't mind you seeing it – in fact they'd want you to see it so you'd know they were kosher.

John had looked at mine and judged me on that. When you're one of three guys sharing a prison cell, you want to know who you're in with.

This guy's deposition said that he was in for raping a young girl and trying to strangle her.

John decided we should pick a piece out of the Scrabble letters bag and whoever got the highest score had to teach the guy a lesson. Prison cells are barely big enough to swing a kitten, let alone a cat, and even less suited to having a fight with a big muscly fucker. I was hoping to get the low score, and I did. So John had to do the deed. And if this all sounds a bit brutal to you, you're dead right – it was. Prison is.

Later that night I was lying on the top bunk. It was about ten to ten. The lights went out at ten o'clock. I assumed that John wasn't going to take him on in the dark, so I was waiting to see what would happen. John was playing Scrabble with the guy, which was a bit odd, but then everyone in prison played Scrabble. Which ain't necessarily a good idea because everyone always ended up arguing because no bastard could spell.

Before boxing matches there's usually a 'big fight build-up' which includes other fights on the bill, the theme from *Rocky*, pretty girls walking around the ring. But I'd never seen a build-up that included a quiet game of Scrabble.

Suddenly John and the guy started arguing about a word on the board – and I could see that John was deliberately making the argument worse. The rapist stood up and started jabbing his finger in John's chest. It was the last move he made. John flew across the table and head-butted the guy full in the face harder than I'd ever seen anyone hit. The guy flew back like he'd been blown off his feet by a jet engine and John ran over and gave him a hard left and right which would've made Mike Tyson proud. The guy slid to the floor of the cell just as the lights went out. His lights went out at the same time.

I woke up the next morning with the sound of that headbutt still echoing round the cell. I looked down at the floor and the guy was still there, in the same position. I thought he must be dead.

The screws tried to open the cell door but his body was behind it. They started banging the door against him, shouting out. We dragged him out of the way. They burst in and we said that they'd hit him with the cell door and knocked him out. They stood there not knowing what to think, not believing us but not really giving a fuck. They pulled him out the cell. He was carried off to hospital and eventually he came round. He was put on '43s', a reference to Prison Service Rule 43, which allows sex offenders to be segregated for their own safety.

So John was a really handy geezer. And not to be messed with during Scrabble.

He was up for bank robbery and in Armley on remand. He asked if I wanted to come and work with him when we both got out, and I said I would. John got off – and I got a guilty. I served another month in Armley and then they shipped me off to Durham.

Durham was one of the worst prisons in Britain and certainly the worst one that I'd been in. It wasn't made easier by the fact that the Geordie screws didn't like non-Geordie prisoners. (They didn't like Geordie prisoners either, but they liked us less.) The kitchens stank of grease, and usually in the soup you'd find a dead sparrow or two.

Fortunately I was there for only a couple of months and then they shipped me out again, this time to a semi-open prison called Wymott in Lancashire.

The dining area was always a good bet for a piss-take. We could have as many slices of bread as we wanted but only one blob of butter about the size of a 50p piece. One evening we had a power cut and all the lights went out. One of the screws on canteen duty was hated by everyone. And when the lights went out there was this strange sound – *pat! pat! pat! pat!* When the lights came back on we fell off our chairs laughing. In the dark everyone had scooped up their blobs of butter on their knives and flicked them at this screw. Not one single shot had hit him – he was surrounded by a mass of butter splats on the wall behind. He stepped forward and left a man-shaped piece of clean wall.

John had finished his stretch and came to visit me. He said he'd pick me up when I was released. He also brought stuff in for me – a block of Pakistani black in a matchbox and a hundred quid in cash. There was a shortage of good blow in Wymott so news of me having this lump soon spread. The cons had such a keen nose for it that they smelt it even before I'd announced it.

In a semi-open you were in a unit where the cell doors were left unlocked, which made you feel less like you were in Colditz, but it was also less safe for valuables. I wanted a bath but I didn't want to leave the dope in the cell, so in the bathroom I found two pipes in the wall with a gap above them. I put the block there, resting on the pipes. After my bath I put my fingers in to get the block but I knocked it and it disappeared. *Fuck!* I banged the wall and it was hollow. That dope had suddenly become the prison's most expensive piece of cavity-wall insulation.

I decided to smash the wall open. I had a guitar in my cell, so I got a mate of mine to play it loudly and sing badly – he was good at both. He banged away on the guitar while I bashed a hole in the skirting board with a bumper that was used for polishing the floors. I put my hand inside but all I could feel was mud. I was sick at losing such a valuable commodity. Dope is worth its weight in gold inside.

Then I felt upwards and my fingers touched a spider's web, a big one. Now I don't like spiders, but I didn't like losing this block even more. I edged my fingertips forward and, right in the middle of the web, I found the block of dope. This spider must have had the world's worst case of the munchies. I bet it had a lot of spider mates too when word got round what had landed in its web.

So there I was, trying to nick back my cannabis from a stoned spider.

Diana finally came to see me one month before my release, probably to try and get on my good side. David was only one at the time and called me 'Dad', which was cool.

10. Going Almost Straight

Bank jobs, true love and the world of pawn

True to his word, John came and picked me up outside the prison gates in his brand-new Jaguar and we went for a drink at the Monica snooker hall. When we got there, John sat down and I went to the bar. The owner, Arthur Greenwood, came over to me, his eyes still on John.

He said, 'Welcome back . . . Dave.'

I said, 'Now then, Arthur, put the kettle on, son. Me and John are going to have a game of snooker.'

We went down to the far end of the club to play a frame. I'd always played any challengers in this place for my last money. Trouble was, I could never get enough money bet on myself, and I needed money at stake to make me try hard. The more money at risk, the better I played.

I once played Carl Adams with 28 points start and he beat me by three frames. But then we played for £1,000 with no handicap and I beat him, which just showed that I needed pressure to perform my best.

Even though I'd planned on going straight when I came out, I was tempted by John's job offer. Every other way of making money was a long slog for little reward. I was either burning my money down the bookies or winning as much as I could at poker and pool and snooker.

I'd yet to find a way of making a big jump in gambling to get to the next level of earnings. Prison had put my poker life on hold.

John said he'd pick me up next day, and that we were going to do a bank job. It had already been planned while I was inside and there were two other guys involved. I didn't know them but he said they were sound and that was good enough for me. I didn't expect he was going to put his freedom at risk with guys who weren't up to it. Including me. A bank job carried a long stretch.

It might seem like a strange road to go down but I'd just come out of nick and had fuck-all in every area – no money, no life, no girl, no family that I could see, no prospects. I didn't have much going for me, and even less to lose. John had a new Jag and a big house and money to burn, so I thought, why not? Deep down I knew, as always, a big part of the attraction was the buzz. The same with poker. The hit of the win and the all-in, and beating everyone at the table was what it was about for me. But I hadn't been able to get the poker buzz for a long time so the withdrawal symptoms meant I needed a big hit. And hits don't come much bigger than robbing a bank.

John left the Monica and all my mates came over to me. When I'd first walked in they'd said hello and then left us alone because I'd said we needed to talk. Now they were all looking at me as though they wanted to ask something. One of them spoke up.

He said, 'Dave? Err, that guy . . .'

I said, 'Yeah, I *know*.'

I slept easy that night. I always did. I guess it was just

natural that I didn't suffer from nerves. Or maybe I'd burned out all my nerve endings already. I'd always been into everything before anyone else – mischief, stealing, fighting, girls, gambling. I got used to risks when I was young. It served me well in poker. Some guys broke out in a sweat if they had every penny riding on a hand. With me, whatever the situation, I could hold my hand out and it was rock steady, never wavered.

Next day I was supposed to meet John on Cottingham Road. I stood by the phone box but no one turned up. There was no sign of him. I rang his house and his missus answered. She was calm but sounded worried. She said that the Regional Crime Squad had picked John up a few hours ago. He'd been followed. She said she thought he would go down again. Then she said something I'll never forget.

'They want him so bad, Dave,' she said. 'You're much better off getting along with what you do.' I wondered what she thought I had to do. Actually I had nothing to do.

I never saw John again. But, once seen, never forgotten. And, one way or another, he changed my life. He wasn't the only one. It turned out to be a good week for good luck because four days later I met someone else who would change everything.

I was going into town with the boys one night and the bus we were on went past our stop. So we got off outside a pub we'd never been in before. Rather than walk back, we went in. And that's when I first saw Mandy. There was a ladies' darts match going on with a team from Mandy's work. She wasn't playing, just sitting looking quiet and reserved. Not my usual type, but then I was guessing I wasn't her usual type either.

So, putting on all my best airs and graces, I went over to talk to her. I couldn't drop the bombshell that I'd only just walked out of prison so I told her I was a truck driver. Which I had been, in the past. I did have some intentions of going back to it now that my bank robbery career had come to an abrupt end. The driving would give me some money until I got my poker back on track.

I escorted Mandy home and she invited me in and we listened to some Simon and Garfunkel and had a glass of wine. It's amazing how quickly life changes. There I was in a nice house with a pretty girl and a glass of wine, listening to music and talking to someone I liked. It couldn't have been more different from my life for the last year – lying on the cold floor of the block in Armley, listening to the generator and eating prison slop.

Mandy and I started going out and we fell in love. I knew she was the best thing that had ever happened to me. It made me determined to knock the old life on the head and do something new. But old habits die hard. I'd still do the odd 'touch' or crack the odd safe on the side. I'd sometimes have to 'work' at night but I'd make the excuse that I was making some overnight deliveries. I had to be careful because Mandy's family were so nice and straight that I knew if I was ever pulled for anything dodgy it would be the end. Although me and her dad, John, got on fine, her mother Susan took an instant dislike to me. I wonder why.

Even though I'd been driving since I was sixteen, I still

didn't have a driving licence. Not a kosher one, anyway. Mandy insisted that I do my test. So I did, and I failed – wheel-spinning out of the test centre might not have been a good start. Over the years I'd picked up loads of bad habits, like accelerating whenever I spotted the police, so I had a few lessons to iron them out. Next time round, I passed.

Now I had a kosher licence, and was giving up my 'night jobs'. It looked like I was finally going straight. It was an odd feeling to think that my life might be changing. But I loved Mandy, we were good together, and I wanted to do right by her.

Her dad was a successful businessman. He spotted that Turner's, the last pawnbroker's in Hull, had shut up shop. We used them when we were kids, as did a lot of the estate families. They were part of life. My mate Kenny Hocking, who was a devout gambler on the horses, had a brother, Don, who was a trawler skipper. The second that Don went on a fishing trip, Kenny would grab his brother's best suits and run down the pawnbroker's with so many in his arms that you could barely see him. He'd pawn them for betting money and then go down the bookies. When he heard that Don was on his way home, he'd run round like a headless chicken trying to get money to get the suits back before Don got back from sea. He always just managed to do it.

With the last pawn shop gone, there was a gap. I had already moved into a little house in Mayfield Street with Mandy, so we decided to do it up, sell it, and put the money into a pawn shop.

But I'm the world's worst decorator – I couldn't repaint a white wall white with a tin of white paint without making it black. So I went down to the snooker hall and played a few cash games until I'd made two guys skint. I asked them to pay me back by decorating my house. Then every day I'd rush home about ten to five, chuck them out, pull on some overalls, slap a bit of paint on my face and Mandy would come home and say, 'You've been busy!'

None of this domestic stuff and the fact that I was loved-up meant that the gambling stopped. It was too deep in me. But it did change. For one thing, I started trying to plug my biggest leak: the horses. When betting on the horses there is some room to get an edge, but you have to put in a lot of time studying form.

You can't do any of those things at, say, roulette, or most casino games, because they're closed systems with limited ways to influence them. And even if you can influence them with your own skill, for example if you card-count in a casino, they'll just throw you out.

At least my weakness for the horses was the kind of betting that I could try to have more influence over. I'd passed enough cash over bookies' counters over the years. I figured it was time to start getting some coming back the other way. Plus, if I bled a lot less money to the bookies I'd be removing the major drain on my poker winnings. I decided that my time would now be split 70 per cent poker, 30 per cent horses.

Mandy's father was smart enough to know that I was a good card player and he said that he'd take a piece of my action in card games – meaning that he'd stake me in return for a share of my winnings. So if I ever needed money for a game, I had it there. John was as sharp as a tack so he wouldn't have offered unless he'd had a lot of faith in my ability. I'd sit down and shuffle decks for him and deal him out straight flushes and Aces from any part of the deck. I didn't realize it at the time, but it was a bit like an audition. I must have passed.

The reason my own dad didn't mind me playing poker was because I used to win so much. I'd have more money in my pocket than him and he used to work all the hours God sent.

Come to think of it, poker had been the only consistent thing in my life that hadn't let me down, betrayed me, grassed me up, stolen from me, kicked me in the teeth or run away. I'd kind of taken it for granted. I guess if my game had been a more physical one, like football, by thirty I'd have been a wasted talent. But there's no age limit on poker.

So now the thought of owning a pawn shop gave me the idea that it might also be an opportunity of a different kind: to use poker as my way out of trouble and my way into money. That gives some idea of the kind of life I'd lived up until then – that poker was an honest way out! For most people, poker would be a big move in the wrong direction; for me, it was like stepping onto the straight and narrow.

So, between the money from the house, the money from a few last touches I'd done, and a fair few quid I'd just won in a poker game, we got together £13,000. That's what we had to our name. I saw this old cobbler's shop on Division

Road for sale and decided it looked just the job for a pawn-broker's. The interior of the shop was covered in fine black dust from the shoe heels being sanded down there for thirty years. It was like the inside of a miner's lung. Coincidentally, the owner wanted £13,000 for it.

I said, 'Look, mate, I'll give you ten grand cash,' and put the cash on the counter in front of him. I don't think this ol' fella had seen £10,000 before. He said he'd take it.

So now I was a shop owner and local businessman. When you think about it, I'd always been on the edge of the jewellery trade anyway, since the safes I'd cracked were often full of it. I knew all about gold, silver, carat weights and hallmarks. I'd just come into jewellery from the wrong side.

Going straight isn't as easy as you think when you've been on the other side of the tracks. You think that people will be glad that you're making a go of it, but you forget that they also look at you as high risk. I couldn't get a licence to lend out money because of my past. But I found a loophole which said it was legal to lend up to £30 without a licence. So I got some tickets made up and lent out £30 at a time. If they wanted £300, I'd just give them ten tickets. That went on until Mandy, whose past was rather less colourful than my own, was granted a licence. She even made me get a TV licence. Finally, I was legit.

We got the shop open quickly with the help of my two builder mates, Jim and Ron, who ran Kirkland Builders. They loved playing cards too, so they wanted it up and running as quickly as me. And it was a success straight away.

1. Devilfish at the World Series of Poker in Las Vegas in 1997.

2. Devilfish and Mandy on their wedding day in Hull in 1985.

3. Devilfish on the opening day of his pawnbroker shop in 1985.

4. Devilfish as Grand Champion of the Jack Binion World Poker Open with Isabelle Mercier at the World Poker Tour in Tunica, Mississippi, 2003.

5. Devilfish pictured with Mimi Rogers in Las Vegas.

6. James Woods and Devilfish.

The Devilfish leaps to his feet in triumph as he wins his World Series of Poker gold bracelet. Gary, his companion and driver for ten years, celebrates beside him

7. Devilfish winning the WSOP in 1997.

8. Devilfish in Memphis with Ben Affleck.

9. Devilfish with Ricky 'Hitman' Hatton.

10. Barry Hearne, Devilfish and Steve Davis in 2006.

By now I'd been playing cards around Hull for over fourteen years and, though I always used to do well at the game, I'd never really concentrated on it until now. But now I'd been painted into a corner by a few things – my would-be fellow bank robber being picked up by the RCS, my other partners in crime grassing me up, meeting Mandy. As my other life had gone tits-up, luckily I had another one waiting to take over. Full-time gambler.

The difference was that I now had a bit of a safety net. Before, when I'd thrown away everything in the bookies, I'd have to crack a safe to get money to fund the gambling. Now I didn't have to do that.

I played cards with my brother and I'd win off him, so then I'd have him do some work for me in the shop. Then I'd play him again and win some more. That kept the wage bill down. So much for brotherly love.

I quickly got a poker game going above the shop. We mostly played 5- or 7-Card Stud, which were my best games. But then it was my joint. I'd played plenty of dives in Hull so I wanted to make it better than that. I was going to be playing there a lot, for one thing, so I made it a little home from home. Mandy would put out a great spread of food to keep the players happy and playing – it always feels a little bit easier losing on a full stomach. I even shared out a magnum of champagne among the players. It never hurt to have a bit too much alcohol in the other players' systems. It's rare for the house not to take a cut – the house usually takes a share from each pot: the rake – but I didn't charge a shilling. Word got round and players came over. All I had to do was beat them.

Not charging rake meant that I had to rely on winning, which meant that I was always outnumbered because it was everyone against me. I had to beat them all to not lose. But it's impossible to avoid anyone in a small game, so it's nice to have an edge if someone decides to hit and run – bail out early with a big sack of winnings. And this is where the dogs came in. If someone decided to leave too soon I'd say they had to go out the back way. That was through a yard patrolled by my two hounds, a Rottweiler called Roxy and a Dobermann called Sultan. Early-leavers tended to return to the table.

We'd usually end up playing through the night and still be going the next morning when the shop opened.

It was interesting, being a pawnbroker. Every oddball in the area seemed to have something to sell. We had every mental case, chancer, con artist and vagrant stepping through the doors – it was a human zoo. Opening a pawnbroker's is a good way of meeting a wide selection of people . . . that you might never want to see again. Most of them offering things you definitely don't want to see again. I mean, what was I going to do with a glass eye or a false leg?

I didn't miss an opportunity to have a bet with customers, especially if I knew the odds beforehand. I used to have a curling bar behind the counter – a little weight-lifting bar. I'd practise with this thing to the point where I could do about fifty. And whenever the gypsies came to Hull they'd come into my shop to wager on curling the bar. I'd make sure that I only just managed a few more curls than they did so they'd come back for more. One of the travellers was a huge hairy geezer who looked like Hagrid in the *Harry Potter* films. He talked really fast and mostly in swear words. He made me sound like Mother fucking Teresa. He just couldn't get his head round the fact that I was half his size but beat him at bar-curling, so he came back again and again.

The shop became a cross between a jeweller's, a drop-in centre, a psychiatric ward, a comedy show, a three-ring circus and a parole board meeting. My kind of place.

The reason I had a good name was because I never dropped anybody in it, ever, and always stood up in a fight. So even though the shop was full of valuable gold and diamond jewellery, I didn't get any trouble from the hard cases or the thieves . . . I was friends with most of them, and the dogs took care of the rest.

I met up again with my good mate Pete Robinson when he got out of Armley. Pete had been accused of planning a wages job on a big factory and he did a year on remand but eventually got a not guilty. He was a handy little tool with a massive heart, and I trusted him with my life. There were only two things that scared Pete: my dogs and my driving. He was a ballsy fucker but he wasn't stupid. He never stroked them but they got used to him – and they decided not to eat him. The only time he probably felt less safe was when he was out in a fast car with me.

Mandy bought me a beautiful cream Jaguar convertible. It looked the bollocks. I took Pete out in it one day when he had a bit of trouble over the river, so we went over the Humber Bridge. We sorted it out but we had to get out of the area fast. I drove back with the top down at 120mph. Pete clung on for dear life to the arm rest.

I said, 'What do you think, Pete?'

Eventually he said, 'Dave? . . . It's fucking scary, man.'

There was always money to be made from something other than ordinary work. The only nine-to-five I could handle was the odds on a horse. I played for both a snooker team and a pool team, and I'd hustle with both games to raise poker cash.

After I'd opened the pawnbroker's, I took my brother Paul under my wing and had him working for me. I was also managing a snooker player called Kev Ashby. He'd come to Hull to play one day, and his 141 break was one of the best I'd ever seen. I signed him up. I knew he could be professional. It could be a way into big money. A lot of the snooker guys were discovered playing in backstreet dives – Alex Higgins was the biggest backstreet snooker street fighter of all, and he won two world championships. And one day Ken Hooper, a regular at the club, bumped into Higgins in a local bookies and actually brought him into the Monica in disguise to hustle some matches. (Not too good a disguise, obviously.) Higgins played Les Talbot, and Les still hasn't recovered.

Kev always played better when he was behind rather than out in front. Some players can chase well but panic when being chased. I'd seen guys in poker make a final table and then panic all their chips into a hole because they couldn't stand the pressure of the bigger league. My problem was I couldn't stand *not* being in a bigger league and I'd lose my money trying to generate more action.

I brought Kev to the Monica and I introduced Kev to a good friend of mine, Eddie Lilly. We used to call him Fast Eddie after Fast Eddie Felson, the famous American pool player. So when I offered Eddie fourteen points' start against Kev, everybody there wanted some of the action.

Kev beat Eddie. So then I had Kev give Eddie a start of twenty-one points. I had to do that to get people to shove their money in again after the first game. Everyone wanted Eddie to win and twenty-one looked a good start. But wanting something to happen counts for nothing in the first frame.

Fast Eddie made a break of fourteen. Then Kev stood up and cleared every ball on the table and went on to win the match 5 to 4.

I got Kev travelling round playing cash games, even down to London. When you've got a player as talented as Kevin, you have to keep moving to avoid being caught hustling. It isn't really cheating – there's nothing wrong in disguising a good player – but if people feel they've been conned they'll react badly.

It was something closer to home, though, that screwed everything up. We went over the bridge to a match in Scunthorpe and Kev lost, which was unusual. Afterwards he confessed that he'd been threatened in the toilets by some guys who supported his opponent. That's when I dissolved our partnership. If Kev couldn't believe that I'd look after him, then he was no good to me.

Soon after, the snooker hustling came back to haunt

me when two guys came hunting for me in the shop. They'd been sent down by a club owner that me and Kev had hustled out of a lot of money. Afterwards, he'd found out about Kev's history and now, according to his two money collectors, he wanted his cash back. They threatened me with all sorts but I surprised them with a re-raise: I said, 'Okay, I'll shut up the shop and take the both of you outside.' They looked at each other and started backing off, literally, until they ended up outside, then they fucked off.

The geezer phoned me up and started throwing more threats at me. I happened to have a gun in the shop.

I said, 'Listen, son, if you send anyone else down, they better have bigger balls or thicker vests,' and I held the receiver out as I fired a shot into the settee. It sounded like a cannon going off in the room. I'd definitely killed the settee. I think on the other end of the line he shat himself.

I told him to meet me at the local William Hill's if he wanted to take it further. I said I'd be there in one hour. Me and Boothy went down there tooled up, but nobody showed.

All that was left to do was explain the smoking hole in the furniture to Mandy.

The shop did well enough to move to new premises in Hessle Road – the fishing area. Dock towns tend to be rough and this was no different. But, despite what you might think, I ran a straight shop, no dodgy business. There were a lot of nice people around us, good working-class folk who worked hard for their money but sometimes needed a little breather.

I got a new safe for the new shop. It was a massive Chubb Banker, major league, and it was sunk in concrete in the floor. To open a Chubb Banker you had to drill holes in the side of the safe around the main barrel of the lock and put a little camera in to see inside and then put prods in to get at the lock tumblers and reset the combination . . . not that I knew anything about that kind of thing: I'd never opened anything anywhere near as big.

By now, me and Mandy were married with a child, another boy I was proud of, Stephen. So I had my new life, my new wife and a new boy. And the freedom to do the thing I'd always really only ever wanted to do, which was play cards.

Things were still far from perfect, though, as usual in my life. Sue had left Liverpool with Paul and Kerry, and I hadn't been told where they'd gone so I couldn't get in touch.

They say that behind every successful man there's a good woman. Well, behind every successful poker player there's either a really pissed-off woman or a very understanding one. I was lucky with Mandy – she was understanding about the kind of life a gambler has to live. She didn't create a fuss and she always had faith in my poker playing. Even when I went broke and raided the safe. If you've never gone broke then you've never really played. However good you are, things can always go wrong. So I'd have to start all over again.

This was still at a time when gambling was seen as

dodgy and disreputable. Poker was something that was played in the shadows in either little illegal backstreet joints or late at night in local casinos. It was always behind the scenes or underground. That's why poker players led such strange lives – when other people were getting up for work, we were just going to bed; when people were going to bed, we were just going out.

Like vampires, gamblers are always on the nightshift.

11. Gunning for Aces

A widening circle of fuck-ups

There are different kinds of prison. Like the nine-to-five. Like sitting behind a shop counter all day long. There were plenty of interesting times there, but I couldn't stand being confined in one place. I felt like an animal in a cage. In prison you don't expect anything else, but here on the outside I felt like I was watching the world go past.

I wasn't working alone for too long – thank God. Though Mandy was pregnant, she had a good job and stayed there for as long as possible as we needed the money. It was great when our son Stephen was born, I felt better having my wife and son with me.

Stephen was so good-looking he won the Bonniest Baby in Hull competition. (I know what you're thinking, but, yes, he was definitely mine.) Soon our next son Christopher arrived and we had two lovely boys knocking fuck out of each other around the shop.

But, although life was great, I was becoming bored with the role of full-time shopkeeper. Now Mandy had her licence and was working at the shop, I had an escape clause. I could get out and play.

I became much stronger at poker this time. The restriction of the shop had made me focus. I couldn't run around playing every game, so I concentrated on cleaning out the games I could play in. Even before the shop opened I was able to beat just about everybody. It's nice when you've got back-up, though. And not just financial back-up: people who stand behind you. It's always nice when you can gamble and you know you won't end up homeless or have an empty fridge; it's the fear of losing that stops you progressing by not being able to take the risks that you need to take to learn. So it wasn't until I got married and went straight that I could really go for it, and as a result I started to win big – I was mopping them all up.

I still ran a private game from our house behind the shop. And I'd still carry it on right through to the next day. That could mean rich pickings for me and though I ran it as a straight game, it gave me a certain amount of control over . . . circumstances, shall we say. A friend of mine, Phil Gittens, used to come round to play, and he loved a drink, did Phil. He was great at pool, even when drunk, but he wasn't a very good poker player. He'd usually lose but one night he played for two hours and he caught every card in the deck. He couldn't miss. No matter how bad a hand he was holding, he was catching miracle cards and outdrawing everyone.

He won all the money and then said he wanted to go. The dogs were asleep so I couldn't even use the backyard trick. I said that he should hang on a bit and maybe give the lads the chance to win their money back but he said he wanted to go because there was no more drink. We were clean out of booze. I asked Mandy if there was anything left in the house and she said there was a magnum of champagne left over from our wedding.

I broke out the champagne for Phil and the lads, but made sure Phil got most of it. I handed out champagne glasses to all the boys, and that was a weird sight – a roomful of red-eyed, rough-looking, wasted poker players holding dinky little champagne glasses like they were at Ascot.

Phil got a half-pint of champagne. He did lose all his money back, but I'd never seen anyone so happy to do it.

Remember, once the game begins . . . no friends in poker, baby, no friends in poker. You can go back to being friends after the smoke clears and the dead have been buried and the wounded have crawled away. Or been sent home in a 57 Taxis minicab.

Whenever I did get charitable in poker, I just ended up getting fucked over.

One night a few years earlier a game had started up above my friend's café. I would have loved to have played, but as usual back then I'd done my money on the horses. I was messing around on the pool table, playing for £20 a time. Now the other players had built the poker game around this guy from the casino who didn't know what he was doing, he'd somehow managed to win £6,000 on roulette, more by accident than design. So some of the lads in the casino had brought him round for a game. Which is a bit like a herd of hungry lions asking an antelope if it wanted to go to dinner.

I was knocking balls around on the pool table, watching. The lions' den was in full effect. This wasn't a con because it was a straight-up game, so the guy wasn't a mark, but he was in the middle of a fucking big hustle. Then again, hustling is like card-counting, it ain't illegal and it ain't cheating. I knew the guy was about to be eaten alive and I was trying to see how I could get some of the action. Not exactly easy when you're not even in the game.

He'd lost about £5,000 when he decided to go for a piss. The only piss he should've been going for was the 'off' kind, but he'd obviously decided to stay. I did feel a bit sorry for the guy. Not being in the game had given me time to think. And remember, even though they were all mates in the game, we were all still enemies at the poker table.

I followed this guy into the toilet to talk to him, which isn't an easy thing for a man to do if you're not George Michael. But there was £6,000 involved here. He was obviously a well-brought-up bad gambler because he was washing his hands.

I said, 'You know you've got no shot at winning in that game, don't you?'

He said, 'Yeah, I know.'

I said, 'Why don't you let me play for you?'

He said, 'Well, can you play?'

I said, 'I can play fucking better than you, mate.'

He said, 'OK. Can I sit behind you when you're playing?'

I said, 'Course you can. You can sit on my fucking knee if you want. Shall we talk about what percentage I'm gonna get?'

He said, 'Don't worry, I'll look after you.'

A so-called streetwise kid like me should have found out exactly what that meant.

He just looked relieved that he wasn't going to lose everything. So I sat down at the game and took over his seat, much to the disgust of my fellow players. Then the Ulliott magic kicked in and I won all of his six grand back. Much to the even greater disgust of my fellow players, who looked at me as though I'd just pissed in their soup. Which in a way, I had – poker style.

The guy now had his £6,000 back, and he gave me . . . two hundred quid. I couldn't believe it. I thought his 'I'll look after you' would mean at least a grand.

I thought how I could manoeuvre this back to a payday. I asked him if he wanted a couple of games of pool. We played for £100 a game and I managed to build up to £500 before he realized he had less chance at pool than he did at Stud poker. So now I had £500 to play with. One of the card players there was a little guy from Glasgow called Hughie, who looked a bit like Dr Crippen: skinny with round glasses. Hughie asked the guy which card game he liked and he said his favourite was 3-Card Brag. Now just because something is your favourite game, doesn't mean you're good at it. And that was the case with this geezer. In fact, I don't think he had a game in him that he was good at, except the losing game and the pissing me off game. He was pretty good at both those.

Hughie and I offered to play him at Brag. It took us about half an hour to take his remaining £5,500. He was totally skint, which is what he deserved after he'd only given me two hundred quid.

He started getting desperate. He said, 'Do you want to give me some money back so I can have a game with you?'

I said, 'What's the point in that? What have you got I can buy off you?'

He said he had a TV in his flat. So I gave him some money back as payment for his house contents and we played again. And he lost it all back to me too. Now he looked worried. He knew I could go around to his gaff and clear it out. I said that I didn't want to see him go home skint but as he'd only given me two hundred quid, I was going to give him two hundred quid back – plus I wouldn't take any house contents. But on one condition. I said that any time I wanted to use his place to crash after a game, or any time I wanted to run a poker game there, he'd have to let me use it. He said that was OK. I knew where he lived and it was a posh area so it was a real touch for me to get a time-share.

There were a couple of other occasions when I won all the stuff in someone's house. It's amazing what people will bet with when they get desperate. I was playing with a bloke called John down in East Hull, and both him and a mate had gone there to try and fleece me. My reputation was getting to the stage where people saw me as a challenge. Bragging rights were already part of the pot.

They hadn't properly taken into account the full scale of the Ulliott magic. I not only won their money, but won John's TV, stereo, sofa, dining table, and just about everything I could carry out of his house bar his wife, his kids and the dog. At one point he tried to raise me with the dog.

The next morning, after we'd been playing all night in his house, this guy's wife and kids came downstairs, and the kids started asking if they could watch the telly. I couldn't take any of his stuff. It wasn't made easier by the fact that I now had three kids of my own with Mandy: Stephen, Christopher and Michael. Michael had been born in January, the best New Year's present.

It's unbelievable what people will risk when they just want a chance to get their money back. It never occurs to them that if they were any good they wouldn't be in that position to begin with. When you beat people out in that way it always seemed to be someone you didn't want to do it to. Some people you wouldn't mind being in debt to you, but I could never find a six-foot, leggy blonde Marilyn Monroe lookalike stripper who played poker.

Gambling can drive people to that kind of desperation; that's just the way it is, and the way it'll always be. I'd been down and broke and on my uppers, too. Everyone at some time gets down in the hole. But I'd always scrapped and fought my way back out. Some never do. But I'd never had any money offered back to me by a casino or a bookie. At least I had some sympathy for the loser.

My play had improved to the point where I couldn't get a game locally. I was taking too much money off the local gambling fraternity. In fact, the cheeky bastards started arranging games and not telling me where they were. I had to find out and just turn up. But it was a blessing in disguise because it drove me out of Hull in search of other games.

I found out about a game in Leeds and one Friday night I drove across to the Stakis Casino with my mate Shaun.

Shaun could handle himself, and was a fearless gambler, so we made a good team.

Straight away I liked the vibe of the place. I'd always felt at home in casinos. For much of my life they've been like a second home . . . that is, if your home is full of pasty-faced gamblers, smoking, drinking, arguing and losing all their money and bitching about it.

I didn't know it at the time, but I made an important discovery in Leeds. Up until then I'd been playing 7-Card Stud, 5-Card Stud, 3-Card Brag, various forms of draw poker . . . and Snap. But I learned that to survive in these dealer's-choice cash games you had to learn Omaha (4-, 5- or 6-Card), 7-Card Hi-Lo, Irish, Paduki, Omaha Hi-Lo, and lots more.

Watching the play in Leeds opened my eyes. I noticed a Greek guy, Bambas, playing a big pot against a guy called Jeff Crone (Big Jeff). And because the stakes were higher and the games were bigger it meant that on a good night you could win what it might take you a week to earn in Hull. These kind of big wins would have emptied the tanks of too many of the players back home.

So I'd found the bigger games. And I also had another Big John kind of a moment when I risked upsetting someone I really shouldn't have. A seat came free on a table so I sat down opposite this guy I thought looked South American. I started calling him 'Pedro the Bandit'. I'd always given verbal to other players equally: everybody got it.

Pedro just smiled back at me. I could tell he wasn't happy at all. He wasn't big physically but he was a little pit bull and I could see he'd be a proper handful. I noticed some of the other players glancing at me.

I took a break from the game and a guy who had been watching us play came over to talk to me. This was the second important thing that would happen to me in Leeds because this guy was Gary Whitaker who would become a really good friend of mine and end up travelling the world with me playing poker. As he told people later, when Gary had first seen me walk into the casino he'd wondered who this cocky-looking fucker was, and then he'd seen me play and how aggressive I was at the table. So he came over to say hi and give me a heads-up about Pedro. It was a valuable bit of advice, as it happened, because 'Pedro' was actually a Moroccan called Mulla, and not at all a man to be messed with. He ran a lot of doormen and a local security firm and he knew all the faces in the area, mostly because he was one.

What Gary was telling me was that Mulla would be a lot better to have as a friend than an enemy. Winding him up was clearly a hand that had no value. Mulla did have the look of a heavy dude about him, and it turned out to be more than just a 'look'.

So I got talking to Mulla and we got on really well. I'd even end up playing private games at his house. He was a respectful guy if you were the same to him but he obviously wasn't someone to cross. Over the years I'd found that once I got talking to people, whatever walk of life they were from, I'd find something in common with them, even if it was just having a laugh.

So Leeds was an eye-opener. Sometimes you need

exposure to new challenges to be able to improve your game. And there were some strong players there like Bambas, Mulla, Kareem and Max, Chris Walker, Big Jeff, Manchester George and a guy I nicknamed Norman the Tatter, because he was a scrap metal dealer.

Things didn't always go smoothly, but when in my life had they ever? I played every Friday in Leeds – usually driving down with Shaun – and at first ended up donating most of my money because these new games were tricky until you mastered them. After a few months of learning, I started going with Gary to different venues like Napoleon's Casino in Bradford, where I played in a few tournaments but mostly in bigger cash games. A lot of the Leeds crowd went there as well, and there was a new set of players to play against, like George Weinberg, Andrew Chambi, and a good friend of Mulla's called Michael Georgiou, who was a gentleman and one of the fixtures of the local scene.

The trouble was, the casino reserved all the dealers for blackjack, roulette, etc., everything but the cash poker games. So the poker players would end up sitting there like lemons, itching to play but unable to because they couldn't find us a dealer. One night I got so pissed off that I staged a walkout; about ten of us left to go and play at one player's house. The manager wasn't happy about this so he stopped me at the door and said that if I walked out and took everyone with me, I'd never play there again. I just laughed, so he banned me. I knew it was fixable. I rang Mulla. He said he'd sort it out – I think it involved a confrontation in a car park and someone being put in a headlock – and the next thing you know, I was back in the casino. And we had some cash-game dealers.

Nowadays Napoleon's has more poker tournaments than most casinos, and looks after its players. It was in Bradford that Mulla and me became closer – I'd had a disagreement with some of the locals and Mulla asked if I needed any help. I put his hand on my jacket so he could feel the gun, and winked. I'd earned his respect.

We'd often end up going back to someone's house to play anyway. We would meet at the casino for a tournament, play a bit of cash, and then set up a house game. These didn't usually start until about three or four in the morning. Whoever was with me, Gary or one of the other fellas, would kip on the sofa while I was playing. When the sun came up and the game broke up, I could go back to Hull with a fresh driver who wouldn't fall asleep at the wheel and slam us into a motorway bridge. Sometimes I'd kip in the car. A lot of the time I was still buzzing, especially if I had a brick of notes in my jacket. The further I travelled out of Hull the less I could go back there to play. So if I wanted another game, Gary would drive to another city.

Eventually, I'd get back into Hull. When everyone else was going out to work, I'd go to my favourite café and have a full English breakfast. The place would be full of workers and commuters and truck drivers having their fry-ups and teas and reading the morning papers; I'd be sat there in the corner in a black leather jacket, shades on, with a good few grand in my pocket, just getting ready to wind down and go home to bed when everyone else was gearing up for the day.

As I said, poker players often live like vampires. Whenever I saw a film about Dracula, I'd think I know just how you feel. I didn't get to bite any virgins, but then I didn't have people trying to put a stake through my heart either, so it was swings and roundabouts. But round our way there weren't that many virgins around. On the estate you'd see a banner hung outside a house saying 'Happy 21st Birthday Grandma!'

My reputation meant that I'd always been able to play poker in Hull without it being too dangerous for me, but moving out to play in Leeds, Bradford, Birmingham and Manchester was far more risky. These cities had areas and games as tough as Hull's, but no one in them knew me. Most of the street fights I'd had before and the danger I'd faced had had nothing to do with poker, it had been in town and in pubs and clubs.

But now the danger from the street started moving into the games.

12. Have Gun, Will Travel

You don't have to have a gun to play here — but it helps

One night I went over to Bradford looking for a game and ended up in a Pakistani-run game in Manningham at a place called Pappa's. The entrance was down a dark alley. Gary was with me and he wasn't too happy about this, but I'd heard there was money flying around. When it came to playing cash poker games, I didn't care where they were. I'd have been the last guy off the *Titanic* if there'd been a game going on.

It was the middle of winter and even the icicles had icicles. We climbed some rickety stairs to a door that looked like it had been attacked by a madman with a machete. We walked in to the smell of damp and gas fumes. Good combination. If the killer mushrooms didn't get you, the gas leak would. It was so cold and wet that there were fish in the mousetraps and the rats wore fur coats over their fur coats. This was the first 'dive' I'd been in that was so damp it had a lifeguard.

The place was full of mostly Asian players crowded round a table or crashed out on old sofas. I got a seat to play. Everyone got £100 in chips and put the rest in cash on the table. I quickly started to clean up. But it looked like I'd have to beat every player in the area because every time I bust one guy, another guy would appear and sit down. Everyone but me was smoking. So between the gas fumes and the cig smoke, if Gary moved more than two feet away I couldn't see him. The other players all spoke Punjabi and only changed to English if they wanted to have a go at me. They probably thought I was an easy mark but I was breaking them all at two, three, four hundred quid a time. By the end of the night I'd bust about fifteen of them.

The only two other non-Asian guys I saw play the game were George Weinberg and Norman the Tatter. He was a good old boy, was George. When we first met we didn't see eye to eye, probably 'cos I was taller than him. But we came to get on just fine. He was like me because wherever there was a money game, George (and Norman) would be there.

Pappa himself was the skinniest guy I'd ever seen, like a pipe cleaner on two matchsticks. He rattled in the wind coming through the keyhole. He was always there, watching over things. Except one time when he went to Pakistan for a couple of weeks to see his family. When he came back, he was all bandaged up – he'd been shot in the leg.

'Pappa,' I said, 'that guy must have been the best fucking shot in Pakistan if he managed to hit your leg. I hope they've got that guy on your Olympic shooting team.'

One night, Gary was so tired from all the travelling we'd been doing that he needed to sleep. Pappa pointed to a bed with just a bare mattress in the corner of a back room. It looked like a herd of cows had already slept on it and shat on it. There was also a blanket standing

against the wall and a pillow doing a slow crawl across
the floor.

Anyway, Gary looked at this bed, looked at me, then
looked at Pappa and said, 'Err . . . I've woken up a bit
now . . .' There's nothing like the thought of getting TB
off a diseased mattress to perk you right up.

As usual, no one had massive money in the game but
as soon as one chair emptied it would be filled by someone else jumping in. So the total money going across the
table built up to a healthy stash. I won well. It was chips
and cash, mostly cash. By the time I was changing the
chips up at the end with Pappa it was five on a winter's
morning and everyone else had gone.

We went to leave, walking through the little kitchen
area to get to the back fire escape. I had a feeling something wasn't right. I stopped at the back door, told Gary
to wait, and turned the light off. I waited until my eyes
got used to the dark before I opened the door. As we
walked out onto the wooden staircase I could hear whispering in the alley. Gary was right behind me.

He said, 'Dave?'

I whispered, 'Quiet.'

He whispered, 'What?'

I whispered, 'Shush.'

He whispered, 'Why we whispering?'

I put my finger to my lips, then I turned back to face
the alley, put my hand inside my jacket, pulled out my gun
and squeezed a shot off into the air. The massive bang
echoed down the alley like a fucking thunderbolt hitting
a stick of dynamite. I was expecting it – and it still shocked

the fuck out of me. Everyone hidden in the alley ran like mad, knocking over dustbins and tripping over each other. Then I heard a thud behind me.

I turned round and Gary was practically sliding down the door having a heart attack.

I'd had the gun on me before but I'd never pulled it out and Gary didn't even know it existed. But he did now. We ran down the alley and jumped into the car. The sound of the shot was still echoing over half of Bradford. I winked at Gary, blew the smoke off the end of the barrel and in my best John Wayne voice said, 'Let's git rollin', boy!'

He said, 'Where the fuck did you get that?'

I said, 'It's a "need to know", son.'

He said, 'Right. OK. So where to now?'

I said, 'The next game.'

There was still money to be won. After sitting on my arse in Pappa's for hours on end, breathing in the stench of cigarette smoke, gas fumes and other people's sweat, there was no way on earth I was letting my winnings go. I would have fought every fucker in that alley hand to hand with nothing more than a dustbin lid and half a kebab. But if firing one shot into the air can save you all that trouble then it seemed silly not to. I know it was a bit lazy, but gimme a break – I'd had a long night.

We went straight over to Leeds to a game in Chapel-town, which wasn't the kind of area you wanted to go jogging through at night. Not unless you were a world-class sprinter. With a bulletproof vest.

I didn't always take a gun to games because I didn't always have to. Because if you flashed it about the odd time, then word got round that you were sometimes carrying. And if anyone was going to rob anyone then they'd not choose you. Also, I had a good posse of guys who used to ride shotgun for me – Gary Whitaker, Gary Young, Les Houseman (the Stud player), Tony Booth (the boxer), Pat Hughes, Scotch Sandy and Shaun.

Most people who get robbed at card games are set up by someone in the game or someone watching. It's never an unconnected raid. They always know what or who they're looking for. The problem is, you don't always know what or who you're playing with.

After my first encounter with it, I soon picked up Texas Hold'em. It was actually easier than other poker games I'd been playing: Omaha was a lot more complicated, especially 6-Card Omaha, because you had so many combinations, plus you've got to use two of the cards you're dealt to make your final hand, so Omaha was a hard game to get your head round. I'd developed into what I thought was a pretty good Omaha player . . .

Actually this modesty thing doesn't suit me, does it? OK, I'll start again: I'd developed into a fucking good Omaha player. One of the best. I'd take anyone on. And I knew I probably had room to get even better. So I knew if I could master Omaha, then Hold'em would be easy.

Tournaments weren't a big deal to me but they were good places to find players to generate cash games. One of the first tournaments I ever played was one that I also won – I went over to Liverpool and entered a 7-Card

Stud tournament. The winnings were only a few thousand, but the real action started afterwards in the cash games. A lot of players would have been satisfied with the tournament win but to me the winnings were only a stake for the cash games.

Poker looks easy when you're not doing it. I knew from the off I was never a lucky poker player – some players are and some aren't – but I was aggressive and I was good. Like every other player, I was always gunning for Aces, hoping those bullets were gonna come down for me. But I soon learned that they were a curse for me – I'd get them, the money would go in, and I'd hardly ever win with them. They're a curse because they have to be played.

A lot of my drivers and guys who rode shotgun with me got into poker and then found it wasn't exactly easy and found it difficult to get out. It can become addictive.

But being a good player is like being a good lover, you need stamina as well as technique. Fortunately I had both. It wasn't unusual for me to play cash games for three solid days at a time. And, before you ask, no, I didn't take anything to keep me going. I'd had a bit of weed in prison but the only Coke I knew came in bottles with bubbles. And no player I knew of did it either. It was just strength, stamina, buckets of coffee, matchsticks under the eyelids and the natural buzz.

I'd get into marathon games with players like Sammy Farha, a Lebanese poker player. Sammy was always great value in a game, he'd set a game on fire for you with aggressive play. So it was a miracle that the matches we were in together lasted as long as they did. Over the years me and Sammy would have many wars at the table.

Now I was travelling even further for even bigger games. I hit London, and as well as the Christmas Cracker tournament at the Victoria Casino I started playing other events like the Festival of Poker, the Spring Classic, the European Open and the October Festival.

When I wanted to track down a cash game, I was like a bloodhound. I'd travel anywhere and at any time. For example, if someone had said to me that there were five different games in five different cities all in one night, I'd have probably said, 'Yeah, I'll do that.'

But that's mad, isn't it? I mean, who would really do that?

13. Midnight to Midnight: the Five-City Run

I love it when a plan comes together

You gamblers out there, the proper ones – you know who you are – you can sit back and enjoy the ride for the next few pages because I know that you know what I'm talking about, and you know that I know you've been there. Everybody else? Buckle up for a bit of a steep learning curve. This ride may not be suitable for small children, tall dwarfs, pregnant ladies, fat lads, people with weak hearts, bow-legged women, knock-kneed men and anyone with a side-parting.

You've got to remember that gamblers like *action*, it's what they live for, and I was an action gambler. I knew there were games going on out there and I wanted to be in them. I wanted to be in all of them. I knew I was more than good enough to clean those games out. And when you get better and better at something, your world gradually gets bigger and bigger. Your little home-town world expands. That's how it was with me and poker: the better I got and the bigger I played, the further away from home I had to go to get any action.

The action is where it's at. In the way that sex addicts search out sex, junkies search out drugs and women sniff out chocolate, gamblers search for action. On the nights that I didn't go out playing, I'd be thinking about the games I should be playing. The pots out there that I could be taking down.

Get this straight – gamblers gamble. It's not rocket science. I've known gamblers who if they couldn't find a card game then they'd bet on horses; if every horse dropped dead they'd bet on dogs; if the dogs all got rabies they'd bet on cats, and rats; and if the cats ate all the rats and died of plague, then they'd bet on two flies fucking on a cherry on a cream bun. You've heard of gamblers who'll bet on two raindrops running down a piece of glass? Well, that's nothing, that's only a two-drop race (with no chance for an each-way). We'd bet the whole window – it was like the Raindrop Grand National.

Don't forget: gamblers don't bet for the money, they bet for the betting. They bet for the buzz. I'll give you a for-instance: an ordinary punter might get lucky and turn £100 into £1,000 but then he'll quit because he's nine times up on his original stake, and he'll be really happy. He quits because he starts thinking:

1) what it would be like to lose £1,000;
2) what he could buy with £1,000;
3) how long he would have to slave at work to earn £1,000.

And that's where ordinary punters clock off. Mentally, they cash in their winnings very early. They do the smart thing for a non-gambler: they quit while they're ahead. They can't take it any further because they'd start leaving their normal life too far behind and might not get back to it. And that's scary. But it isn't scary if you've never had a normal life. And that point – the sensible punter's quitting point – that's where a gambler is just getting started. A gambler doesn't have a normal life to leave behind.

You see, a real gambler would look at that £1,000 only as a bankroll for winning £10,000 with an eye to turning it into £100,000. It's a start, not a finish. And what bothers the ordinary punter doesn't bother him at all.

He doesn't care about losing £1,000 because he's done it so many times before, and, anyway, however many times he's lost before, a gambler's brain will only let him remember about one-tenth of the true number.

He doesn't care what he could buy with £1,000 because in the grand scheme of things £1,000 is fuck-all and what use are things that you buy anyway – try dragging a washing machine into a bookies and see what it'll get you: a bad back and some funny looks.

And how long it would take him to earn a grand at work doesn't even enter into it because gambling *is* his work. So any gambler who *didn't* try to turn that £1,000 into £10,000 or more would just be workshy. Or, worse, guilty of not thinking big.

The buzz still meant more than the money. When I used to climb over roofs to empty safes it was for the buzz as much as anything. The money wasn't *really* important. I only needed the money to gamble more in order to chase the buzz. That was the drug. The buzz could come from anything exciting. I realized I'd always needed it and sometimes even put myself in dangerous positions to get it. At least gambling didn't carry a prison sentence, though it could be just as dangerous.

I loved the anticipation of a night out and the ritual of getting ready. I'd get dressed, count out my bankroll, lay out my money and my knuckle duster. And the gun if I was taking it. I'd phone round and see what was going on, who'd popped up. I'd see who was going out, who was broke, who was flush, who was in jail, who was up for riding with me. Sometimes there'd be no one. But I absolutely loved it when I walked outside and climbed into my car. Most times Gary would pick me up, but sometimes I'd jump in the car and just drive off alone.

The circle I travelled to get games was widening. The level of play was getting better and the stakes higher, which was good because it forced your game to improve, and it also meant that when I won, I won big. I'd now entered over twenty tournaments at the Victoria Casino alone and had money finishes in ten of them. In 1996 I had my first decent tournament win when I got first place and £11,325 prize money in the Pot Limit Hold'em European Open Championship. Not bad for £100 entrance fee. I got third the next month in the No Limit Hold'em European Open and won £15,600.

But I hadn't yet left all my old ways behind. I was still a bit of a maniac for going on what I called the smash-and-grab raids around the north. I'd hit these lower-stakes poker games hard and fast most weekends and try to hoover up as much cash as I could. Gary would pick me up and we'd start out on yet another game hunt. One particular night, though, turned into something a bit mental, even by my standards.

When we set off from Hull that Friday evening it was already dark because it was winter and it was freezing and slashing it down with rain. Typical cheery English scene, then. If we'd been in America, we might have been heading down Route 66 with the top down. Instead we were aquaplaning down the M18 with the heater on.

As usual Gary was driving and, as usual, I was talking ten to the dozen on the phone, ringing ahead to find a game. One hour and sixty miles later we were in Bonapartes in Sheffield. But it was an action game, and that's all that mattered.

I sat there with rain steaming off me for the first five minutes, and over the next few hours I hammered the fuck out of every player there. Poker players are not the most attractive bunch at the best of times but they all look as pretty as a picture when you're leaving them behind potless at a table you've just cleaned out. It's not about how you carry the wins, though, but how you carry the losses. Big wins can make you walk on water; big losses can hammer you into the ground like a tent peg. But only if you let yourself care. As long as you realize that *money means nothing*, you're ahead.

We left Sheffield at midnight with me about three grand ahead and set off for home. But I knew I had more good games in me, and everything felt right – it felt like one of those times when you should take advantage of how well you're rolling. Gary thought we should call it a night.

I was ringing round everywhere, looking for the next game. I found it.

'Nottingham, Gaz!' I said. He gave me one of those looks. He knew we were going to a Chinese Triad-run game. Their idea of a Chinese takeaway is to get your arms and legs and take them away from the rest of your body. Put it this way: you wouldn't want them running a crèche.

You can see how driving through the night towards this game might have not been first on Gary's wish list, but forty minutes and forty miles later, we were there. The game was being played in a private house around a big table, and the game was 5-Card Stud. 5-Card Stud is the game that's usually seen in old cowboy films – it started out in the Old West – but it isn't played much any more. It was my best game – I'd been playing it for twenty years. Anyway, I'd play any kind of poker with any player, any place. Even in a Chinese Triad kitchen full of knives, choppers, meat cleavers – and an egg whisk. Don't laugh. If it stuck where the sun don't shine – that would be a bad 'beat'.

The place was full of Chinese guys (surprise, surprise), and there's no one on earth with a better poker face than a Chinaman. You could set off a firework in their boxers and they wouldn't twitch a nostril hair. Trying to get a 'tell' of these fellas was like flogging a dead horse. Which, funnily enough, they were already doing in the kitchen.

Everyone turned to look at us, which I didn't mind, it just gave me a better audience when I walked up to the table and slapped down £3,000 in cash. As a sign of acceptance, a woman approached and offered us something to eat. By now I was so hungry I could've eaten the arse off a low-flying duck. We were looking forward to a full banquet of crispy duck, barbecue ribs and dim sum. The full Eastern Monty. Five minutes later she came back with two bacon and fried-egg butties.

The oddest thing about the game was that underneath the table was a huge bucket. When we got nearer I saw it was full of £50, £20 and £10 notes and casino chips. The dealer was the owner of the game, so after every hand he'd take his rake and throw it under the table into the bucket.

A few hours later, there were a few more signs of emotion in the players' faces because I was about £14,000 ahead. I was starting to feel the pace a bit and Gary said that I looked exhausted. I said, 'OK, we can go home now.'

We didn't go home.

Go home after only playing for ten hours straight, only being £17,000 up, and only eating ten bacon butties? I was on a roll and wanted to keep on rockin'. I sent us on a game hunt to Leeds. Sixty miles later we ended up in a backstreet game in Chapeltown, another place you wouldn't want to leave your tank unattended.

This time, we were playing Omaha, which was fine by me. A few hours later I was another £10,000 or so up. Now I needed something new, a change of scene, to combat the tiredness that was starting to kick in.

Half an hour later we were in Pappa's in Bradford. You might think the fact that I'd had to pull a gun in this place before would make it a no-go zone, but I figured that would stand us in good stead for a return visit. Gary took a bit of convincing of the wisdom behind that, though he was happy enough a few hours later when I'd wiped the floor with everyone and put another £8,000 in the kitty.

One of the players there was Norman the Tatter. Now that the action was dead at Pappa's, Norman asked me if I wanted to play him heads-up back at his house in Wakefield. That I couldn't refuse, even after being on the road for as long as we had. The winning streak had to go on until the wheels started to come off. And that didn't feel like it was about to happen. Twenty minutes into the game at Norman's, I was £3,000 up and Norman quit.

By now, I'd raked in £38,000, been through five cities, three motorways, two red lights, twelve bacon butties and seen the sun rise and set again. By the time we dragged ourselves back to Hull, we'd travelled almost 250 miles in a twenty-four-hour period. Midnight to midnight.

The only thing that didn't work out was the Chinese duck. Obviously, the duck was off.

Now I was on the road all the time chasing games. Motorways, cafés, cards – that's all I saw. Occasionally I saw the inside of my eyelids. And my wife and kids. Gary drove me, Pat drove me, Les drove me – I had plenty of blokes riding shotgun. If I were Batman, I'd have had more Robins than Reliant.

It made sense now to hit London big time. If you're trying to win big at gambling then you've always got to follow the money. When you're starting out, you don't try to find the best players, you try to find the worst ones with the most cash. But if you want to improve your game you've got to follow the game. Once you've exhausted the limits of the local games, which I had, and then the non-local games, which I had as well, you've then got to move further. I knew London would help my game progress.

I decided to go to London mainly for the big tournaments: the money prizes in the bigger games were much better, worth sitting down for, and it became one of the first places I'd have decent size tournament wins. Of course, me being me, I'd sit in on a few cash games too. My speciality.

London didn't worry me because I was confident enough to think I could take on the best. The players there didn't necessarily think that, and a lot of them had me down as arrogant. But the good thing about coming from the north of England is that you grow up with an inbred ability to take the piss out of other people.

So I'd walk into a London casino and just do my thing. My thing being to talk and joke and talk some more, and just generally have fun with them. They'd either join in and start firing back, which I preferred because then you'd get some banter going. Or they'd be royally pissed off, which was fine by me too because then they were more likely to start playing loose and go on tilt. So it was win–win: I'd amuse myself, and I might make even more money along the way.

The winnings in London were bigger, but so were the losses. The big killer was the card game Lo-Ball. There were a couple of millionaires who played there who knew their only chance was in Lo-Ball, so the good Omaha players played a round of each to keep the wealthy guys happy and keep them in the games.

One time at the Vic, I got in a big pot in a game of 4-Card Omaha with a famous Irish player, Donnacha O'Dea. O'Dea had been getting very lucky against me. This time he raised with A-A-8-6 and I called with 8-8-9-10.* The flop (the first three board cards) came down 6-6-8. In Omaha, you have to make the best five-card hand using two of the cards you're dealt plus three from the board, so I had him pretty much painted into a corner with my full house (8-8-8-6-6, or 8s over 6s), while Donnacha had only a full house with 6s over 8s. Five board cards are dealt in total, so after the flop there were only two cards left to come – fourth street, or the turn (the fourth card), and the river (the fifth card) – and there were only three cards in the whole deck that he could hit to outdraw me: either of the two Aces or a 6. A roughly 10 per cent chance.

I bet straight out on the flop, hoping he'd put me on a flush draw and put all his money in. He obliged, and we had £65,000 in the pot between us. The turn was a blank. So now there was only one card to be dealt and only three cards in the pack that could give Don a winning hand. Of course, the river was an Ace and he made a full house with Aces. And took nearly all my money off me.

Now you know that it's not like me to moan about a bad beat . . . But believe me, that was a *really* bad beat.

* In hand descriptions, Ace, King, Queen, Jack are abbreviated to A, K, Q, J, respectively.

What's that about the luck of the Irish? I notice there's no saying about the luck of the fucker from Hull.

So, on the turn of one card, I'd lost enough money to buy my house in Hull outright with a nice car on the drive thrown in for good measure. But – and here's the really important bit (because *anybody* can lose, you don't have to be a genius to do that) – it's more important to face your losses than sing about your wins.

I now had only about £4,000 left after the hand with Donnacha. The very next hand I got a full house against Surinder Sunar, and although I badly wanted to play the hand and get out of there, I knew inside that he had me beat so I laid the full house down, leaving me with £3k. But eventually I turned the £3k into £10k. I felt I was back on a bit of a roll and played privately with Ali Sarkeshik at the Metropol and then, the next day back at the Vic, where Ali had challenged me to a heads-up game. We carried on in a private game back at his hotel. The match went on for hours. Eventually I had to say, 'Ali, I'm gonna have to quit.'

He smiled and said, 'I'm glad you're going. There's no way I can beat you tonight, and there's no way I can quit.' He was still smiling, though. Ali was one of the most gracious players I'd met.

So we played the last hand. At the final tally I took £68,000 off the table. I was tired and ready for home.

When I finally left I was back on top by £70,000 overall.

So I'd turned round another tight spot. But at least I'd never killed anyone at a poker table. Not then.

14. Dead Man's Hand

The first time I killed someone at a poker table

You know what they say: if at first you don't succeed, so much for skydiving. Anyway, it's not the fall that kills you, it's the landing – so you may as well enjoy the trip down. Personally, I don't see the point of jumping out of an aeroplane unless it's on fire, and preferably over water.

Now, illegal card games can be dangerous places. I've played in joints where the sawdust on the floor was last night's furniture, the ashtrays were kneecaps and the pattern on the carpet changed according to the blood stains. But most nights the worst thing you might see would be someone throw an insult, a beer bottle or a tantrum. And that was usually me when I got a bad beat.

No one had yet been killed at a card game I was playing in, although I'd murdered a few chip stacks and slaughtered loads of cash. So when I played a late-night cash game in Manchester and a guy ended up dying, it came as a bit of a surprise. Most of all to him, I imagine. There's nothing that can spoil a good night out like dropping dead.

The night of the Dead Man's Hand, my driver was my old mate Tony Booth. I'd first met Tony years ago, when he was a kid, at the Kingston Boxing Club. He also sometimes used to hang round the Spring Bank amusement arcade where I shot games of pool for money. Now he was all grown up – and he'd really grown: he was a professional heavyweight boxer.

Boothy's a Hull lad and a bit of a local legend now after boxing for eighteen years professionally and eight years amateur – when he eventually retired in 2009, he'd had an amazing 166 fights. That's three more than I've had with ex-wives. Even when Boothy was driving me round in 1996 he'd already been a pro for five years. Tony's a tough guy with a lot of heart (but don't tell him I told you that), and he's a funny fucker too.

He's even funny in the ring, and there's not many boxers you can say that about. Boothy, like Ricky Hatton, tended to let himself get out of shape between fights, but unlike Ricky, Tony didn't always get back *into* shape. Or not the shape of a boxer, anyway. More like a really, really dangerous Tellytubby. In his book *Boxing Booth* he talks about when he fought Jon Ibbotson in Sheffield, and when Boothy got in the ring, Ibbotson's fans all started chanting, 'You've NEVER seen a SALAD!'

One night I saw Boothy fight in Southampton. He climbed into the ring and did a bit of shadow boxing . . . and lost. Then, to clear the old airways, he coughed and spat something up that flew through the air like a fuzzy green tennis ball. It took the ring cleaners ten minutes just to get it off the canvas. They even brought in buckets and brushes. I thought at one point the ref was going to step in, count them out, and pronounce Tony's spit-ball the winner. They should have had it on the undercard as a supporting bout.

When the fight started, Boothy's young opponent was moving around pretty well, but not as well as Tony. To be honest, for a big geezer, Boothy was quick on his feet, and one of his favourite tricks was to copy the famous Muhammad Ali shuffle. The crowd thought it was really funny to see him suddenly break into a quick foot-shuffle in the middle of the fight. When Tony did it, it looked like he'd just eaten John Travolta.

But it worked – the other fighter looked down one too many times and Boothy cracked him with a peach of an uppercut and knocked him spark out. The next day, the local paper had an interview with the kid's trainer and he was quoted as saying, 'I *told* him not to look at his feet!'

Funnily enough, Tony's boxing career was finally ended because of his feet – they took him into too many fish-and-chip shops.

Tony made perfect company for me when I was on the road gambling – he could take a drink, he could take a punch, he could just about drive, he could make me laugh, and he could flatten anyone who might try to nick the night's winnings.

We Butch-and-Sundanced it up and down the motor-ways of Britain from one card game to the next. When walking into the kind of places I used to walk into, it helped to have someone watching your back.

If we were going anywhere dodgy, the usual scenario would be for me to have a folded copy of the *Sun* with a cleaver hidden inside it and my gun in my other pocket; Tony would have two big fists hidden in his gloves.

I wore my long black leather coat, and Tony, as well as

having a face like a dented frying pan and a head like a piss pot, wore an expression like a grizzly bear with a migraine. If there was anyone at the game planning on robbing someone, when we walked in they probably decided to pick on the skinny geezer with the glasses instead. There are no advantages in real life to making yourself look like a soft touch. In poker, it's different. You can deliberately make yourself look weak to encourage some mug to bet everything against you. But you don't want to do that away from the tables. Real life all-ins can be fatal.

Things didn't always go to plan. In fact mostly they didn't. On the way back from another all-night session, this time in Sheffield, Boothy managed to get us lost in the countryside in the middle of nowhere. I was half asleep in the back but I started to come round when I heard Tony swearing. It was pitch black, and foggy, and we were driving down a country lane. I couldn't under-stand it – it was six in the morning and I should have been tucked up in bed.

'Tony, where the fuck are we – Cornwall?'

'I don't know, mate,' he said. 'I think I took a left when I should've taken a right.'

I said, 'I think you've taken too many left-rights in the ring. Tell me one thing: Are. We. Lost?'

'Dave, mate, I'd have to know where we are to know if we're lost.'

I said, 'Tone, did you look out the window to see where we were and accidentally bang your empty head on a lamp post? Because that's what it sounds like.'

He said, 'No, but I did have to swerve to avoid the

Eiffel Tower, if that's any help.' Suddenly he hit the brakes, and we found ourselves in a big traffic jam. With my luck, we were probably stuck behind a tractor with a flat tyre and a one-legged farmer with a foot pump. After waiting in the jam without moving, Boothy got out to have a look and disappeared into the morning mist. He came back looking really pissed off. For the last ten minutes we'd been sat in a queue of cars for a local car boot sale.

I used to play at a place in Bearwood, Birmingham, called Barry's. This was an action game, and sometimes big by local standards – you needed £1,000 to sit down on the Friday night. Players who are now big names, like Dave Colclough, Mickey Wernick, Peter Singleton, Tom Gibson, Derek Baxter, Lucy Rokach and John Shipley, were there. So the money was the attraction – they certainly weren't going to Birmingham for the sun.

It was a crazy game. Especially with Dave Colclough in it. Dave's a big-name player now, nicknamed Blondie – which is a bit of a surprise 'cos in the early days he was ginger. He was also a dead ringer for Jasper Carrott. But he didn't play the game he plays now, which is more refined; he used to love getting the money in and re-raising and bullying with some shite hand like J-9-5-6-2 while I'd be sitting there holding two Aces. Now a pair of Aces in 6-Card Omaha, when you're getting four-way action, is worth about as much as a pinch of shit. But we'd end up getting our money in there. It was a bingo type game, whereby a lot of the money was in there before the flop. It was tough to win because a lot of luck came into it. But when I was running good, I was regularly taking a few grand a week out of Barry's. Trouble was, I didn't always run good.

I came out of Barry's with Boothy one morning about nine after I'd been playing all night. I was knackered, and things weren't helped by the fact I'd had a bad streak and lost heavily. Boothy was pissed off too because he was on a percentage of my winnings – so he was due 20 per cent of fuck-all.

It was a bright winter morning so as we came out into the light I put my shades on to stop my eyes from shrivelling up any more. If you want to know what it feels like to have your eyes sucked out and a couple of rotting grapes screwed in your sockets, try playing poker for twelve hours straight in a room full of cigarette and cigar smoke.

We got into the car, which was parked on a steep slope. Tony started backing out into the street. Suddenly a van sped down the road and Tony had to slam on the brakes. The van missed us by an inch and screeched to a stop. Two guys inside jumped out and started marching over to us, one of them shouting the odds. I thought, I *know* what your odds are, matey.

What these guys saw climbing out of our car: me – pale as a vampire's arse, stubble, shades on, long black leather coat, fists balled – and Tony – stocky fucker, face like a bag of files, baseball bat in hand. We were a *Crimewatch* version of *The Matrix*.

Laurel and Hardy stopped in their tracks. I shouted two words. The second one was 'OFF!' And they did.

If we'd been to dodgier games earlier, I'd end up at Barry's still carrying the gun. Derek, who ran it with Barry, wasn't having it, and he barred me. It worked out OK for me in the end because the police raided it the week after and I wasn't there to get nicked with it.

Some of the places I played, if they searched you and found you didn't have a weapon, they'd give you one. When I was travelling to games in Manchester, Bradford and Leeds, the difficult thing was not winning money, but getting back home with it.

Anyway, back to the Dead Man's Hand. Although I encountered it in Manchester, it first got its name in 1876 in the old American West, in a town called Deadwood. I've played a few places like that. The hand was held by the famous gambler and gunfighter Wild Bill Hickok, who always sat at the back of the poker table to guard against an attack from behind – smart move, though I never could figure out where the back of a round table was. It gave Wild Bill a chance to draw his two silver-plated Colts.

On the fatal night in Deadwood, however, all the wall seats were taken. Wild Bill sat with his back to the room and a man called Jack McCall, who had lost all his money to Hickok, took the opportunity to shoot him in the back of the head while he was playing 5-Card Stud. Hickok was holding two black Aces and two black 8s, which has ever since been known as the Dead Man's Hand. Shame he didn't have his own Wild West version of Boothy to do the Ali shuffle as a distraction.

Fast forward 120 years to Manchester – an English version of Deadwood but with fish and chips and worse weather and nightlife. This late-night cash game was run by a good player, Dave Gardner. Dave used to play in Leeds and that's where I met him and he told me about this private game he'd started in Manchester. So I had Boothy drive us down one night and we found it, eventually, down a little backstreet. They even had a betting shop going on in there too. It was a proper little gold mine. Dave was always a bit of a Del Boy entrepreneur. He always had something in the boot of his car he wanted to show you. Fortunately it was never a body – it was usually new suits or videos.

One of the players in the game was an older guy called Charlie Bayliff who ran a pub called the Cock & Bottle in Preston. I'd first met him in Stockport. He was a real action player. We were fighting over a decent-sized pot – about £3,000. As usual I'd put in a big bluff raise, trying to scare him off the hand. We were playing 6-Card Omaha, a game that can be full of wild moves. Betting without the best hand in 6-Card Omaha can be lethal because there is always a good chance that the other guy has the best possible hand – the nuts.

But the way this hand came down and played out, it was difficult for me to credit him with the nuts; and when the last card came down it completed a backdoor straight or flush, so I took a chance and bet the pot. Of course, it hadn't completed my straight or flush – it was a total bluff but, as usual, I made sure it was a big one. Charlie immediately went to push in all his chips, which wasn't good news for me since he'd never do that with a hand worse than mine.

Then, suddenly, he sat up straight, went as stiff as Elvis's quiff, and collapsed off his chair and landed on the floor.

Now as tells go, that's a pretty strong one. Trouble is, I didn't know if having a heart attack meant he had a good hand, a bad hand, or if he'd just had too much cheese before bedtime. Turned out he'd taken painkillers with whisky: not a good combination.

Old Charlie's brother was making drinks, and he rushed over to the table and everybody gathered round. Gamblers aren't the most sympathetic bunch in the world but no one wants to see a man go down at the table, especially a nice old gent. I looked down and saw that as the old fella had fallen, he'd flipped over his cards and he had the winning hand. He had the stone cold nuts. Unbeatable.

Money was a bit tight, and gambling and poker playing was all I did, it was my life, so keep that in mind when I tell you that the next thing I said was:

'So, have I won the hand or what?'

That sounds pretty cold, but that's how I could be then. Because he hadn't called my raise, I asked where we stood. I asked again if I'd won the pot. Everyone looked at me, and then down at the guy on the floor. Unlike boxing, there's no ten-count in poker, so I didn't know what we were waiting for. Then, on a face that already looked dead, the eyes flickered open and he managed to croak out a few words to his brother. He said, 'Call . . . call the raise . . .'

So Charlie won the pot.

I'm not known as being a lucky player, but still, I must be the only poker player in history to have lost a hand to a guy with one foot in the grave and the other on a banana skin.

As an ambulance pulled up outside with its lights on, I started on a world-class bitch to Boothy about how unlucky I'd been. Even Boothy was shocked.

'Are you kidding me? You're not as unlucky as *him*, you silly fucker! That was the only hand he won all night and it fucking killed him!'

I had to admit that he was right. But that's how obsessed I was with poker: everything came second to the game. If that's not a sign of gambling obsession, I don't know what is – and not just my obsession, but the other guy's too. After all, when he came round, the first thing he said to his brother wasn't *Tell my wife I love her* or *Kiss the kids for me* or *Feed the goldfish*. The first thing that old gambler thought of saying was *Call the raise.*

We watched the old fella being loaded into the ambulance on a stretcher. Later I heard that he died the same night. Poor bloke. Actually, not so 'poor' – he did have £1,500 of mine in his pocket.

What a way to go, though. If there's a gambling heaven, that gentleman must be up there right now, saying how he was such a good player he even managed to win a hand while he was dying.

Now if it had been *me* in that position, it would've happened the other way round. Knowing my luck, I'd have lived and lost the hand.

15. The Seven Dwarfs of the Apocalypse

*You can kid yourself that anything is possible
– but try slamming a revolving door*

I'd say £6,600 is quite a lot to pay for a bacon butty. For
that sort of money I'd usually want the whole pig, the
farmer's wife *and* a ride on the tractor. But, on the way
down to London for the Victoria Casino's Christmas
Cracker tournament, that's how much I ended up paying
for a sandwich.

I'd started to do well in London – I'd already won my
first big British tournament there, the Pot Limit Hold'em
European Open at the Grosvenor – so it was worth the
slog down the M1. Gary was driving and we decided we
should live dangerously and eat at motorway services – if
the fat from a fry-up didn't give you an instant heart
attack, the passive smoking would. There's nothing like
seeing a cigarette butt stubbed out in the yolk of a fried
egg to let you know you're in a classy joint.

We pulled off at the next place, just past Rotherham,
and slap-bang next door to the café there was a Ladbroke's
betting shop. I'd never seen one in all the motorway stops
we'd made before. What are the odds on that? I'd got
thousands in cash to play at the Vic, Gary thinks we're

safe to stop on the M1 because there's nothing to tempt me, and then we pull up outside this place!

(It reminded me of when I was in Torquay once with Ziggy and Kev Allanby and met some great mates, Mickey Moran, Alan Vincent, Tony Bloom, Mehmet and Mick The Clock. We had a great time playing snooker and poker all night. I somehow managed to lose everyone and ended up walking home at ten in the morning through the thickest fog I've ever seen, or ever not been seen in. Suddenly, a voice came out of nowhere – 'There going in the traps at hackney!' It was from a tannoy speaker coming out of a local bookies, announcing a dog race. Even in a thick pea-souper, my radar had taken me, half-blind, to the nearest betting shop. And I'd had a really good night playing poker. So I walked inside with my pockets carrying ten grand in cash . . . and walked back out with them carrying ten grammes in fluff.)

Anyway, Gary said, 'Trust me to find the only stop with a bookies.' I persuaded him we should have a look inside just to see what was going on. Famous last words.

It was only a small shop and I knew that if I won more than they had in the safe then I'd have to take a cheque – which I couldn't do because I'd be in London. So this was a 'cash is king' situation. Most of them are. I asked the manager how much they could pay in cash and he said about £600.

I asked Gary to give me just £600 out of the stash. He looked at me with that Gary look that I got in these kinds of situations.

'Look,' I said, 'just give me six hundred, OK? Then go

get us some sandwiches, and don't come back. That way, I can only lose the six, right?' He didn't look convinced but six hundred for me wasn't heavy.

I'll give you three guesses what happened, and if each guess is 'Dave – you lost the lot', then you'd be right. By this time I was betting horses more cleverly than I'd ever done before – only choosing certain races on certain tracks, smaller fields, favourable conditions, and no three-legged ones. But as we'd just dropped on this bookies by accident, I had no chance to study the form. And sometimes no matter what you do, the horses just go against you. You could chisel that in big letters on a million gamblers' gravestones: 'KILLED BY HORSES! – REST IN PEACE WITH EMPTY POCKETS'.

Mind you, it didn't help that every horse I backed seemed to have one of the seven dwarfs riding it instead of a jockey. I got Sleepy, Dopey and, on the last horse, Twatty.

I was about to walk out when Gary walked in – the food was cold by now – wondering what was happening. I mugged him for more money – about £6,000 this time – and proceeded to lose all of it chasing the first £600. Mostly because I managed to pick the other four dwarfs that happened to be riding. I wasn't Happy (too tall for a start).

So that turned out to be one very, very expensive bacon sandwich. And a bad start for me going into the Vic's tournaments. It might have been a bad start but I didn't for a second think it was a bad omen – and that's the difference. It's a mental thing. If you're pessimistic, you might chalk up that £6,600 loss as a bad omen and let it affect your play. It's better if you can wipe the board clean. But not everyone can do that. In fact, most can't.

And this was at a time when money was still tight. The pawnbroker's was doing OK, but losing £6,600 on the horses was a dent that I could definitely feel. Especially if it affected my performance at the tables.

One thing I could draw on was my own self-belief. If people don't like you, they call it arrogance. But self-belief is a powerful weapon to have in your armoury. I'd learned that quite early on when I'd fought gangs, chatted up women, survived prison, worked the doors, or just risked going broke on an all-in.

Anyway, like always, I didn't let losing over six grand bother me. Gary wasn't too happy but then he wouldn't have been Gary otherwise. I even managed to get some sleep in the car on the rest of the journey down the M1. Which was reckless because I was driving.

Even though I had a badly dented bankroll, when we got to the Vic, I didn't alter my play and just steamed straight into the games like always.

Playing in the north for small- to medium-sized pots was one thing; playing in London for big money was another. But I'd always sought out 'action' games and played my best when the stakes were high. I'd discovered that I had the natural nerve for big games. You'll find that under pressure people always return to the behaviour that's natural to them – and if you've got a mountain of money on the table that's worth as much as your house, and you're risking losing it, then that's enough to make a lot of players brick it.

When it comes to poker nerve, you've either got it or you ain't – and if you ain't, then don't get involved in high-stakes poker. Edge-of-the-cliff situations leave you nowhere to go, so you might as well come out fighting.

And that year London had been a good battleground for me: I'd already picked up £26,000 in winnings at the Grosvenor tourneys. Matthew, the latest fine addition, arrived only the week before I'd come down for the Christmas Cracker events – so I like to think I played better because I had another mouth to feed. It's amazing how quickly four kids can eat you out of house and home.

I celebrated Matthew's birth by winning the Pot Limit Hold'em Christmas Cracker, and I also came third in the No Limit Hold'em event. That gave me another thirteen grand for the kitty (and we didn't even have a cat).

Tournament wins were good for prestige and reputation but they didn't pay too big. They certainly didn't pay big enough to start covering too many six-and-half-grand bacon butties.

I wanted to hit the cash games and build up some big money. So over the next few weeks all I did was play tournaments and cash games, mostly cash, and I came out well ahead. Tournament wins were not big news to me at this point; that would come later. There were only two things I was chasing: big cash wins and the buzz.

Most of all, the buzz.

I built up nearly another £40,000 to go with my Vic winnings and give a total bankroll of just over £100,000.

Not for the first time, some of the other players said that my aggressive style of play was suited to Vegas. I was in form, and for a gambler, that's the equivalent of when sportsmen are 'in the zone', where they feel they can do nothing wrong. So much of being a good poker player is capitalizing on your good form and minimizing your bad. Normal people want to quit when they're ahead – gamblers don't, they want to go further. They want to win more. What you should remember whenever you see someone who has won big at poker – he has only been able to do so because he is also never prepared to quit.

That's what a lot of these young kids don't understand. They've grown up playing online with limited risk or where the worst thing that can happen is that they max out their credit card, or their dad's. But playing live and going flat broke – and I mean pockets-inside-out broke – is something every gambler goes through at some point. There's a big difference between playing online and putting your balls on the line.

Mind you, I've heard some ridiculous stories about millions changing hands online. I once had dinner with my mate Tom Dwan in the Bellagio in Las Vegas and he told me he'd lost millions the night before online. How sick is that? Being Tom he insisted on paying the bill.

Not being short of a ball or two, I started to think that I should go out to Vegas for 'the biggest game in town' – the famous World Series of Poker tournament at the Horseshoe Casino. The WSOP was like the Olympics, the Oscars, the World Series and the World Cup all rolled into one massive poker circus – with bells on. And a big fat million-dollar cherry on top.

I knew that luck might be playing a hand when something happened which put me in the wrong place at the right time. I was playing at the Rainbow Casino in Birmingham and I'd just about won all the money off the players in there. Afterwards, I was invited back to a private game at Stevie Au-Yeung's – a guy who would play an interesting part in my life a little later on. I started driving to the game. I was feeling good about carrying on playing because I was running good.

Now, as we've established, there's bad card luck and bad life luck and I'd already had a 'good luck' moment when I'd decided not to visit another game in Birmingham I often played – and that night it was raided by an armed gang. They demanded all the money and said they'd 'do' anyone that was found with cash on them. One player, Mickey, only had a few hundred whereas everyone else had thousands, so he managed to stuff it down his trousers. As the gang marched everyone into another room at gunpoint, twenty-pound notes were falling out of Mickey's trousers. Which made all the other players think they were going to get shot.

This time, I got within about fifty yards of Stevie's house and I suddenly decided not to go in. I thought, what's the point: I already had most of the money and I knew certain people would be wanting to borrow off me.

I turned the car round and went back to the Strathmore Hotel for a drink. The next day I got an early phone call from someone who had been at the game. Not long after it started, a gang of three guys had kicked in the front door and stormed in with shotguns. They'd been looking for me. I was the only geezer who'd walked out of the casino with any money. Someone had called them and marked their card.

Make no mistake, when anybody gets set up after they've left a casino, it's an inside job. Armed gangs don't just turn up on the off-chance, because you might be coming out of the casino or a backstreet game with five quid and a curled-up cheese sandwich.

But I was back at Stevie Au-Yeung's soon enough. You can't let a little armed robbery keep you from a good game. This particular night became memorable for another reason. I was playing my usual game, raising the fuck out of everybody, talking the fuck out of everyone, and generally trying to boss the table. Stevie stood there watching, and then he smiled and said that I was a devil fish.

Now I'd been called some things in my time, but never that. He said 'devil fish' was the slang name for a Japanese fish, the tako fugu or blowfish, which was poisonous to eat if it wasn't prepared exactly right.

I liked the name 'Devilfish', but we just laughed about it and carried on playing. When I left the game I forgot all about it.

Is there any day of the year more boring than New Year's Day? The most exciting thing to look forward to is some turkey trifle, the goldfish dying, or the last of the Christmas sprouts working through you.

I can't remember anyone ever ringing me on a New Year's Day with any kind of dramatic offers, but I bet a mate of mine can. Gary had been riding shotgun with me now for a few years, driving everywhere between games, late at night, early in the morning. We'd been through a lot of scrapes. He was a good fella to have around because he was always having a laugh and, just as important, he was always in your corner. After I'd been thinking for a while about what had been said to me in London, I picked up the phone.

'Gary, it's me, mate,' I said. 'How d'you like to go to Las Vegas?'

16. 'Go, the Devilfish!'

*Four Queens, nine FBI agents, and $40,000 in cash
— welcome to the Devilfish Express*

You learn a lot about yourself when you're alone in a hotel room in another country – how quickly you get bored, how much you're willing to pay for TV porn, and how much money you can blow in five minutes on the mini-bar. If they'd been really smart, they'd have offered the man who broke the bank in Monte Carlo a room in the hotel. He'd have paid back half his winnings on peanuts, chocolate biccies and miniature vodkas.

It was January 1997, and Gary was with me on a reconnaissance trip for the big one – the World Series of Poker championship in April. I'd decided to travel quite light, for me, with only £30,000 in cash so as not to risk all of the WSOP stash I'd built up. We'd flown out of Manchester on a cheap night-flight to keep the expenses down. I think it was Plummit Airways. We weren't exactly travelling in style: the lifesaving equipment was a rosary and a prayer mat. Though I was more comfy than Gary; he was strapped to the wing.

Flying into Vegas at night is an amazing sight. It's a bright blast of light in the middle of the desert. A big neon gamblers' heaven. Pity the fucker who changes the bulbs. Then I thought about how much money there must be down there just waiting to be won.

We were booked into the Four Queens Hotel and Casino, which was in an area called Glitter Gulch in downtown Las Vegas. Downtown is the original part of Vegas, first built by gangsters and gamblers, so I thought that would be a good place to start and somewhere I'd probably feel at home. Even though this was about as similar to Hull as Monte Carlo was to Grimsby. Most of what I knew about Vegas came from Elvis films and gamblers' stories – so Vegas had a lot to live up to.

Just walking into the Four Queens was a blast. It was full of bright lights and mirrors and this amazing sound of slot machines and jackpot bells. The Four Queens was called the jackpot capital of the world because it had so many slots, and slap-bang in the middle of the casino was Nickel Palace, where all the slot machines were. The casino was straight across from Binion's Horseshoe where they always held the World Series, so I could easily go and check it out.

We walked in off the street and out of the heat and into the Four Queens. I was boiling hot because I was in a suit and I noticed that I was just about the only one in the place wearing one. I'd already noticed that Vegas casinos were full of some of the best scruffy-looking fuckers I'd ever seen. It was like Crufts with card tables. A lot of the blokes were wearing sportswear, but it looked like the only exercise most of them got was running up a bar bill.

Gary went straight up to the room and I went straight to the card room. I asked a guy if there were any Omaha games going on. I noticed he looked me up and down

– taking in the suit, the shades and the suitcase – and then he pointed to a game over in the corner. I marched right over and took an empty seat. I thought I'd play a few hands, lock the seat up as mine and then go upstairs and get changed.

As it happens, two poker mates of mine were already sitting in on the game – Chris Truby and Tony Kelly. Both were posher than I was, which didn't take much doing.

There was also a big guy from Texas. Now I like to speak at the table, but I'd learned the art of being able to do it without revealing any information. Actually, I'd not learned it as such, it was something I could just do naturally. So if you can't speak at the table without giving yourself away, then don't say anything. Unless you're playing me, of course, in which case, take a seat and start talking.

But this big Texan player could've talked the arse off Beyoncé. He was taking it in turns to insult every player at the table. 'Trash talk' has its place in poker, and it's mostly used against whoever you've got a hand against, or someone you might have a rivalry with, but this geezer was just scatter-gunning everyone. He eventually got round to me. His slow Texas drawl stood no chance against my machine-gun patter. I'd managed to get out ten sentences before he'd got to the end of his first word. While he was still telling me I looked like an amateur, I'd already insulted him, his mother, his brother, his wife, his dog and whatever cow he'd ridden into town on. If people were nice to me, I was nice to them. If people were aggressive to me, they were going to get it back ten times worse. I'd never liked bullies.

Naturally, whatever I'd said at three hundred words per minute to Big Tex had gone straight over his head. Or whizzed right past his ears. My broad Hull accent probably didn't help.

'What *the hell* did he say?!' he said to everyone. So I told him again what I thought about him. He still didn't get it, and the only two at the table who did – Chris and Tony – were not going to translate. I could tell that by the look on their faces. Big Tex muttered something to himself but he'd obviously got the gist of what I was saying and he decided to leave me alone for the rest of the game.

After the game had broken up, Chris and Tony came up to me looking more worried than pleased to see me. They said no offence but they were going to give me a wide berth for the rest of their time in Vegas. Apparently Big Tex, apart from being a well-known gambler, was also a well-known nutcase who carried a gun in his boot. 'Dodging the bullets' is what we call avoiding being beaten by a player holding Aces, but I didn't want to try it in real life. Having said that, I was so hot-blooded at this time that I wouldn't have given a fuck anyway.

That was another thing I was going to have to get accustomed to in Vegas casinos – taking everything the American players said with a big pinch of salt. I had to get used to them just *speaking*. British casinos, and the Victoria especially, had a strict policy of not speaking at the poker table during tournaments. Which was crazy because talking is such a big part of poker, and it was a part of the game that gave me an advantage. Some younger players today wouldn't even believe that rule ever existed.

But I remember Ali Sarkeshik once being told he couldn't bet any more in a hand because he'd said, 'If I lose this, I'll go back to work!'

In fact, the first time they did a TV poker show at the Vic, I told them that they'd better change their 'no talking' rule if they wanted a good show. They did change it.

It was a big revelation in Vegas to find casino card games were like private cash games back home – big money and freedom to talk. Which suited me down to the ground. It caught me off guard at first but I'm a quick learner where cards and money are concerned. So now I could take my cash style of play from England and bring it to an American casino.

Reading a local newspaper, it made Vegas sound like Hull on a Friday night, so it was no wonder I felt at home. I decided to call it a day for the first day and went to give Gary the reassuring news that I'd just pissed off a big Texan with a handgun.

I started to hit the cash games hard and soon I was doing pretty good. I wasn't that bothered with tournaments, I was playing in big-money games. I couldn't believe how much cash there was floating around and how many bad poker players there were. Poker was practically invented by Americans and everyone thinks of it as the Americans' game, so I thought I'd have to raise my game a lot, but that wasn't true. I found that I was better than most of the home-grown players.

What surprised me was that the standard of Omaha play in Vegas was so bad. Omaha was the version of poker favoured by the British and Europeans, so we had the edge there – whereas Hold'em poker was originally American. I stuck to Omaha games to exploit their weakness. Two Aces, for example – the bullets – is a great hand in Hold'em but in Omaha it's virtually worthless. So I could bet thirty grand and be holding a full house, and my opponent's got two Aces and calls the bet. It never dawned on them that they've overplayed their hand – they didn't think about what you might have – because they're blinded by their Aces. Those Aces might as well be pennies on their eyes because they're dead in the chair.

Immediately I could see that the amount of money moving across the tables and piled up in front of the players was way more than anything in Britain. I'd had to work my arse off for weeks back home to earn anywhere near the kind of cash I could hoover up here in one night. It was unbelievable. I knew I had to get some of this action before these boys wised up. People used to go to London thinking the streets were paved with gold – I'd landed in Vegas and found that it was carpeted with dollars.

We went for a steak in the casino restaurant. And this is where I first ran into Benny Binion. Benny was the son of Jack Binion and grandson of Lester 'Benny' Binion, the Texan who founded the Horseshoe and staged the first World Series of Poker in 1970, one of the legends of Las Vegas. Benny Snr organized what is still the most famous game of poker ever played – between Johnny Moss and 'Nick the Greek' Dandalos in 1949. The game went on for five months. That even beats some of the games I'd been involved in. And it shows you why the Americans say that poker players need a 'leather ass'.

So the Binions were genuine gambling royalty. They went right back to the cowboys, gamblers and gangsters that first made Vegas what it is.

I hit it off with the younger Benny straight away. He was a nice guy and he was interested in the gambling stories I had about playing in England. He had a bit of a fascination for London gangsters like the Krays and 'Mad' Frankie Fraser. I was probably the closest Benny had got to an English rock'n'roller. We'd sit having steaks and I'd tell him stories about the past. The Horseshoe did the best steaks because the Binions had their own ranch. So if they didn't get your stake money in the casino, they got your steak money in the restaurant.

I told Benny that this trip was a tester for the WSOP in April at his granddaddy's place. He said he could see that I was doing well and that I should look him up when I came back.

An interesting guy I met at the Four Queens was a Texan called Bobby Lores. He was a bail bondsman, putting up bail money to get accused people out of jail. We got on so well that when I'd run into him again in a few months' time at the WSOP, I'd lose $60,000 of his money.

I decided to enter the Four Queens Poker Classic Omaha tournament. It was $500 buy-in with re-buys – so you had the chance to buy back into play if you were wiped out. I didn't know it then, but this would be the game that would help make my name, big time – and I didn't even yet know that I *had* a name. By this point I'd forgotten the 'Devilfish' nickname that Stevie Au-Yeung had given me that time at his game in Birmingham. I was Dave Ulliott, not Devilfish, so I didn't give the name a second thought. But someone else had remembered it and was about to remind me.

I seemed to find my best form during this Omaha event and I made it down to the final table of six players. That meant I was now definitely in the money. Sometimes it's enough for some players to reach the final table and it seems like they can't murder their chips quick enough to get off. I'd never been like that. And this was no different: I was in Vegas and I was on the final table of the biggest poker game in the casino.

Soon we'd fought down to just two players – me and a Vietnamese guy called Men 'The Master' Nguyen. Men was a bit of a poker legend in his own right by this point. This geezer had won over $5 million and four gold winner's bracelets at World Series. So going heads-up with this guy was great, the biggest name I'd played. I'd been in more dangerous games, I'd been in games where I'd stood to win (or lose) more money, but in terms of prestige, this was the big one.

Because this was the final head-to-head showdown a lot of the casino floor and other card players were gathered round watching, kept back from the table by a security rail. Men had every Asian in the crowd cheering him on, and I had no fucker except Gary. We were pretty evenly matched to begin with, the chips going back and forth between us. I'd never played in a game this big, but

I felt at home. It felt as though this was where I was meant to be. I had no nerves. Even when I was bluffing Men for a massive pot, scaring him off whatever hand he had even when I had nothing.

I'd played before in rowdy games with blokes shouting and swearing, even fighting, but I'd never played a game like this with such a big *audience*. The crowd were really getting into it, shouting out to me and Men and cheering and groaning when cards were turned over. I started to edge ahead in the match and a supporter of Men's shouted out, 'Go on, the Master!' Gary, who was at the front of the rail, responded by shouting back, 'GO ON, THE DEVILFISH!'

I'd forgotten all about the nickname until Gary resurrected it. I thought 'Devilfish' sounded good now – in Vegas – and when Gary shouted it out it went down really well with the crowd too.

Men didn't like the reaction the name caused, and it was the beginning of a rich streak for me that saw me start to dominate him at the table. By the time I'd finished steamrolling over him I had more chips than McDonald's. Statistically, there was still a slim chance Men could win, but I had 95 per cent of the chips, so his chance was about the same as Elvis being your postman and riding up your path on the back of Marilyn Monroe.

I said I was taking a toilet break. He started complaining and saying how we should play on and finish. He was definitely getting on my tits. So I stood up, leaned forward on my hands, looked over my shades at him and said, slowly: 'I'm taking the break, son. Give you the chance to work out your strategy.'

As soon as the break was over, Men threw his last stack of chips into the pot. I won the hand – and also won my first big American tournament – taking out a big-time poker name and winning nearly $21,000.

Not bad for a day's work (not counting the twenty-odd years of playing that had got me there). That $21,000 would go very nicely with the other twenty grand I'd won in cash games and the ninety grand I had back home in England. I'd have quite a bankroll to bring back out here for the WSOP. If I didn't lose it all by then.

But tonight we had some celebrating to do, so we hit the bars and clubs of the Bright Light City. Vegas is a great place for drinking, eating, partying, playing and watching beautiful, long-legged blonde strippers floss themselves with a G-string. If you like that kind of thing.

Next morning, I was laid out like a starfish in one of the two king-size beds in the suite I'd upgraded us to with my winnings. My Pot Limit Omaha winner's trophy was on my bedside table. Gary had already gone downstairs to enter me into another poker tournament with $2,000 that I'd given him.

Vegas hotels have heavy-duty curtains to keep that desert sun out of the rooms, but I could see a bright line of sunlight down the curtain edge. I was just about to order a barrel of black coffee from room service when suddenly there were three loud bangs on my bedroom door – BOOM! BOOM! BOOM! Then a voice shouted out 'FBI! – *OPEN UP!*'

I thought, you've gotta be kidding me, right – the FBI? Fucking Big Indian? That only happens in the movies. It must be Gary, messing about, so I did what anyone else would do. I shouted back, '*Fuck* off!'

It didn't work.

'*SIR!* THIS IS THE FBI! OPEN UP THE DOOR OR WE *WILL* BE FORCED TO ENTER!'

Fair play to Gary, I thought, for persisting with it. This time I changed my response to: 'Fuck *right* off!' Then I heard a little voice that sounded about halfway down the corridor. It was Gary. 'Dave! It really is the FBI, mate.'

That was still sinking in when the first voice came back again – 'SIR! *OPEN THE DOOR!*'

I staggered out of bed with the duvet wrapped round me, hoping this guy had a volume control button because my head couldn't take any more shouting. I opened the door a couple of inches and was blasted – 'PLEASE KEEP YOUR HANDS VISIBLE *AT ALL TIMES!*'

I thought, this guy should be working on a boating lake.

I raised my hands over my head, letting the duvet fall. When he saw that he just said 'OK, sir' so I could cover myself – he was obviously feeling inadequate.

It turned out I'd been playing in the casino with counterfeit $100 bills, or at least, that's what they said. The FBI agents came into my room with a worried-looking Gary and a couple of cops. Gary had been picked up downstairs at the cashier's desk with bills that were identified as forgeries. The casino had called the Feds. They wanted to know if I had any more money that they could check. Straight away I had a picture of the $40,000 in winnings that was downstairs in a security deposit box and, because I'm always happy to help with police enquiries, I said, 'No. That's all we've got – the two grand.'

I didn't want them to go through the other money and take out all the dodgy notes. I could end up left with $50 in cash and a $500 mini-bar bill. If I had any moody bills it was only because people had passed them on to me in the casino. I figured I deserved a chance to recirculate them. My bit towards recycling.

We both gave a statement and Mulder and Scully left my room. We knew we'd have to go through the $40,000 in the security box. Gary said he knew exactly what the counterfeit ones looked like. When we did go through them, we found that we had over $17,000 in dodgy bills. I decided the best thing to do was take them downstairs, play cash games and try to wash the dirty notes through the games until they came out clean. Even if I had to lose seven grand through playing them quickly, ten grand good was better than seventeen grand bad. That's about a 40 per cent loss, which is probably less than you'd pay a money launderer, so I figured we'd be ahead. Even more so if I won. I believe that's what they call a win–win.

It was a strange feeling, playing with money that you actually *wanted* to get rid of. Some of the other players couldn't figure out the way I was playing. I was taking long shots that I wouldn't normally play, but when they paid off I got lots of new money back, some of it clean. Eventually, I ended up with ten grand of clean money. Then, one of the older players, who had been looking a bit puzzled, asked me why I was throwing all the old notes in and keeping all the new ones. I asked him what he meant by 'old'.

'Well,' he said, 'there's nothing wrong with these. All they are is old bills . . .'

I looked at Gary. I asked if he was sure. He said he was 100 per cent sure. I went over to the cashier's cage and I handed over a few of the 'dodgy' bills for them to check. The bloke looked them over and said, 'Nope – nothing wrong with that, sir.'

So I'd just fucked off seven grand in cash that was healthy all along. I'd just 'laundered' $7,000 of clean money. It was now clean enough to buy sex off a nun. I'd like to say we laughed about it but I'm still waiting for that particular laugh to kick in. But that's poker. Anything can happen and it usually does. Still, it could've been worse – I could have been banged up by the FBI as a suspected counterfeiter. There are far worse things to lose than money – your health, your car keys, the control of your bowels in a jacuzzi. Sometimes money is a small price to pay for experience.

One thing that made up for it was the headlines I was making in the local papers. After the early morning knock from the FBI, and then 'cleaning' the money through the poker tables, we finally got to sit down for a beer and a steak. One of the British poker players showed me a morning edition of the local newspaper. The sports page headline was all about my tournament win over Men 'The Master' Nguyen. It said: 'DEVILFISH DEVOURS THE MASTER!' I thought, I'm really glad they worded it that way and didn't put 'DEVILFISH DEVOURS MEN'.

*

So what should have been a fairly simple trip to Vegas turned out to be just about business-as-usual for me in terms of making a bloody big drama out of a big bleeding crisis:

1) Picked a fight with an armed Texan – *check*
2　Befriended a Binion – *check*
3) Got raided by the FBI – *check*
4) Threw away over $7,000 – *check*
5) Won over $100,000 – *check*
6) Won a Poker Classic tournament – *check*
7) Made headline news in Las Vegas – *check*

I could tick all those off my holiday 'To Do' list, then. Job done. Now all I had to do was get home without the plane bursting into flames and crash landing on a dynamite factory.

I'd never even been abroad on holiday until I'd met Mandy. Until then, a holiday was soggy fish and chips on Bridlington front.

But when I finally arrived I found that I slotted right in. Me and Vegas were definitely a good fit. I saw the place as a big game that I wanted to get my teeth into. And I absolutely loved it – the games, the action, the money, the nightlife, the poker. I just swam in it. Which was appropriate because as well as making my mark on the Vegas poker scene, I'd also made my name – my new name: 'Devilfish'. You could say I'd made a big splash.

This was the start of a lifelong relationship with Vegas. Playing in Las Vegas in the middle of the Nevada Desert couldn't have been more different from playing in cold, rainy Hull if I'd stepped off a flight on to the backside of the moon.

Speaking of which, I knew it was time to go back home and touch down on planet earth. I also definitely knew that I'd be back out here in two months' time for the World Series of Poker. What I didn't know about yet was something that might have made me think twice – because when I returned to Las Vegas, I'd have much bigger wins, but also much, much bigger losses than any I'd ever experienced before.

17. Holding Gold – Viva Lost Wages!

A lot of guys come to Vegas expecting to lose,
and they're rarely disappointed

I flew back into Britain with over $100,000 in cash. At Customs I walked straight through 'Nothing to Declare'.

Being back in England was a relief but also a come-down – it was January, it was freezing cold and it was miserable, especially after the light and heat of Vegas. The rectangular shades I'd started to become known for wearing had orange lenses, which helped make Hull seem a little bit warmer. But only for about the half-second before the cold hit my bones and took a bite.

It felt like we'd been away for much longer than two weeks, even though when we were actually there, the two weeks had flown by. Weird how time works on you.

In terms of my professional life, going to Vegas did one major thing – it killed England for me. After seeing the amounts of money flying round over there, and how much you could win in an hour, I knew I couldn't come back to slogging up and down Britain's motorways. It also woke me up to the fact that I could never settle down to working in the shop when I knew it would take me ten years to make what I could win in one night. And that, in a nutshell, is where gambling really grabs you: they say that money won is sweeter than money earned. And if you add the fact that you might win a month's or even a year's wages in one night – you can see why I kept going back to the tables. That first win I'd had in the bookies when I was fifteen . . . in a way, I'd been chasing it ever since.

I was really glad to be home, of course, to see Mandy, and Stephen, Christopher, Mike and little Matthew. Four boys tearing round the place were definitely enough to let you know you were home. The eldest ones wanted to hear about Vegas. There was no danger of me glamorizing gambling because they saw the other side. And I definitely didn't want them going down the gambling route. You always want better for your kids, and professional gambling is too hard a route to take even when you choose it.

Coming home with a big bag full of cash allowed me to take my foot off the gas, gambling wise, for a few days and just be at home with the wife and kids, which is something that most gamblers don't do enough, and I wasn't any different. There's also nothing in the world like being back home in your own bed – especially when it's warmed by your missus. So for the next week I slept like the dead.

The pawnbroker's was going well and Mandy was more than capable of running it with her sister Wendy, while I was away. In fact, she did a better job than me because she had loads of patience – it still felt too much to me like the nine-to-five, or prison. Which is the same thing to a gambler. I'd done both and I didn't like either. Gamblers are meant to play all night, sleep all morning, and take all bets. The days I'd enjoyed working in the shop were when I'd turned the place into a gambling joint anyway: taking on bets from travellers and gypsies, or taking a punt on some object that someone had brought in to sell.

Gary went home to Doncaster to recharge his batteries and dream about Vegas strippers, and I started to prepare for going back out to America for the big one – the World Series of Poker in April.

The annual WSOP is the Olympics of poker, and whoever wins the WSOP Main Event becomes the champion of the poker world for a year. It's a bit like winning the Best Actor Oscar, except that whoever wins it also takes home a boatload of money.

The WSOP was first started in 1970 by Benny Binion – grandfather of the young Benny Binion I'd become friends with – at old Benny's casino, the Horseshoe. Times had changed since those early days when only six players entered the first event; by 1997 there were hundreds of players paying $10,000 to play in the Main Event. That meant the WSOP Main Event winner got a $1,000,000 payout – the only million-dollar poker prize in the world at the time.

I knew that the previous year the Main Event had been won by an American player called, believe it or not, Huckleberry Seed. Now, you wouldn't have got out my school in Orchard Park alive with that name – if the kids hadn't killed you the teachers would. But this Huck Seed survived his childhood to go on and win the World Series of Poker. Mind you, his final table heads-up opponent was called Bruce Van Horn, so a guy called Seed probably thought he'd got off lightly.

At the age Huck Seed won it – twenty-seven – I'd been

working on the door of a local disco and living on a council estate. A million dollars would've looked pretty good to me then.

All poker's biggest names had played at the World Series – Johnny Moss, Johnny Chan, Doyle Brunson, Stu Ungar, Bobby Baldwin, Scotty Nguyen, Phil Hellmuth, Jack Keller, Berry Johnston, Dan Harrington, Jim Betchel – and they'd all won the Main Event. In time, I'd end up playing against most of them. In my opinion Chip Reese was the best player ever, though he never won the Main Event. True gentleman.

With my cash game and tournament winnings in England, and the stash I'd brought back from Vegas, I figured on taking out about £120,000 ($200,000) to the WSOP. I could hit the casino cash games and enter a lot of the tournaments that are played in the build-up to the Main Event. It would be a big poker circus and I knew there'd be lots of different rings to jump into, and a few to jump out of.

Flying back into Vegas felt really good. We flew in during the day this time, our flights paid for by the last visit's winnings. A bird's-eye view of the place in the sunlight made it look a lot less attractive than it does at night with the neon blazing. The town is basically just one big neon sign, so during the day it looks like Las Vegas unplugged. I couldn't wait to get back into it, though, and I had reason to be confident after the last trip. The Devilfish Express was steaming back into town.

This time, I'd booked us into Binion's Horseshoe itself,

home of the WSOP. I'd always liked being near the big-time action and this time I'd be sleeping above it. And action was one thing I knew there'd be plenty of over the next three weeks: the World Series would consist of twenty big poker tournaments, building up to the million-dollar Main Event on 12 May. I'd have to buy my seat in that with the $10,000 entrance fee, along with 312 other players from around the world, the biggest field yet for a WSOP. My mate Benny comped me a suite. I let Gary have a look round before he went to his pokey little room – how I spoilt that boy.

There were a fair number of Brit players around, and also my old mate Men 'The Master' Nguyen, probably still trying to heal the scars from our last meeting. Men had finished fourth in the Main Event the previous year. Huck Seed was back to defend his title (though I didn't see his brother, Bird), and Ali Sarkeshik was there too.

If I'd told you it wasn't a buzz to be there, I'd have been lying. The gambling capital of the world was host-ing the biggest poker game in the world for the best poker players in the world. Being an arrogant sod, I thought I was one of them. Better still was the fact that anyone could enter if they had the entrance fee. You couldn't say that about the World Cup or Wimbledon or the heavy-weight championship of the world.

So, I was wearing my suit, my rings and my favourite orange shades. I had $200,000 in my bag. What could possibly go wrong?

Now . . . I figure you could just about fit that across a gravestone if you chiselled the letters small enough:

WHAT COULD POSSIBLY GO WRONG?
DAVID 'Devilfish' ULLIOTT
1954 ~ 1997

Loving Father and Unlucky Fucker

Could you put 'Unlucky Fucker' on a gravestone? There are plenty of people in cemeteries who would qualify, probably most of them, so I don't see why not. Every year people are killed by falling trees, or struck by lightning, or killed by falling trees struck by lightning. And I think *I'm* unlucky? Though it's probably a good thing we don't have honest headstones or there'd be plenty of wives burying husbands under 'Lazy Bastard', and 'Not Really the Father'; and plenty of wives lying under a stone saying 'Tart', and 'Thank God – Peace at Last'.

Me, I always liked the comedian Spike Milligan's idea for what he wanted on his headstone – 'I Told You I Was Ill!'

The first day of play at the WSOP wasn't too funny, though. I lost $20,000 of my bankroll in two cash games, then I entered the $2,000 Texas Hold'em event and got knocked out with no payout, then I lost another $18,000 in an evening cash game, $27,000 through the late-night/early-morning cash game, and then I lost my $1,500 buy-in to the 7-Card Razz event when I got knocked out with no prize money.

Not exactly a good thirty-six hours. I'd be heading home next day at this rate. I'd lost nearly two grand an hour, on average. That was me $68,500 down. But, that's poker. You can be in form one minute and out of luck the next. If you panic at this stage you may as well go home. Me? I didn't even go to bed.

Gary was getting a bit worried, but then Gary always did. It's not as if we hadn't been here before – in both senses – in Vegas, and on a losing streak. Just not both together. That was a first.

We went to the Horseshoe restaurant and met Benny Binion for lunch. It was good to see Benny again, and I caught up on some of the news since I'd last been there. The big news at the WSOP was that Stu Ungar was in the Main Event. Stu was an interesting kid. He was a great poker player with a high IQ, but had had a tough fifteen years. He'd won the WSOP Main Event here in 1980 and 1981, which made him one of only three players to win it in consecutive years (Doyle Brunson and Johnny Chan were the others). If Ungar won it this year he'd become the first three-time winner in history.

We left Benny in the restaurant, and as we walked across the casino floor Stu Ungar walked by. I was surprised that he was such a tiny geezer but you could immediately see why they called him 'The Kid'. I was wearing my square orange-lens glasses, Stu had on these big round shades with dark blue lenses, like the kind John Lennon wore in the sixties. They looked even bigger on Stuey's face because he was so small.

After my big cash losses, I decided to bide my time and wait for the next day's $1,500 buy-in Pot Limit Omaha event. Trouble was, the way I decided to bide my time was by playing more cash games. By twelve midnight, another \$53,000 of my stash had been blown. This time the hourly average loss went up to \$5,800. At that rate, I might as well pay Whitney to sing me to sleep and Madonna to tuck me in.

It's not that I was running into better players this time, so much as the fact that I just wasn't getting any cards – absolutely *nothing*. And the more I lost, the worse I played.

I needed to get out of the casino, so I went outside into the streets with Gary. Even at night the heat can hit you – the night was warmer than an English summer day. Night-time Vegas is a fantastic sight, especially outside the Horseshoe in Fremont Street. This part of Vegas was given the name 'Glitter Gulch' because of the amount of neon here. Then they decided to build this huge dome roof over the whole of Fremont Street and make the underside into an enormous light show – they said it was the biggest in the world. Anything in Vegas to do with lights has to be the biggest in the world. I think it's the law. Another example: the light beam that shoots out of the top of the pyramid hotel, the Luxor, is the brightest light beam in the world. It fucking well would be. My arse was so hot from the spanking I'd just taken at the tables that if I'd dropped my keks they'd have seen it glowing from space.

I'd like to say that all this wasn't wasted on us, and for a few minutes it wasn't, but mostly I was thinking about how to get the Las Vegas Devilfish Express back on the rails before it ran out of steam and ended up upside down in a ditch. Gary decided to do some really serious thinking about the whole situation . . . in a nearby strip joint.

I decided not to go to bed. What was I gonna do there that would help? Nothing. I hadn't been to bed for two days anyway and now I'd got to that place where you're past sleep. I just needed a little inspiration. I decided to look for it back at the tables. There were always cash games going on, and things could only get better.

Next morning, I realized that I'd come up with another good epitaph – 'THINGS CAN ONLY GET BETTER'. Because that night I'd lost everything. Every cent. The very last $78,000 of the bankroll. In three days I'd managed to get myself into a $200,000 hole. And the sides are pretty steep on a hole that deep.

The bad thing about gamblers living out of each other's pockets – and they do – is that other players are often hitting you for loans. The good thing about gamblers living out of each other's pockets – and we do – is that I saw some fella in the casino who I knew I could hit for a loan.

He subbed me $3,000, enough for the buy-in to the Pot Limit Omaha event at noon. The payouts in events like this depend on how high up the field you finish. I was only a couple of spots away from getting into the money placing. Then I got into a heads-up confrontation with a Turkish player who had such a low forehead that his hair looked like one big eyebrow. Or maybe his wig had slipped forward. Anyway, I went all-in and pushed all my chips into the middle. He called, and pushed in his chips. We turned our cards over – there was one card to come. Everyone at the rail watching shifted forward a bit to see better. I saw that I was way ahead and that he only had two cards in the whole deck that he could catch to beat me – that's about a 19–1 shot, or 5 per cent chance of it happening. I couldn't believe he'd even called with the hand he had. So I didn't even need to get lucky here, I just needed to not get *un*lucky. Forty unknown cards and he could catch just two.

I got unlucky.

The Human Eyebrow saw his 5 per cent ship come in and I got bounced out of the tournament.

What I needed now was to get as lucky as the woman who'd walked into the new New York-New York Hotel Casino about a week ago. The local papers were still talking about it. She put a coin in the casino's Megabucks slot machine, pulled the handle, watched the big drums click round, and then heard the alarms go off – she'd won the jackpot of $12,000,000. Biggest ever slot machine payout in history. Now $12,000,000 ain't a bad haul for a fruit machine, is it? It's a fuckload of coins to try and carry up to your room, that's for sure. I don't know how long the odds were against the jackpot falling, but it just proved that the long odds eventually do come up for someone.

But just imagine how the poor fucker felt who had been playing that slot machine just before the jackpot dropped. Right now, I felt about as lucky as that guy.

On the fifth day of the WSOP I got my first run of good play, in the $1,500 Pot Limit Omaha event. Out of 250 entrants, I managed to scrap and fight my way into the last twenty; and it *was* a fight, because I was catching bugger-all cards. I knew things could be worse, though – those last twenty players included fellas with the names 'Marlon', 'Rupert', 'Manfred', 'Hilbert' and 'Tomko'. It must be awful when you're a baby and your mother suffers a brain injury just before she chooses your name. Fucking awful.

By the time we got down to the last thirteen, I knew I was only four places away from the final table and only twelve places away from winning the event and picking up $169,000. That would solve an awful lot of problems in one fell swoop. But, unlucky for some – and it was for me – I got bounced out in thirteenth place and picked up only $4,230 in prize money. Four thousand two hundred and thirty bucks. So, that was Gary's hotel mini-bar bill covered, then. What a relief. I might have just enough left to buy us a couple of steaks.

I needed to do a lot better than this and I knew it. It wasn't just bad luck either: it was that I was playing badly, which you can easily do when you're chasing losses. And, believe me, I could chase for England. I was on the chase now.

When you're on a big losing streak, things can seem a lot different, but you can't let it get to you. The noise of a casino when you walk through it, for instance – that noise of the chips being moved about and the slot machines rattling and the roulette numbers being called – all those sounds sound different when you're losing. When you're winning, it's the sound of somewhere where you want to be; when you're losing, it's all just a constant reminder that you ain't winning. Then I heard something that I didn't mind hearing:

'Dave? Dave!'

I turned round and there stood Bobby Lores, the Texas bail bondsman I'd made friends with last time at the Four Queens. Some people you meet you just hit it off with, and Bobby was one of them. Over the last three days I'd seen Bobby in cash games and tournament events and we'd even played on the same tables. I gathered he'd been quite a big winner in some of the games. He said we should go and find Gary and then all go out for dinner. Gary had been keeping out of my way since I'd gone $200k down, as well he might because I wasn't in the best of moods.

As a bondsman, Bobby had the job of posting bail for criminals, and then tracking them down if they skipped. He was also a gambler, as lots of Texans are – Texas is a big gambling state.

Over dinner I was telling him a few bad-beat stories, as poker players do, but I genuinely wasn't after anything from him. I'd only really just met the fella, after all. So I was surprised when at the end of the meal he said he'd loan me sixty grand. Out the corner of my eye I saw Gary look at me and when I turned to him he looked like his arse was chewing the seat. He was obviously thinking, *No, don't do it – you might lose*. I asked Bobby if he was sure about this.

'Positive,' he said. 'I know you're good for it, even if things go bad, but I remember how you played at the Four Queens and think you've got it in you to win big. I know you have. I've been around poker players all my life, son.'

I thanked him for that. And paid for the meal, obviously. Talk about 'the least I could do'.

A bloke I didn't know too well staking all that money on me might seem like an odd thing to people who don't gamble. I've found that non-gamblers find it very, very difficult to understand how gamblers deal with money. How they lose it, and risk it and lend it out, and then win it back only to risk losing it again. Gamblers are a breed apart. Normal people wouldn't give 6op to a guy who lived on the other side of the world at the drop of a hat, never mind $60k.

And non-players always say the same thing – why don't you quit while you're ahead? The simple answer is this – if you quit while you were ahead, if you quit at any time, then there'd be *no more playing*.

What I'd first thought years ago was still true: *you had to* not *care about money in order to win it.*

I knew that the next few days would bring cash games galore out there, and three other major WSOP events to play in.

I had $60,000 of Bobby's cash in my pocket.

Over the next two days, I lost every single cent of it.

18. Two Hundred and Eighty Thousand Dollars Bad

Quick death or victory: life on Death Row

Right now, money wise, I was freewheeling on an empty tank. You know that sound when a car's running out of petrol – that whining sound of the petrol pump when it's sucking up nothing but air? That's what I was hearing when I opened my wallet. There was just a sound where air was being sucked up instead of money. Me and Gary were potless. Flat. Fucking. Broke. Mind you, Gary was broke when he arrived, so if you count the 150 thongs he'd seen then he was still on a winner.

There's a lot of bad luck out there – in life and in poker – and eventually we all get our share. Sometimes it feels like we get an unfair share. What's important is this: not the bad luck itself (fuck the luck) but how you deal with it. That's when you find out what you've got in you. And Vegas was the kind of place that found you out.

I could win in one night in Vegas what it'd take me a year to win in England. Donnacha O'Dea said to me, 'I'd sooner be lucky in Vegas than London.' But it wasn't only the winnings that were bigger – so were the losses.

Here's the thing, and I don't want this to sound too sentimental, *but* – if it's only your bank account that's been emptied out and not your heart, then you've still got a chance. That might sound soppy, but the toughest boxer will tell you that heart is what makes champions. You need the heart to get back up and get back out there, and as long as you've got that, you've still got a fighting chance.

I had all the heart, I just needed the cash. Because when you did the sums, Heart + Sod-All-Money = No Game. And I couldn't rip out my heart, throw the old pump on the table and say, 'I'm all in!'

So, I was 5,000 miles away from home, $200,000 of my own money down, $80,000 (all told) of other people's money in debt, with nothing in my pockets but the lining and fluff, nothing in my wallet but fresh air, and no money to get back on track. And definitely no $10,000 to enter the big one – the million-dollar WSOP Main Event.

Vegas is the absolute worst place on earth to go broke. The place just goes cold around you. You're in the middle of the desert but you might as well be in the Arctic. The place exists to make money and to generate money, so it's just like Hollywood: it has no time for losers. When you're in Vegas, and you're playing and winning, you feel like the brightest bulb on the Strip. But when you lose, and lose big, it's as if someone's yanked out your plug. And if there's one thing that ain't welcome in Vegas, it's a blown bulb. It screws up the whole vibe.

Vegas is really just a big wet dream being sold to gamblers about what they might win if they get lucky. As we know, most of them don't. And even when you had a talent for something, like I had for cards, you could still get royally screwed.

I could see that Gary felt much worse about that than

I did. I knew I could live to play another day. At that moment, though, every bridge we might have used as an escape route had been burned. There was no way back or forward. Gary had said to me earlier that I was on the poker equivalent of Death Row. With every minute, Hull was starting to look more and more like the next destination for the Devilfish Express.

There were a large number of Brits out there at the World Series, more than I'd thought, and more than there had ever been before. Poker was becoming more popular and the World Series was getting bigger every year. That was a bit of a touch for me because it meant I ran into a couple of guys I knew from playing in Manchester. I borrowed $2,000 off them.

I used it to enter the next Pot Limit Hold'em tournament. The buy-in for the event was . . . $2,000, so I really was playing in the Last Chance Saloon. And that did make me want to go to bed a little early. So, I got my head down at one minute to midnight. Who says poker players can't have early nights?

The $2,000 Pot Limit Hold'em started at noon, as all the WSOP events did. There were 247 entrants, a prize pool of $494,000 and a first prize of $180,310. It was one of the biggest first prizes other than the Main Event and had attracted one of the biggest fields. All the poker big boys were in there to slug it out – Johnny Chan, Stu Ungar, Phil Hellmuth, Chris Ferguson, Scotty Nguyen – so it definitely wasn't going to be a tickling match, it was going to be a war.

In tournaments such as this, the players are split into

tables of nine. As players are knocked out and the number at the table falls, those still in are moved to other tables. Where you're drawn, or where you're moved to if your table breaks, can make or break your tournament. You might be moved from a table where you were dominating the play to a table full of some of the toughest players in the event.

I got through the first half of the day OK, about evens, and by the time I made it to the second break in the afternoon, I'd built up a decent stack. I was definitely playing cagier than normal – it's not my style to play tight to just get in the money. I've always got to play to win. But I knew I had to tighten up my game at least until the loose players had been squeezed out. If anyone was going to take any money off me, they were going to have to earn it.

In this tournament, the top twenty-seven finishers would be paid, though most of them wouldn't get paid much:

27th to 19th got $2,964,
18th to 16th got $3,952,
16th to 13th got $4,940,
12th to 10th got $5,928.

Ninth place, which is a pretty good result in a strong field of 247, only paid $7,904. None of those sums were any good to me. They seemed even smaller compared to the amount I was trying to earn back. I tried not to think too much about the fact that even if I came third I'd only win $43,930 – not even enough to pay Bobby back his $60,000, let alone the other guys. It felt like I was trying to climb Mount Everest on roller skates.

I was aware of Gary prowling about the place. Sometimes he'd come up to the rail to watch, and sometimes he was just too nervous to look, so he went off for a wander. I didn't have the luxury. I had to sit there and grind it out.

The end of the first day came round slowly but the number of tables and players had been reduced drastically. Towards the end there had been a lot of brutal beats and eliminations. Some big names had gone. I'd handed out a few of those beats and I was feeling like I was back up to speed. Time was called on the first day's play at 11 p.m. with thirty of us still left in.

I decided to go straight up to my room to get some kip. I knew with the time difference between Vegas and England that just as I was packing up for bed, the kids would be coming home from school. That was a weird thought, because England now felt much more than 5,000 miles away, it felt like another planet. And I seemed to have been in Vegas for a lot longer than I actually had. But then a losing streak tends to slow time down, like a winning streak speeds things up. Tomorrow I'd be looking at the tournament in the same way that gladiators used to think about fighting in front of the crowds – they wanted either a quick death, or victory.

Next day, soon after noon, the first three of the thirty fell, so we were down to the twenty-seven money places, which might have pleased a lot of the players, but it meant absolutely jack to me. Most of the money placings were worth sweet FA.

In the money were two English players, one French

and one German; all the rest were Americans. Which sounded like a cue for a bad joke: 'Two Englishmen, one Frenchman, one German and twenty-three Americans walk into a bar ...' Funnily enough, the other English player was Chris Truby. He was one of the two English guys who'd been at the first table I'd played on at the Four Queens back in January.

There was a good crowd building up now as we got further into the afternoon and nearer to the final table, and punters started to flood into the casino.

By the time all the blood had been wiped off, we were down to the last nine for the final table. And I was one of them.

Cards were in the air – meaning the game started – at four o'clock in the afternoon. I was fourth in the chip count with $64,000. The chip leader with $131,000 was Stan Goldstein, who eventually finished fifth. Chris Ferguson, aka 'Jesus' because of his long hair, was the tail-end Charlie with $23,000.

Over the next three hours the chips moved backwards and forwards. The price of the blinds started to rise, which meant the action got bigger and the play quicker, and that suited me down to the ground. I was chip leader now. I seemed to be the table assassin. I iced 'Eskimo' Paul Clark with Q-4. Now, with only three of us left, the next faller would be the big one – the one that would leave two players fighting heads-up for the tournament. I couldn't wait to get to the heads-up. It only took three minutes for me to take out the American 1983 Main Event winner Tom McEvoy, with my pair of 8s to his 5-4.

So, at last, after everything that had happened, we were now down to just two players – Chris Truby and me. Two Brits in Yankland playing for a WSOP title. I didn't know it at the time but it was the first time in WSOP history that two Englishmen had gone head to head for a title. We were about equal in chips, me with $265k to Chris's $230k. I didn't know how long this was going to last, but I saw that the tournament officials were gathering, and the announcer with a microphone, and the crowd had grown bigger. No one wanted to miss a quick kill. They were right. When the end came it was quicker than I'd thought – only twenty minutes and seven hands into the heads-up.

We were both dealt our two hole cards. I bent up the corners of mine and saw that I had A-4, both hearts. I immediately raised the pot to $20,000. Chris re-raised $20,000. I called. The dealer 'burned' the top card (put it to one side), tapped the table (as traditional) and turned over the next three cards. The flop came down:

5 ♥   7 ♥   3 ♠

I knew this was going to be it, one way or the other – death or victory time: I had two inside straight draws *and* a flush draw. If a 2 came I had Ace to 5, and if a 6 came I had 3 to 7. Or if another heart came I had the nut flush. But at the moment I had nothing. Chris must have something on the flop, or more likely an overpair, because he bet $60,000.

But I had a potential monster out there, and I was hoping he had an overpair so that my Ace might be good too. But even if he'd made a set (three of a kind) with a pocket pair of 7s, 5s or 3s it would still be almost a coin-flip, although he'd be slight favourite. All I had at the moment, though, was Ace-high. But still, this was it, baby. Hold on to your hats . . .

I re-raised the pot.

The crowd gasped, and then cheered. Everyone looked at Chris. I knew he was calling. And he did, straight away, he pushed in his chips. If I won the hand, I'd win the tournament.

This was it. Everyone was cheering. Over the noise I could hear Gary shouting, 'Come *on*, Dave! *Come on, Devilfish!*'

The dealer said, 'Gentlemen', meaning we should turn our cards over. The crowd quietened. Chris flipped his first, and then I did the same. He had a pair of 7s. He'd flopped top set.

This wasn't the best of news for me. A set on the flop is a very strong hand because if the board pairs, it gives you a full house (or quads). And a full house beats a flush. If the turn card was a 3, 5 or 7, I was finished.

The dealer paused, tapped the table, and turned the fourth card:

K ♦

For just a split second, when I saw the red of the diamond, I thought it was the heart that I needed for a flush. That didn't do the old ticker any good. The King helped neither of us improve, but it did help Chris because it meant that for me, one chance had gone. He was ahead and I had only one chance left.

Now even though I say so myself, I'm a ballsy fucker. That isn't bragging, it's just how it is. I'll sit across from anyone, and I'll play anyone. But, all things considered, at this point ... when all my bankroll's wiped out ... when my $200k winnings are all gone ... when I'm chin-deep in debt ... when I'm halfway round the world ... I'll tell you, waiting for that last card to be turned over even made *my* heart start doing a quick drum roll. And waiting to see that last card was about the most brutal few seconds I'd ever had at a card table.

The British in the crowd, led by Gary, started chanting, 'TWO, SIX, HEART! TWO, SIX, HEART!' Even in the middle of all the noise and the shouting, when it gets down to this stage of a match it always seems like the whole place goes quiet – and I felt as though I could've heard a fly pissing on cotton wool.

The dealer tapped the table, paused, and then she turned over the last card:

2 ♠

I looked again. Yep, it really was a 2. *A fucking 2!* That gave me a winning straight – Ace, 2, 3, 4, 5, *baby*. My supporters just erupted – Gary, Bobby and the two Manchester boys I'd borrowed from. I stood up out of my chair and punched the air, and Gary shouted out louder than anyone else in the room and then jumped over the rail like Frankie Dettori leaping off a horse. The whole place went mental. Gary jumped on top of me, shouting with happiness and relief. A real Hollywood card.

But when the press wrote the next day about 'Devilfish catching a miracle 2', they were wrong; they just didn't understand poker. I actually had two shots at three 2s, two shots at three 6s and two 1-in-4 shots at catching a heart – which meant I was around evens to win the hand when we flipped our cards. But who cares?

Nobody but Gary and me really knew exactly how much that last card meant. That's why in the photograph taken just after the last card was turned, I'm out of my chair with my fist in the air (not something I usually do), and Gary is just behind me, shouting his head off. He'd seen me get in these spots so many times before and I think he just couldn't believe that I'd got us out of it once more. Talk about Houdini.

I flipped the dealer a $1,000 chip as a thank you, and I started to think about the party we were going to have that night – and for the next two weeks I had left in Vegas. And if only I'd known then what was in store for me over the next two weeks, the partying would have been even bigger.

But whatever happened from here on, I now had my first World Series of Poker champions' gold bracelet and no one could take that away. I later learned that I was only the third Englishman in WSOP history to win a tournament bracelet. I also knew what I was going to get engraved on it. It would be 'Devilfish'.

In the poker world, that's who I was now – Devilfish.

19. The Devilfish Express

Get on board – the money rush starts here . . .

I woke up the next morning with five things:

1) A fucker of a hangover.
2) One part blood to nine parts vodka still chugging through my veins.
3) A mouth like a gravedigger's armpit.
4) A WSOP bracelet engraved with my name.
5) The British Prime Minister's wage under my bed in a bag . . . *in cash.*

Let me explain.

The previous night, while I'd been playing my backside flat at poker, someone had been watching the news on satellite, and they'd learned an interesting bit of information. Turned out that the day that I was coming back from the poker dead and making that Ace-to-5 straight was exactly the same day – 2 May 1997 – that Tony Blair had just been sworn in as our new Prime Minister back in Britain. And Tony Blair's salary for the year, apparently, would be £102,000. Pretty good. But in a two-day Hold'em poker tournament, I'd just won the dollar equivalent of £112,000. And I hadn't had to shake any hands or kiss any babies or arses to get it.

Not bad for a kid who'd left school with no exams, no

11. Lester Piggott with Devilfish.

12. Devilfish and Lyle Berman (with gold brick).

13. Devilfish pictured with Mike Greco and Stacey in Las Vegas.

14. Devilfish with Ronnie Wood and Jimmy White.

15. Devilfish and Frank Lampard in Las Vegas in 2006.

16. Devilfish pictured with Steve Davis.

17. Devilfish with his dad Stan and his mum Joyce.

18. Devilfish with Roy Hilda, Stacey and Freddie Foreman in London.

19. Devilfish at home in Swanland, Hull, in 2010.

20. Brian Hughes, Devilfish, Sonic and Andy Holland in Hull in 2009.

21. Devilfish with Tony Booth and Dave Pride.

22.
Devilfish
with his
son Dave.

23.
Steven,
Mandy,
Chris,
Mike and
Matthew.

24.
Devilfish
with Paul
and Kerry.

plans, no future, a jacketful of woodwork tools, and a kick up the arse.

First order of the day was an English fry-up, or the closest thing Vegas could do to one, which ain't that close. Their version has 'eggs over-easy' – which sounded to me like a fertile woman who can't say no.

Then I met up with Gary and went for my WSOP bracelet fitting. I decided to celebrate with a spending spree in the casino boutiques and picked up $4,000 worth of suits and shirts for the two of us. On the way back to our rooms, walking across the casino floor with armfuls of shopping bags, we happened to pass a table near the foyer that had a seat free – seat three.

I said to the dealer, 'Deal me in, pal. How much is it?'

He said, 'It's a $5,000 table.'

An hour later I was up $83,000. Not bad for an hour's work.

I had nearly two weeks ahead of me before the million-dollar WSOP Main Event began on 12 May. Between now and then there were another eleven World Series tournaments of all kinds of poker – 7-Card Stud, Texas Hold'em, Omaha Hi-Lo Split, Deuce-to-Seven Draw, etc., etc. I could play all those styles, no problem. There was only one tournament event that I couldn't enter because it would've cost me far too much: the Women's 7-Card Stud event. I thought that sex-change surgery was too high a price to pay to get a sit-down at that table. Not that you'd be sitting down much after an operation that would rob you of your stone cold nuts.

Anyway, over the next two weeks I was less interested in the WSOP events than in the card room cash games. I did what I'd have done back home: I went on a massive cash-game hunt. The difference was I didn't have to do five cities in a day; all I had to do was get into a lift, press 'GROUND', get out, and walk across a casino floor.

I didn't want to disappoint all those gamblers who'd come out to Vegas expecting to lose. I saw players with $10,000, $20,000, $30,000 stacked in front of them. And these were guys who weren't even considered big players. So you could sit down and win $100,000 a night. Back home I'd wiped out five cash games in one night and still only bagged about thirty grand, and it was a fuckload of work. In Vegas you could suck up $100k in a few hours – and without the petrol costs, the fights, the threats, the raids, the frostbite, the rising damp and the crap food that all got added on to your bill back home.

They say the best way to end up with a million from gambling is start off with two. But I was planning on going the other way.

It wasn't all machine-gunning caged animals, though. I did some genuine big-game hunting too. There's no point going home with a bag full of squirrel heads to mount on your trophy wall. You need some lions. This is where a well-known American player called Lyle Berman came in. He was older than me and had been playing for longer. He was known as a high-stakes cash game specialist, and a good one. He already had three WSOP event bracelets to his name. He was a respected player. Probably the most recognizable Omaha player.

I asked Lyle whether he fancied a game and he agreed. He'd obviously heard the rumours going round about me and probably thought I was some flash-in-the-pan that he could turn the heat up under. Depends what's in the pan, though, doesn't it?

From a distance it didn't exactly look like an even match, with the odds stacked heavily in Lyle's favour. I sat down – a gabby, smart-arse motherfucker in shades with a freshly minted WSOP bracelet. Lyle sat down – a quiet, grey-haired gentleman with glasses. He was a successful businessman and wealthy. I'd been lucky enough to win a WSOP event, clearing all my debts. For the two weeks since that win I'd been riding high in the cash games. I now had $240,000 all told, so I was $40,000 up on the trip.

So I'd gone skint, borrowed, gone skint again, borrowed, gone skint, borrowed again ... and finally won. *But*, I was still willing to risk everything I had in a heads-up game with a guy who could buy me out a thousand times over. There was no risk to him. And, yet, I was still willing to put it all on the line. Everything. That's the sort of guy I was.

Lyle started off with about half a million and I had my near quarter-mill.

Sitting behind him, Lyle had support from a huge Texas fella called TJ Cloutier, who was a famous ex-American football player and now a famous poker player. And – get this – laid out in front of Lyle, on the table next to his cards, was a massive solid gold bar. You couldn't help but keep looking at this big yellow bar shining under the lights. He said that he kept this gold brick as a reminder. A reminder of what, I didn't know. Maybe of all the gold teeth and fillings he'd won off other players.

In only a few months, I'd gone from playing in the backstreets of Bradford, Manchester and dark old London casinos – and often playing against Brits with limited bankrolls – to playing in the Nevada desert in the gambling capital of the world against a millionaire businessman with mineshaft pockets full of cash and a solid gold brick as a lucky charm. That kind of game change, and the amount of money at stake, would cause a lot of players to produce their own bricks of a different kind.

I don't think Lyle or TJ were too worried about the competition. From their side of the table, what they saw were two pasty-faced Brits from Britland.

All we had was my belief in how good I was. And Gary's belief . . . in how good I was.

I had one other believer on my side, the British player Ali Sarkeshik, who knew from experience how good a player I was heads-up. He must have had some faith in me because he had 15 per cent of my action.

Before you knew it, I was $100,000 up against Lyle. I kept changing the way I played and I was doing everything that he wouldn't expect me to do. I checked the nuts right to the end and got a big bet out of him before I re-raised. I was doing all sorts of moves. It was like poker gymnastics. I bet aggressively one minute and then changed the next. I knew, from Lyle's point of view, this wasn't how it was supposed to go, but, for me, this was exactly how I'd seen it panning out.

At one point, I got Aces, which, as I said, in Omaha can deceive you into thinking you've got a better hand than you have. Even when the flop came 2, 3, Q, giving me a straight draw, I still had a bad feeling about it and I threw the hand away; he'd re-raised me on the flop and even though usually I'd go to war, this time I folded and waited for the next hand.

At this stage, I can't imagine that Lyle liked me too much. No one likes getting beaten. Especially by some English guy with a chip on his shoulder who keeps having a go at everybody.

Eventually, I ended up getting $168,000 off Lyle. I was just sorry that I couldn't get him to the point where he'd push the gold bar into the pot. That would've looked good sitting in the pawnshop window. But he was smart enough to realize this was not his day.

News travels fast when you take a lot of money off someone heads-up in Vegas. People like heads-up play because it's real man-to-man stuff, like gunfighters facing each other down the street. And news of me taking on all comers had even made it to New York. I knew this because the card room manager at the Horseshoe, Tony, rang me and told me that some fella from NYC had just flown in to play me. Said he wanted to play me half his game – which was Razz – and half my game – which was Omaha. He obviously thought he was flying in to bust me.

Like a lot of New York guys, he looked like he was part of the Mafia. But as long as his money was good he could've had horns for ears for all I cared. The beautiful thing about the game Razz is that it's very similar to London Lo-Ball, which I had played. London Lo-Ball is played Ace-to-6 and Razz is played Ace-to-5; that's the only difference, and apart from that, they're the same. In Razz the best hand is called 'the wheel', which is Ace, 2, 3, 4, 5.

So things were pretty much in my favour: I was good at Razz, which was his game, and (from what I could learn) he wasn't too good at Omaha, which was my game. Heads he loses, tails I win.

I told him I'd never played Razz before, which was true, it wasn't a hustle, because I'd only played a very similar game (London Lo-Ball). I was able to bluff him on so many Razz pots because he thought I was frightened of the game and that I didn't know what I was doing.

By the time we'd finished the Razz part of the match, I'd already got most of the money out of him. So playing Omaha was a freewheel downhill. I had him completely beaten. By the end, I'd taken nearly sixty grand off him.

Next in line to try and take down the Devilfish was a player called Doc Jennings. There's an old gamblers' saying – never play poker with a guy named 'Doc'. Which is a good reason to not listen to old gamblers. He was supposed to be the best Deuce-to-Seven player in Las Vegas. Maybe he was. He was a biggish guy with kinda curly hair and glasses, another Southern player.

Like the New York guy, Doc came up with the idea of playing heads-up with me, half my game – Omaha – and half his game – Deuce-to-Seven. I said that was fine by me. I wasn't in the mood to lose to anyone. We played Omaha and Doc started to get in front. Doc spoke in that slow, drawn-out drawl. At one point, when he was winning, he turned to me and said, 'Devilfish. Ah think ah *liiiike* this *Omahaaaa*!' Then we moved on to playing his game, Deuce-to-Seven. About two hours later when I'd broken him and he was getting up from the table, I said, 'Doc. Ah think ah *liiike* this Deuce-to-Seven!' He took it like a pro.

By the end of the game, I had about $300,000 on the table, and I didn't think it could get any better. Who happened to be walking by but Walter 'Puggy' Pearson. Puggy was a proper poker legend. He'd been a pool hustler, a sports better, a card player, a poker champion and a gambler who'd bet on anything that moved. He wasn't difficult to spot in his loud patterned shirts and stripy trousers – to me, he always looked like he'd been in a fight with two deckchairs. And he chuffed away on big Cuban cigars.

Puggy had won four WSOP bracelets, including the Main Event title in 1973 against Johnny Moss. This geezer was another member of the gambling royalty.

Gary had already told me about Puggy Pearson's mobile tour bus which he travelled round in from tournament to tournament, and which was famous because it had a gambling quote of Puggy's painted down the side of it in big letters. Everyone seemed to know this bloody van. It was more famous than most gamblers.

So this was too good a chance to miss. As Puggy walked past in a cloud of blue cigar smoke – I knew it was him because through the smoke I could see deck-chairs fighting – I shouted out to him.

'Hey, Puggy! How about me and you playing heads-up?' He turned round to look at me.

I said, 'Come on, Puggy! You're always telling everyone what a great gambler you are, so let's play!'

Like Doc, he was another good ol' Southern boy. He walked over to me, smiling, and in his lazy drawl, he said, 'Devilfish. Son, I wanna *show* you somethin'.'

I told Gary to watch my money. Puggy asked me to walk with him across the casino. Outside the Horseshoe we crossed the road to the car park. Then I saw his van, which wasn't exactly a van – it was a massive touring mobile home. It looked like it needed two engines to move it. The kind of thing you only see in America because it wouldn't fit most other places. In Britain, this vehicle would've had its own postcode, street name and seventeen wheelie bins.

On the side, in big letters, were painted the words 'PUGGY PEARSON – ROVING GAMBLER' and underneath that, something else was written, which Puggy pointed at and started to read out loud. He said, 'As you can see, it says: *I'll play any man from any land any game he can name for any amount I can count*,' and then he lowered his finger to point at some really small writing at the bottom of the bus: '. . . *Providing I like it!*'

Then he turned to me, and to answer my challenge, he said, 'And ah don't *like* it, *Devilfish*! Ah don't like it *at all.*' He stuck the cigar back in his mouth and I started laughing. It was really funny. He was a clever enough gambler to give himself a get-out clause.

Puggy lived in Vegas and later he would die in Vegas,

which tells you plenty about the man. And if he died broke, it was probably the mobile home petrol bills.

He was also smart enough to know when to avoid a good player on a hot streak. That was quite a compliment to me, when I thought about it – Puggy Pearson, a four-time bracelet winner, WSOP champion and a member of the Poker Hall of Fame, didn't want to play me heads-up, even though he'd 'play any man from any land', because when he thought about playing me, he 'didn't like it'.

The actual Main Event of the WSOP turned out to be a bit of an anti-climax for me after all the action I'd been getting. I got knocked out early, but then I was exhausted from all the cash games I'd been playing so I hadn't given myself much of a chance.

Eventually, the WSOP got down to the last six players (including Stu Ungar) and five of those were classed as Las Vegas residents, which says something about the town. The only finalist not from Vegas was a London player and mate of mine, Mel Judah.

That final became one of the biggest stories in poker history because Stu Ungar – in his blue John Lennon shades – won it and became the 1997 WSOP champion, sixteen years after his last win. He was now the only person in history to win it three times. Everyone was calling him The Comeback Kid.

Within a year Stu Ungar would be dead, and there's no comeback from that. A terrible waste of a great talent.

For me, things were definitely alive. On only my second trip to Vegas, I'd become known. I realized that when I walked into the Four Queens and ran into Johnny Chan. Johnny was a bit of a poker legend. He'd won the WSOP Main Event in 1987 and 1988, and was runner-up in 1989.

Being the cocky fucker I am, I walked right up to Chan and said, 'Now then, Johnny boy!' He barely nodded.

This was getting to be a bit of a surprise trip: I'd outgrown Hull, outgrown the north of England and then outgrown London; the last thing I thought would happen would be for me to outgrow Vegas. So the only place left for me now was the rest of the world. But first, there was somewhere I had to go that was more important than the rest of the world. Back home.

20. 'Apart from the $742,000 in Cash – Anything to Declare?'

Homeward bound . . . only to bounce off round the world

Putting your feet up in the first-class cabin of a flight home, while you're being served champagne and steak, is a pretty good feeling. Especially if you know you've also got a bag under your chair crammed with over three-quarters of a million dollars. Well, you didn't think I was gonna put it in the hold, did you?

Before flying, I decided that carrying so much cash round in duty-free carrier bags wasn't a particularly good idea. So at the airport mall I picked up a black leather holdall that looked like it would hold the cash, and took it to the till. I put it on the counter and then lifted up the duty-free bags and dumped all the cash straight into the holdall. There was a young kid serving behind the counter and when he saw all these bricks of cash tumbling from one bag into the other, his jaw practically smacked onto the floor. He was still in a bit of a daze as I paid for the bag, and because I'd enjoyed his reaction so much, I winked and gave him a $100 tip. That cut the strings on his jaw for the second time.

I'd brought the money on board as hand luggage and hung on to it like a guy with a bad heart carrying a spare pump in an icebox. These days, I'd probably be singled out as a potential terrorist and stabbed in the eye with a biro. I realized that clinging on to the bag could look a bit suss, so I put it in the overhead locker. If I got any sleep, I'd do it with one eye open: that was an awful lot of money to put in a plastic locker with a crappy lock. This Vegas trip had been the roller-coaster ride of my life, no doubt about it.

This was the second time in four months that I'd taken off from Las Vegas to fly back to Britain. This time the winnings were much bigger, and so was the splash I'd made. I'd now played some of the big name poker players, and beaten them. If that was a surprise to them, it wasn't a surprise to me. I know that sounds a bit flash but it's also the truth, so that makes it OK. Anyway, what do you want from me – modesty? At this point in my life if I'd been twins I'd have married myself.

Then again, if I was modest, how could I tell you about all the great things I've done? (I'm laughing when I say this, by the way . . .)

The thing is this: poker players are like boxers, you hardly ever hear one praising their own. It's something to do with the way you have to think about yourself to go into battle. It's a warrior thing. I'm not comparing boxing to poker in the danger stakes, obviously, because I know that stepping between the ropes is a dangerous job – you might come back out on a board, or flying through the air. When you're in the ring you really are on your own.

So, flying back home first class with Gary and my shoes kicked off and my feet up and my champagne and my gold WSOP bracelet and my bags of cash . . . it felt to me like I'd earned every penny. I'd certainly risked enough to get it. And I'd played long enough and hard enough in enough shitholes to earn my stripes. I didn't blame Puggy Pearson for taking one look at me and deciding he didn't like it – I wouldn't have wanted to play me either.

Being home was strange. I'd only been away a month but it seemed much longer. A lot had happened. Sometimes it's not until you're home that it hits you how much you've missed it; and it's weird also how soon after getting back, you want to hit the road again. My theory is that every gambler, especially a travelling one, needs to check back that the rock is still there. And by 'the rock' I mean the stable things in your life – your wife, your kids, your house – basically, your home. If your home life is sorted out you can deal with the world's shit. Exactly the same as when you're in prison. Every gambler knows that if your home is settled, you can more easily leave it. And the weight of any losses you carry are easier to bear. This time, I wasn't carrying any losses. I was carrying a big bag of wins.

It was great to see Mandy and the kids. The boys loved seeing the gold WSOP bracelet with 'Devilfish' engraved on it. My mother and father only ever really knew bits they read in the paper about my wins. I didn't go round bragging about them. I enjoyed treating them to whatever they wanted. So they knew one way or another. It's nice to be able to send your mam and dad on holiday. Their only experience of holidays had been the same as mine when I was growing up – Bridlington.

I went round to my dad's and showed him the World

Series bracelet. He was an old tough guy, my dad, so there were no hugs or back-slaps. But I could tell he was pleased. I think he realized that this poker thing was paying off, and compared to what I'd been up to before, me being a gambler was more like being on the straight and narrow. Which says a lot. I mean, it's come to something when parents are pleased that their son's a professional gambler. It must have seemed almost respectable.

I bought myself a new Lexus and paid the mortgage off on the house. And we were up and running.

From blazing Vegas to dull Hull. Don't get me wrong, I love Hull, it's my home. I just wish I could turn the dimmer switch up on the sun.

A really good thing that happened was when I went with Gary back to the casino in Leeds where we'd first met about seven years before. Gary had first gone home to his family in Doncaster. He called me one night and asked if I fancied meeting up again at the Stakis casino in Leeds. When we walked into the Stakis card room, the punters and players all stood up and applauded as we walked across the floor. They'd heard about the Vegas exploits and the bracelet win. Poker wasn't mainstream news at this time, but the gambling grapevine was there.

It felt pretty good, to be honest, getting a reception like that. It happened a few times because Gary was such a good storyteller and he'd tell everyone about what had happened over there. Word got round pretty quick. Like I'll say a hundred times, gamblers aren't sentimental folk (especially the Brits) – a gambler's life is selfish and independent and you sacrifice a lot – so it's a big deal to get that kind of acknowledgement from other players. I knew I was a bit of an upfront, in-your-face kind of guy but I think they respected that I'd gone out there and risked everything I had.

When I thought about it afterwards, I think I realized for the first time that when I'd flown out to Vegas, I'd sort of been carrying the Vegas Dream for a lot of the guys who stayed behind. I guess a lot of the players were either too broke, too unskilled, too inexperienced, too scared or too unlucky to follow me out there. At one time I'd been all those things – except scared. Fear had never held me back.

It was a strange night in Leeds, because I knew I was going to be seeing a lot less of these guys in future. I was moving on to other things. And you can't take everyone with you.

London, of course, was still worth hitting, big time. There's nothing better for a northern gambler than taking money off southerners. Providing you could find them down there. London casinos had such international punters it was like a European pick'n'mix. You might end up round a table with an Arab, a Greek, an Indian, a Turk, a Chinese guy, a Pole and a Brummie. So, basically, no one whose first language was English.

One reputation that I'd picked up over the years, apart for being an aggressive player, was being a good reader of other players. That is a massive weapon to have on your side and it can't be taught. It's much more instinctive. I got a lift from accurately calling other players' hands; and if you do that a few times at a table, it puts everyone on notice that they need to have a good hand to go against you. It's a good leg-wobbler – it gets other players scared.

It came in handy when I got involved in a big tournament at the London Vic. This was when I first met Jesse May, who would go on to become a famous poker commentator. Every game needs its ambassadors, and Jesse was a kind of world poker missionary. He was American, but I didn't hold that against him. You'll know him if you see him at a tournament: he's the smiley short-arse who looks like he's had his hair combed by Stevie Wonder.

Anyway, in this game at the Vic, against John Shoreman, I had the third best hand you can get in poker: four of a kind. That is a very difficult hand to lay down. I know players who would rather lay down on railway tracks than lay down four of a kind. But I knew that my opponent had a straight flush, which is the best hand in poker after a Royal Flush. It's difficult to accept that you might be behind, even with a real peach of a hand like quads. But if you're behind, you're behind. So I laid the hand down. And I turned it over and showed what I'd done. That caused a big ripple to go through the crowd. I looked at the other guy, and I could see that because I'd laid down the quads, he felt like he almost owed it to me to show his hand. Sure enough, he had the straight flush. There was a burst of applause from the spectators.

Afterwards, when he'd heard about it, Jesse May said, 'I don't know of any player in the world other than Devilfish who would be able to lay that hand down!' Which shows that Jesse should get out more.

*

After not being long in the UK, I went straight out to Amsterdam. My old mate from Armley, Pete Robinson, decided to come out with me, along with Paz who'd just got out of the nick. Pete was terrified of flying, so we wound him up all the way.

In Amsterdam I went to Marcel Lüske's private gambling club. I had my first heads-up game with a German guy called Markus Golser. I knew he was a very aggressive player, and he'd come to Marcel's place just to play me. The cameras were rolling so I played my 'A' game and managed to break him. After that game we became good mates – and when I played at his club he'd usually take a piece of me.

When I got into the airport on the way home, I wasn't exactly inconspicuous. It didn't help that everyone else going through Customs seemed to be a white-haired five-foot-two pensioner. It made me look like a Mafia assassin on a retirement away-day. I was a strong odds-on favourite to get searched. I might as well have been carrying a fluorescent gun-shaped balloon with 'STOP ME' written on it in fresh blood.

Did I mention that I was also carrying cash – £50,000 and $80,000 – in a bag? So it was no surprise when one of the Customs officers asked me to walk over to be searched.

Now at this time, before the euro, if I'd been all round Europe I might have half a dozen different kinds of money: French francs, Austrian schillings, English pounds, Dutch guilders, German marks. I was a travelling bureau de change. The only currencies I didn't carry were Monopoly money and chocolate coins.

The Customs guy opened my case and found the hundred and thirty thousand – in thirteen small bricks of cash – and then he opened my passport and saw that it had been stamped on more times than a circus ring full of elephants. He slowly looked me up and down.

He finally said, 'You're not a hit man, are you?'

I told him I was a poker player. From the look on his face, I might as well have stuck with the first option. This was still at a time when most of the public didn't know you could actually be a professional poker player. So saying that made you sound like a liar, a lunatic or . . . a hit man.

For me, anyway, it was never a job. That didn't sum it up. I did it to *escape* doing a job. It was always more of a lifestyle. You certainly couldn't live this way unless it was naturally in you; and if you tried to force this life on someone, it would kill them.

The Customs guy finally gave me the all-clear after calling the casino I'd been playing in. And if you're leaving a country then you're soon going to be someone else's problem, not theirs.

By the time the flight arrived at Humberside it was late enough for there to be only one guy on the arrivals desk, and he didn't seem that bothered. I hate it when you walk through Customs and there's no fucker there – it just makes you think about all the stuff you could've brought through. Shame life doesn't have a rewind button.

Over the next twelve months I flew more miles than I'd done in the first forty-two years of my life. I went back to America three times, to France three times, and to

Amsterdam. I entered over forty tournaments and got a money finish or a win in twenty of them. It's not that I'd got a taste for airline food, but the winnings were bigger abroad. If I was going to sit at a table for hours and put everything into it, I wanted a pay-off. The bigger the better.

I carried my Vegas form through to the card rooms of Europe for the next year. It became quite a roll: at the Vic I came second in the European No Limit Hold'em Championship and picked up £22,062.

Then in Vegas I got $16,000 at the Pot Limit Omaha Hall of Fame Classic and second in the Omaha Hi-Lo.

In Paris I won first prize and $10,902 in the Pot Limit Courcheval and $30,399 in the Pot Limit Omaha Euro Finals of Poker.

Back in London I got second place at the Vic's Hold'em Christmas Cracker (where I'd always done well).

And in Amsterdam, a fifth place in the Hold'em Classic.

Vegas gave me a second place. And I got another first place and $18,936 in the Pot Limit Omaha tournament in Paris.

And at home I won a game of snap with a mate who stutters.

I probably had more sleep in aeroplane seats than I did in my own bed. But the year went by fast and before I knew it, it was time for the World Series of Poker again in Las Vegas.

But big prizes aren't only found at the card tables. At this time, I had probably the biggest win of my career, and it was absolutely nothing to do with poker.

After splitting up with Susan and her going to Liverpool with the kids, apart from the visits I'd made there, I hadn't seen my daughter Kerry and son Paul since. I'd been told that they had moved to Greece with their mother. I'd been told wrongly, as it turned out, because they were still living in Liverpool. Kerry, when she'd got older, had decided to get in touch with me. She'd gone to the trouble of finding me through the family tracing service of the Salvation Army. When she telephoned, I was away, but Mandy had taken the call. Now some women might not like the idea of children of a previous marriage suddenly appearing out of the blue, and I've seen that happen to other men, but Mandy is so genuinely kind and such a diamond that she wanted Kerry to get in touch with me as soon as possible.

I was in the Aviation Club casino in Paris, so Mandy rang me with the news and gave me Kerry's number. It was great to hear Kerry's voice and to know that she and Paul wanted to see me. It was better than flopping any royal flush. We talked, and then arranged that when I got back to Britain I'd meet with both Kerry and Paul.

So I guess sometimes I did get lucky in casinos – out of nowhere, I'd got two Aces.

21. Vegas Normal

Playing the world

Being back in Vegas for the 1998 World Series of Poker was a good feeling. Like how I felt when I'd played poker well for the first time or the first time I'd walked into a casino. It was a long way from the Fifty-One Club in Hull all those years ago.

I turned out Devilfish style: black suit, orange shades, WSOP winner's bracelet and two brand-new rings that I'd had made. The truth is, I'd asked a guy in Vegas to make me another 'Devilfish' bracelet but I didn't like the result, it was shite, and I asked for my money back. He said he couldn't afford to, but he had a mate who was really good at making things. I said it was a shame I hadn't had his mate make my bracelet then. Now I had to come up with an idea of what to make.

So I came up with the idea for two gold rings – each ring covered two fingers – with 'DEVIL' and 'FISH' spelt out in diamonds. They melted down the gold from the bracelet, but kept adding more to the rings, and they kept getting more expensive. In the end, it was worth it – they looked the dog's bollocks (if your dog had diamond-studded gold bollocks). They complemented the WSOP tournament bracelet. What I didn't know then was that the rings would go on to become famous in their own right. They'd even get their own fan mail.

So the rings were kind of an accident, like a lot of things in my life – it was another case of right place/right time. My favourite combination.

In 1997 I'd walked off with the winner's bracelet in the $2,000 Pot Limit Hold'em tournament. In 1998 I was going to enter the same tournament, the $3,000 Pot Limit Hold'em tournament and the $10,000 Main Event. I also planned to play as many cash games as I could squeeze in.

I crapped out of the $2,000 Pot Limit Hold'em, so I didn't manage to hold on to my title, but the $3,000 tournament was still alive. The prize pool was just over half a million dollars, and first place $206,000. It turned out to be a better run for me.

Out of a field of 172, I got through to the final table. And of those nine finalists, three were British: me, Steve Rydel and my old adversary from London games at the Vic Surinder Sunar. True to tradition, the other five were American, and had the kind of names you could only have in the States and not get killed for at school – Taz Kampf and Lenny Barshack, for example. I thought Lenny Barshack was a character in *The Simpsons*.

Out of the $516,000 total chips in play between us, I was the shortest stacked at only $11,000. Steve Rydel was chip leader with $118,000. My chips were going down faster than the Three Tenors in an elevator.

I was short stacked and getting shorter than Ronnie Corbett and Kylie Minogue's love child by the minute, so when Andre Boyer went all-in, I called with my A-10.

He put his cards on their backs and it was bad for me, he had A-K. The flop was K-8-6, so I was out of my chair. Then a 9 followed by a 7. I'd made a 6-7-8-9-10 runner-runner straight. Finally I was a lucky fucker. And Andre Boyer went straight to the foyer, kicked into touch in eighth place. He lived in Vegas so at least he didn't have far to go.

I'd always said the English were better at pot-limit poker than the Yanks and it was proved true when the last three in the game were me, Surinder and Steve Rydel. The Brits always had the advantage in pot limit, basically because we played it more; pot-limit is more skilful than no-limit because you could control the pots and there's less of that all-in bullshit.

Surinder had got his stack up to $100,000 and I was still the shortest stack of the finalists. But I weakened Surinder during one hand, and then knocked him out in third place with my K-Q a few hands later. Now we were heads-up at last. Me and Steve Rydel. Steve had more than a two-to-one chip lead on me – $361,000 to my $155,000. This was war. In fact, because we were both Brits, one of the commentators described it as civil war.

I wanted the bracelet *and* the cash. In this case there was $206,400 first prize and $103,200 second. And it would be great to pick up two WSOP bracelets back to back, both in a Pot Limit Hold'em tournament. Last year I'd become only the third Englishman to ever win a WSOP gold bracelet, so now I wanted to add to that.

As the final started, I immediately got busy and started mixing my game up with a lot of calls to see flops, re-raising, bluffs and all-ins. His game was more to wait for a strong hand to pay off. More like a baseline player in tennis.

In fact, afterwards one commentator described the final: 'It was Bjorn Borg against John McEnroe at Wimbledon. The baseline slugger against the serve-and-volley specialist. One would dink, drop shot and dive to the net, the other would stay back and bang it cross court. Devilfish is as deceptive as they come. You can never know if he's bluffing or slow playing the nuts.'

Well, I never had the nuts. One dealer gave me a 2 nearly every hand for thirty minutes. In the end I was turning the 2s over and showing the crowd every time.

Well I dinked (whatever the fuck that is), played drop shots and dived for the net for the next hour, trying to claw back some of that lead. But you can fight everything except the cards, and after a few all-ins, I eventually got beaten on just a high-card hand with Steve's Q-9 against my J-6.

He had been chip leader from the get-go and was playing well and catching cards, and that's a difficult combo to beat.

It was a bit sick, to be honest, to get so close to a second winner's bracelet, and I didn't realize it yet but it was going to set a bit of a trend. But the $103,200 second prize was good compensation. I learned that in his non-poker-playing life, Steve was also a jeweller, so the final of the tournament had ended up with two jewellers fighting over a bracelet.

It was weird in Vegas: you could play your best game, hack through loads of other players in a tournament and still end up with fuck-all. You had to raise your game to get anywhere. The kind of stakes I was playing now were way beyond anything I'd started out playing in Hull and bigger than most of the games back in the UK.

As the WSOP Main Event got bigger and attracted more entrants, it turned into more of a crap shoot. So some of the smaller poker events were considered a kind of unofficial Main Event because they attracted a smaller field of much better players. The Pot Limit Omaha tournament was one of those games. Because of the strength of the field it was considered to be the prestige poker event outside of the Main Event. There was TJ Cloutier, Doyle Brunson, Huck Seed, Erik Seidel, Donnacha O'Dea, Scotty Nguyen, Jay Heimowitz, Bob Laws, Phil Hellmuth, Bobby Baldwin, Sammy Farha, the Hendon Mob (Joe Beevers, Barney and Ross Boatman, and Ram Vaswani), my old mate Surinder Sunar and, of course, the one and only me.

One of the commentators said, 'Dave "Devilfish" Ulliott is one of the most feared high-stakes players in the world. He's prepared to win or lose hundreds of thousands of dollars a day playing cards. But this is a tournament. The re-buys are over . . .'

Which was true. We were now down to pure match play. The other bit was true too: since last year's win in Vegas I'd played more high-stakes cash games in one period than I'd ever done before.

Because there were only eighty-four entrants in the tournament, you had to make the final table of nine players to get paid. And you had to cut your way through the best players in the world. Which I really enjoyed. To get to be king you've got to take heads. I enjoyed being executioner.

I'd burst on the scene last year out of nowhere and made a name for myself, and I loved beating players who were bigger names than me. I'd found out that they were only bigger in name, not in game. They were probably thinking, *Who is this guy?* But I knew I'd paid my poker dues over the years and I didn't give a flying fuck what they thought.

In one way, poker was my life, because I lived it – but poker *wasn't* life. I knew enough about life to know that much. Poker couldn't kill you or imprison you or grass you up or leave you – so the risks I took at poker were nothing to me. I'd already run much bigger risks on the street. The only thing I was bothered about at poker was running out of ammunition before I'd machine-gunned everyone at the table. Not literally, of course, that wasn't allowed.

It was hard play getting there, but the field of eighty-four eventually thinned down to only two tables of players. I did my fair share of knee-capping and busting people on the way. These last two tables were considered the two most star-studded tables of poker players to play in any WSOP event. Mine was the toughest table. Any other tournament and this table would have been the final table with everyone on a payday, but the field had been so strong that we were still fighting to get there.

A lot of these guys were rich already and their investment was in the title, not the cash.

Huck Seed, Berry Johnston, Jay Heimowitz, Scotty Nguyen, Surinder Sunar, Steve Zolotow, Allen Cunningham and David Tavernier all got knocked out before me, meaning there were now ten players left and only one more to be eliminated to leave the final-table nine. In poker terms, we were 'on the bubble'. Some players in this situation just keep their heads down and hope someone else gets knocked out, but that's never been my way and I was in danger of getting short stacked and killed on the blinds. I had a 3, so when the flop came 3-3-5 I went all-in. TJ Cloutier called me. I had a set of 3s and I was on a draw to quads, a full house, an open-ended straight and a flush. Actually, I didn't have a draw to quad 3s because when TJ flipped his cards, I saw that he had the last one – and he also had an Ace and I didn't. The next two cards didn't help either of us, so I lost to a set of 3s with a better kicker. The Devilfish took a bite at the money and ended up with fish bait.

That's what's known as a bit of a bastard – getting knocked out on the bubble and going home with nothing. At least I'd been beaten by the eventual champion, because TJ Cloutier went on to win the event. Which meant that Cloutier became one of the top ten earners in WSOP history. Better to be beaten by an experienced player in good form than by some spotty-faced teenager in a hooded top and headphones who's younger than some of the cheese in your fridge.

I entered the big one, the WSOP Main Event – still the only million-dollar poker game at the time – for the $10,000 buy-in. The big news that year was that two

Hollywood actors, Matt Damon and Edward Norton, were entering the tournament. Apparently they were in a new film about poker called *Rounders* and it was good publicity for the film for them to come to Vegas and play.

Not such good publicity, maybe, when they both got bounced out of the tournament on the first day, but then neither of them was a professional, so they did OK to hold their own. In fact, they did better than me, because I *was* a pro and I got knocked out on the first day too. I played as well as an actor.

Getting knocked out just gave me more time off. All I'd been doing was gambling, gambling, gambling. I'd met a player called Jake who was from Oceanside on the West Coast. When he got knocked out of the Main Event too, I decided to change my plans and postpone my flight home so I could leave Las Vegas with Jake when he set off for home. And see a bit more of America.

Oceanside was about halfway down the coast between LA and Mexico. Jake said it was only about seventy miles from LA, so I could easily pop up to Los Angeles if I wanted. 'Pop up' there? Seventy miles? That's one of the differences between the UK and the US: when we say we'll pop to the shops, we mean a walk to the off-licence at the end of the road in drizzling rain and coming back smelling like a wet dog; in America it means driving seventy miles down a straight empty highway in baking heat with vultures circling above you and being followed by a serial killer.

It was about a 250-mile drive down to Oceanside so

we set off early. Well, when I say early, I mean Gambler's Early, which is later than Normal Early because gamblers only see 6 a.m. from the back side, not the front. It was weird driving out of Vegas and into the desert. I'd only ever seen it from inside a hotel or an aeroplane, and it felt very different from how I'd imagined. Las Vegas is a bit like an old showgirl – better at night with the light behind her.

I knew a few Oceanside players: Big Billy, Asian Tony, Mal and Geoff. Jake had said Oceanside was a nice place, but often the casinos in even nice places were in the not-so-nice areas, and I knew I'd be going onto LA afterwards, which wasn't exactly Disneyland either, so I decided to box-off most of my stash in the safe at the Horseshoe. Even though I was in America, where it was legal to carry a gun, I didn't have mine. I guess I could always stop at a corner shop and buy one.

I decided to take just $50,000 with me. Which would be a good payday for anyone who mugged me at gunpoint, but not as good as it would have been if I'd taken the lot. The casino in Oceanside, Jake said, was named Ocean's Eleven, after the Frank Sinatra film. I'd also learned from a gambler back in Vegas that until recently gambling in California had been pretty much unregulated, but this year they'd decided to tighten all the laws up. Typical, I thought, I've just missed out on all the good stuff. I'd say that so far, 80 per cent of my poker playing had been 'unregulated'. That's one word for it, anyway.

The new gambling regulations meant that a lot of the poker rooms had gone legit. In fact, Jake said there were even standalone poker places where nothing else was played; that's something you'd never find in Britain or Europe, where all card rooms are inside casinos. At least, the legal ones.

Some of the freeway trips in the US might not be any longer than some motorway journeys in Britain, but they certainly seemed it. The national speed limit of 55mph didn't help. I go that fast backing out the garage.

I'd heard that only a minority of Americans have passports because they don't ever travel outside the States. And you could kinda see why – America's a bit like a world in itself. Even the sky is bigger. (Christ knows how that works, but it's true.)

As we got nearer Oceanside, we passed big signs for Camp Pendleton, which Jake said was the biggest US Marine base in the States. I bet that made for a rowdy Saturday night in town when the beer started flowing. Come to think of it, if you could get a card game going in that camp you could probably mop up thousands of Marines' wages. I'm not saying you'd get out alive, but that's never stopped me before.

Oceanside had a harbour, a boardwalk, white beaches and surfer chicks. It was a beautiful place to chill out for a while – it made Vegas look like a cross between a pinball machine and a multi-storey car park.

So I decided to have a couple of weeks playing at the Ocean's Eleven before I went up to LA. The only thing about the town that bugged me was that you could never get a taxi. Even though legs run in my family, I'm not exactly a big walker. But I was so pissed off at not being able to get about that I decided to buy a pushbike. It seemed like a good idea at the time. Or maybe I just had heatstroke. I'd not been on a bike since I was a kid, but you don't forget, do you? It's like riding a bike.

So one afternoon I started walking to a bike store. I was so used to the air conditioning in Vegas that I'd forgotten how hot America can get – and the low-level Spanish-style towns didn't throw any shadows. I was sweating so much I needed wiper blades on my shades. When the temperature rises in summer in New York, the murder rate rises too. I could understand that. If I got to this bike shop and it only sold kids' bikes and unicycles, some fucker was going to die. And it'd probably be me, from heat exhaustion.

When I got to the place, it was even worse than I'd feared – the shop was closed. There was a note on the door saying the owner had gone to an auction. I hoped he'd gone looking for a new heart valve or a kidney. It was even hotter coming back. It only got this hot back home if somebody burned your house down.

When I finally saw my hotel, I felt like one of those guys who come walking out of the desert saying, 'Water! Water!' And speaking of water – there was a big blue rectangular hole full of the stuff at the side of the hotel. As I walked towards it, I could see there was a girl in a yellow bikini floating on a lilo and a fat guy in a straw hat on a lounger. I walked towards the pool, winked at the bird on the lilo, and then still fully dressed and wearing my shades, I walked straight off the pool edge and dropped into the water.

I could imagine there was a little cloud of steam rising from the surface where I'd gone in. I sank to the bottom and sat there cross-legged for a second. The girl on the lilo dipped her head under the water and looked at me like I was some new kind of idiot that she hadn't seen before.

I clambered out the pool and scrambled in my pockets for my mobile. Too late, water was leaking out of it. I had a watch that I could wear to a depth of sixty metres but a phone that wouldn't go down four feet. I don't understand why someone hasn't yet made a waterproof mobile. People who are drowning could call for help. I should patent one.

It was time to move on. I'd had a few good wins at Ocean's Eleven, topped up my tan, dropped in the pool, bought a new phone, said goodbye to Jake, and put a brick through the bicycle shop guy's window. My work here was done.

I hired a car and drove up Interstate 5, which runs right up the coastline to Los Angeles. On the way I passed something called John Wayne Airport. Only in America. I couldn't wait to tell my dad that one. He was a big western fan but even he'd think it was odd naming an airport after a cowboy.

I'd never really thought of LA as a casino kind of town, but there are casinos there. I'd heard there was a big game at a place called the Bicycle Club. Locals called the place the Bike. I hoped I'd have more luck with this bike than the last one.

It was in an area called Bell Gardens and it was surrounded by some dangerous places like Compton and Watts, proper hardcore street-gang country. I'd heard some dodgy reports about the club, so I decided to leave most of my stash back at Jake's. Outside, gangs of gangbangers were hanging round: they looked like they'd slit your throat for five dollars and sell your blood for ten. It had a kind of happy-go-fuck-ya vibe. So I fitted right in.

Some of the games in the club didn't seem to be quite kosher – too many locals who knew each other. But, still, I got the feel of things and settled down. That's the great thing about poker, it's like a bank you can take anywhere and open up any time for a withdrawal. Whatever the country, the people, the language, the customs, the weather, if you could find a game then there was always the possibility of poker paying you off.

After playing for a few days I managed to come out ahead. From LA I flew back into Vegas, and it was good to look down and see the old town again from the air, lit up at night like the world's biggest fruit machine, ready to pay out. It was a long way from Hull: there wasn't one of Paddy's cars burning in the street and I didn't have to climb in through my hotel window to avoid the police. God bless America.

Vegas takes something that for a lot of people is still a secret – gambling – and makes a big song and dance about it. And shines half the light bulbs in the world on it. So all the gambling freaks in the world can go to Las Vegas and feel normal. Vegas Normal.

And Vegas Normal ain't *normal* normal.

For example, not long after I got into a poker game at the Four Queens. Everything was fine until an earthquake started shaking the whole building. People were running in all directions. The dealer at the table was shitting himself. He looked at me.

He said, 'What shall I do?'

I said, 'Deal . . .'

22. Bright Lights, Late Nights and Fame at Last

OK, let's get it on

In early 1999 I got a call from a British TV producer called Rob Gardner who wanted me to play in a televised poker tournament. Poker had never been shown on TV before, but Rob's idea was to put a camera on the players' cards so people would know what they were holding. As invitations go, it didn't sound too attractive. It was about on a level with having a boxing match wearing oven gloves, playing snooker with a stick of celery, or throwing darts blindfolded. In other words, a non-starter and a hiding to nothing all rolled into one. Why would a poker player want to show his cards?

But then Rob explained what the programme was going to be like and how the cameras were going to be used. I thought about it, and told them to count me in. The thought of being on TV was quite a thrill and I'd always been a bit of a show-off. I was now the top player in Britain in tournament wins – nine firsts, seven seconds, three thirds, and five fourths – and after my showings in Las Vegas, I was the only English guy with a gold WSOP bracelet. Apparently, Rob Gardner was a bit of a fan of mine. The show was going to be called *Late Night Poker*.

It wasn't all good news, though – they were filming it

in Wales. I turned up looking like the nuts, of course, in a black suit, orange shades, WSOP bracelet, gold and diamond 'DEVIL' 'FISH' rings. The line-up was really strong: Liam Flood, Dave Colclough, Joe Beevers, Surinder Sunar, Ram Vaswani, Malcolm Harwood, Barney and Ross Boatman, Dave Welch, Peter Evans, Ali Sarkeshik and Charalambos Xanthos. Every heavyweight poker player from the European scene. I knew most of them either from tournaments, casinos, cash games or illegal poker dens.

We'd be playing No Limit Texas Hold'em, which made sense for TV because it was an action game that encouraged betting, bluffing, bad beats and all-ins – it was a drawing game and it was simple to understand. Lots of times in Hold'em, the money's all in, the cards are on their backs, and it's in the lap of the gods who wins. People like to see all the chips get shoved in the middle and a big showdown.

There were a total of forty players who would play five eight-player heats, and the winner and runner-up of each heat would go through to a ten-player final table. The prize money for first was £40,000 – which was nothing compared to what I'd been winning in cash games and in Las Vegas but it was a pretty good prize for the first ever TV tournament. The winner also got a free buy-in to the World Series in Vegas, which was worth another $10,000.

Jesse May and Nic Szeremeta were the commentators, though Jesse was also playing in one of the heats under the name Mickey Dane, so how that was gonna work, I didn't know. Maybe he'd commentate on his own play and predict what he was going to do.

Also playing was Sir Clive Sinclair, who'd invented the first small calculators and made some of the first home computers. He looked like a scientist, with his little grey beard and glasses, but I didn't know him from a hole in the ground. I'd never played against a 'Sir' before – I'd played against 24-carat cunts, 100 per cent fuckers and total dyed-in-the-wool bastards, but never against a Sir. It caused a bit of a stir when I called him 'son'.

It was Joe Beevers who told me all about this Clive bloke. And here was a strange thing – Joe said that when he was a kid, his dad (who was a gambler) had taught him all about probabilities and percentages in betting, and to teach him he'd used something called a ZX computer. And this ZX computer was actually invented by Sir Clive Sinclair. So years later, Joe had now found himself playing poker with the geezer who had invented the computer he used as a kid to learn how to play poker!

The big innovation for this game was the use of cameras under the tables to see the players' hole cards. The hole-cams. They pointed up to a piece of glass that was set into the table, and when the player laid his two hole cards face down the viewers could see what he had. It was a genius idea, really. In one fell swoop it solved the big problem of televised poker – that no one knew what the hell was going on.

He was only a young kid, Rob Gardner, in his thirties, but he had the smarts to see how it could work. Before his hole-cam technology, watching poker on TV would have just left the audience wondering what was happening. *Why did he do that? Why did he fold then?* Now they could see for themselves why players were betting, folding, slitting their wrists. And the commentators could explain the thinking behind every move.

It was strange, seeing the cameras for the first time. It went against everything that a poker player learns how to do – to protect your cards, never to reveal what you've got, to play against the odds when necessary. Most of all, to bluff. A big part of my game was bluffing. I knew I had a strong table image and I knew I didn't give a toss about taking any player on, and I knew that they all knew that about me too. Which puts you in a strong position to bully people off hands and out of pots. This show, though, was going to reveal how we all played and when we bluffed and when we didn't. I knew that being on TV would make any player with an obvious tell vulnerable in future. Because the show's audience wouldn't only be casual poker players: plenty of professionals would be tuning in, and every player involved in the show would watch it back to try to pick up clues.

So in some ways it felt like a risk, but then I thought that it could just as easily work in my favour. If other players saw me bluffing them off hands, it might make them more likely to go up against me in future when I was actually holding a strong hand. I knew I wasn't easy to read as a player, so I could use that.

Another thing in my favour was that I tried to play different people in different ways. It depended on the player: some people you'd have to check to 'em to get them to bet. Others you have to bet into them and hope they decide you're bluffing, or you hope they've found a good second-best hand, and then come over the top of you with a re-raise.

Anyway, poker had never been on TV before and this was going out late on Channel 4, so none of us really expected it to set the world on fire. It would be a start, that's all. Each of the five heats would go out at 1 a.m. on a Saturday night (well, Sunday morning, if you want to split hairs), for five weeks, and then the final would be shown on the sixth. It seemed to us that everybody would be out pubbing and clubbing on a Saturday night, but what did we know?

Still, getting some time on TV would be good for me, and I could finally show my mam and dad and Mandy and the kids what I'd been doing for all those years when I used to disappear.

The first heat included Ram Vaswani and Dave Colclough, who were both knocked out, as was Sir Clive Sinclair. So that was the ZX computer theory down the pan. The heat was eventually won by Liam Flood and the runner-up was Pete 'The Bandit' Evans. Even though the programme went out so late, it got good viewing figures – a few hundred thousand. The next Saturday the second heat was shown. Surinder won it and Joe Beevers was runner-up (so, a bit of a recovery for the computer theory). This time the viewing figures doubled to nearly half a million, which seemed to surprise even Rob Gardner and the production team. They'd judged the market better than even they'd expected.

What was happening was that people were coming home from the pub – from students to young guys to older blokes – and instead of watching the kind of crap that's usually put out on a Saturday night as a punishment for not going out, they had all started watching *Late Night Poker* instead. And got hooked on it straight away and told all their mates.

At first it seemed odd to me because it was just a poker game. But when I watched it back on the telly I could see exactly what they'd done with it. They'd made it look like a dark little poker club, not a big studio. And the hole-cam thing was great for showing who was bluffing, who was slow playing, who was trapping. When you saw it edited together it was like a scene from a film. But it was better because you had Jesse May and Nic Szeremeta building up the drama with their commentary; Jesse would be going mad, shouting as if he was watching heavyweight boxing, and Nic's commentary would be much quieter. I could see why people were hooked.

The next Saturday was my heat. By now I knew that even more people would be watching. I was playing against Nicky Katz, Tyrone Pooley, Charalambos Xanthos, Barney Boatman, Mo Gibbins, Richard Baldwin and a middle-aged lady with grey hair and glasses called Beryl Cook (no, not the famous artist, another Beryl Cook). She was the least-likely looking poker player I'd ever seen. She certainly had something going for her because the heat ended up with all the other players getting knocked out and just me and Ma Baker left. I felt like I was heads-up with my granny.

Apparently the ads for this heat during the week had shown some clips of me in action, so the audience was expected to be the biggest yet. Afterwards they said it was nearly a million people . . . so thank Christ I managed to win my heads-up confrontation with Beryl, because 'OLD LADY DEVOURS THE DEVILFISH!' was a headline I didn't want to see. Anyway, as winner and runner-up we both went through to the final, so there was still the chance for her to shoot me down.

People had now started coming home from bars and clubs specially to watch *Late Night Poker*. We had a bit of luck in the build-up to the final. The following week there was a gangster film due to be released called *Lock, Stock and Two Smoking Barrels* and the film had a big card scene, so the adverts started to make poker look cool. (The 'poker' scene in the film actually turned out to be 3-Card Brag, but to most people it was just poker.)

The next two heats were won by Jin Lin (while drinking a gin sling) and Malcolm Harwood, so we now had a full line-up of ten players for the *Late Night Poker* final: Me, Surinder, Liam Flood, Joe Beevers, Dave Welch, Malcolm Harwood, Pete Evans, Joe Fernandez, Jin Cai Lin and Beryl Cook. Altogether we had a WSOP bracelet winner from Hull (and a handsome bastard to boot), an Indian-born Englishman, an Irishman, a young Brit, a middle Brit, an old Brit, Bandit Pete, a Yank, a Thai guy and Ma Baker. It was like poker pick'n'mix.

The hype that had grown during the heats now got even bigger in the run-up to the final. We were pulling in over a million viewers, on Channel 4, at one in the

morning. It was crazy. Fifteen years ago the police would
have kicked my door in for running a game like this, but
now local coppers in Hull were pulling me over to say hi.
And to ask what was in the boot.

The final kicked off. I had on the suit, the shades, the
rings, the bracelet, and I was a ring of confidence. I didn't
think even Beryl could stop me.

Unusually for me, I did start to catch some cards and
hit some flops, which made up for the last ten years when
I couldn't hit a barn door with a bucket of shit. No Limit
Hold'em is a tough game to play in tournaments, especially these one-table satellite situations on TV. You've
got to make the most of what you get when you get it. I
got out the blocks well by beating Surinder's straight with
my flush. Surinder never did have much luck against me,
so he probably wasn't too surprised. Then, by only the
third hand, I knocked out Old Mother Riley with a full
house – she left asking where Kitty was. I started to get
the feeling even more that this might be my night when
I got quad 10s against Joe Beevers. I was now out in the
lead and had a pile of chips like the New York skyline.
I'm dangerous when I'm behind but I think I'm pretty
unstoppable when I'm out in front.

'Gentleman' Liam Flood is a very good player so I was
happy to take him out. Liam went all-in with A-7 but I had
him well covered with my A-K. When Surinder got shot
down next, there were only three of us left: me, Dave
Welch and Pete Evans. And Pete was from Birmingham,
so that meant there were only two of us who spoke English.
But it was against Dave that I had the next big hand.

I got A-9, different suits. Pete folded whatever he had. That left Dave. Now A-9 is a good hand to have heads-up but it can easily get you into trouble against a pair. Dave bet £3,000. He could be slow playing a big hand and tempting me in, but I didn't think that was the case. I thought, fuck this let's find out what the geezer's made of, and I put in a raise of £20,000. Everything seemed to stop. I knew this was a big one. If he took me on and won the hand, he'd take over the lead from me. Welch paused to have a think. Out of the corner of my eye I was aware of a camera that had the red light blinking on top of it to indicate the camera was on – it was pointing at me. So were Dave's eyes.

He folded.

It didn't end there. Again Pete folded, and again I was heads-up with Dave. He threw in a raise of £3,000.

The hole-cam showed the commentators and everybody at home that Dave had got a pair of Jacks. That's a pretty monster hand heads-up. Over *one and a half million people* were on the edges of their sofas watching us. Jesse May went all Jesse May and said, 'Oh my GOD! Welch has got pocket JACKS! If Devilfish goes all-in it could be all over! WHAT cards does Devilfish have!?'

No one but me knew what I had.

The audience didn't know. Even Jesse and Nic, the commentators, didn't know. And this was another genius move on *Late Night Poker* – during a big hand the cameras only showed one player's hand. So everybody watching, including even the commentators, had to try to guess the play from the players' reactions.

I called Welch's bet. The pot was now £6,500. The flop was dealt and came down 5-A-10. The cameras still didn't show what I had. At home everyone could hear Jesse and Nic trying to guess.

Welch bet another £4,000. I just flat called. And now the cameras showed for the first time what I was holding. Two Aces. Giving me a set of Aces with the one on the flop. Jesse May nearly had a heart attack when he saw what I had – I'm surprised I couldn't hear him shouting even in the studio. Nic Szeremeta said, 'Devilfish has him strangled!'

Jesse May said, 'We're about to find out why they call him "Devilfish"!'

I might have been strangling him but he wasn't dead yet, it wasn't exactly a cold deck and I didn't quite have the nuts: but the only way I could be beaten was if the next two cards dealt were the other two Jacks or a King and a Queen, to give him a runner-runner straight. I didn't know that at the time, of course, but I did know I was a huge favourite and wanted Welch to go all-in so I could get heads up with Pete Evans.

I didn't want to alert him that I had him beat so I checked the turn card, which was a blank. He checked as well. There was only the river card to come now. I hoped I'd slow played the Aces enough for him to doubt I was holding anything and was on a bluff.

I said, 'I'm going to put you all-in, son.'

At home one-point-five million arses all shifted a little closer to the edge of their seats. On the commentary, Nic said, 'I've never seen a hand played so well.' And Jesse

May said, 'I'm STAGGERED! Ninety-nine out of a hundred players with £40,000 at stake and holding two Aces would put all their chips in BEFORE the flop and not leave the chance for Welch to get lucky later!'

When I moved all-in it didn't look like I had even one Ace because I hadn't re-raised. After a long dip in the think tank, Dave called me all-in, and got bounced out of the final in third place, talking to himself.

Nic Szeremeta and Jesse May were both shouting how they'd never seen anyone play Aces as well as that, but 90 per cent of professional poker players worth their salt would probably have played it the same way. I had two Aces and was a lucky fucker.

Those were the two big hands. I was now a big chip leader and I thought as long as 'The Bandit' didn't draw two pistols and shoot me dead, I had a great chance. Pete's a strong player and we later became great mates. But, sure enough, I managed to beat him on the day.

So I became the first *Late Night Poker* champion. Out of the £40,000 winnings, I tossed the dealer a £1,000 chip.

It was weird reading about myself afterwards. Before now my name had only appeared in court depositions. Now I was being mentioned in the *Sun*, the *Mirror*, the *Guardian*, probably the *People's Friend* too, and on TV.

By this stage of the book you know I don't do modesty, so here's what the *Independent* said:

Dave 'Devilfish' Ulliott and Pete 'The Bandit' Evans are not famous. If you saw one of them standing in a checkout queue in the supermarket, you would not give them a second glance (although if you saw Devilfish behind you, you might think about moving to a different queue). They are not famous, but they should be.

Evans and Ulliott were the last players standing, or rather sitting, at the climax of Late Night Poker (C4) in the early hours of this morning. Forget the men's final at Wimbledon or the snooker in Sheffield. This was the most enthralling head to head of the summer, and more to the point, it was also brilliant television.

They call him Devilfish, in case you were wondering, because the Devilfish is famous for its sting. Dave Welch thought he might be bluffing. If ever anyone needed to Phone-a-Friend, it was him, but there are no lifelines in a high-stakes poker game. Don't do it, Dave, viewers will have yelled from behind the sofa, as he pondered whether to keep betting. He thought long and hard, and then he did it. And he got stung. For everything.

And so did Pete the Bandit, after a few more hands. His opponent, who is a generously built man, shook his hand, and then tried to find enough pockets to fit in all the cash. Then, without so much as an interview, the Devilfish was gone. Please, Channel 4, make him come back soon.

In the bad old days, when someone on the other side of the street had shouted, 'Oi, Dave!', I knew it was time to find an alibi. Now it was just people wanting to meet me and talk about poker and ask if they could see the rings. I got so sick of disappointing people when they found out I didn't wear them 24/7, that I started carrying them round with me.

So all this attention was obviously a problem, wasn't it? Sod off, I loved it. Who wouldn't? I was becoming famous for the things I was best at – playing poker and showing off.

Things changed quite a bit after *Late Night Poker*. I was in newspapers and magazines and interviewed on radio and TV, and featured in a BBC documentary called *Jackpot*. I knew it was because I was close to people's image of what a poker player should be. Even if they didn't know about poker, they knew enough to see that I was the real thing.

Put it this way – if I hadn't been like I was, then I wouldn't have had the life I'd had; and if I hadn't had the life I'd had, then I wouldn't have been on *Late Night Poker*; and if I hadn't been there, then I wouldn't have won it; and if I hadn't won it, then everything would have been different. And if it had been won by some softly spoken short-arse in glasses and a cardigan, *Late Night Poker* wouldn't have taken off like it did.

That series opened the floodgates for every poker show that came afterwards. American TV producers had been tuning in to see how the hole-cam technology thing worked and by the time of the final they'd already decided to import it to the States. And because they do everything bigger in America, soon there would be poker shows popping up everywhere, on TV and in films.

Suddenly poker was the new rock'n'roll. Which was fine by me because I loved both.

Poker was about to go massive worldwide. And all because of a little British programme called *Late Night*

Poker. I like to think I did my bit by being the player every-one wanted to tune in to watch, and by being the cocky bastard who then went on to actually win.

We took poker out of the casinos and backstreets and showed it to the world.

So to all you poker players who have ever had a go at me, and to all you snotty-nosed kids who are playing poker now, and even to all you saggy-arsed old bastards who are still playing poker . . . *you're welcome.* I wouldn't go so far as to say you owe me a living but you owe me a big drink. And you owe it even more to Rob Gardner, so read up a bit about him. I know Jesse May would agree with me on that. Rob was another example of a good guy who didn't get lucky. He would die of lung cancer at only thirty-six. Rest in peace, Rob. And sometimes life and poker are exactly the same in that way – it's better to be lucky than good.

So, two Englishmen and an American reintroduced poker to the world in a way it hadn't been seen before – and it took off like an astronaut with a rocket up his arse.

23. The World Is Your Lobster

The Devil goes fishing

Winning *Late Night Poker* had given me a free ticket to the $10,000 2000 World Series of Poker Main Event in Las Vegas, not that I needed an excuse to fly out there. All gambling roads lead to Vegas. Or it may be that the millions of light bulbs in Vegas turned all gamblers into moths.

The second *Late Night Poker* tournament had just finished, and I'd won my heat and made the final again. I thought it would be quite an achievement if I could win the first two back to back, and after the first series' viewing figures I bet the producers were willing the old Fish to win it again too. But it wasn't to be.

Anyway, the WSOP in Vegas was alive for me. It was even madder and more of a circus now than it had been last time. The number of entrants for the Main Event had nearly doubled and the first prize money had gone up from $1 million to $1.5 million. Leading up to the Main Event there were even more tournaments, this time twenty-four. I could have entered every one but there's only so much poker a man could play – even this one.

Walking across the casino floor in Binion's Horseshoe was as exciting as it had been the first time. The difference now was that it took me a lot longer because of the number of people I knew to say hello to, or who stopped to say hello to me. In no particular order, this included pit bosses, floor managers, security guards, bodyguards, showgirls, singers, cowboys, strippers, coin-flippers, bookies, rookies, photographers, TV presenters, actors, waitresses, wheelers, dealers, wheeler-dealers, groupies, croupiers, fans, grans, some German called Hans, world champs, chimps, chumps, money loaners, moaners and casino owners. And a dwarf.

One of the people to shake my hand was Puggy Pearson, the poker legend I'd met here during my first World Series. He'd stepped back from playing me then because I'd been steamrolling over everyone. But we got on well and he was a good old character. This time he greeted me with, 'Devilfish, how are you? Are you ready to skin 'em?' I smiled and nodded.

Britain's biggest selling men's magazine, *Loaded*, had sent a writer out to Vegas to do a feature on my progress in the WSOP. Which sounded like the kiss of death. And out of the hundreds of poker players there, I was one of the few priced at odds as short as 25–1 of winning the Main Event. Another kiss of death.

Things got off to a shaky start when I ended up hanging off the outside of the Horseshoe Casino building. The photographer from *Loaded* wanted a shot of me standing *behind* the famous Horseshoe neon sign above the main entrance. It didn't look too high when you were on Fremont Street looking up, but it seemed a bloody sight higher when you were up there looking down – especially when you knew you were standing on something from the 1950s. I felt as if I could drop through the floor at any minute. And that was the last thing I needed to see the next day, a front-page newspaper report: 'DEVIL-FISH KILLS TOURIST!'

I entered the $2,000 No Limit Texas Hold'em tournament the next day. I looked at the list of 396 entrants and saw that some of them were already a hell of a lot unluckier than me just by the fact of the names they'd been lumbered with – there was Buddy Pitcock, Dan Dang, Lin Poon Wang, Hung La, Freddie Deeb and Rudy Stanko. I mean, come on, the poor fucker's already called Wang and then his mam goes and gives him 'Poon'. How cruel is that? If I ended up on the final table with those guys, I wouldn't be able to play a single hand of poker for taking the piss or pissing myself laughing.

As it happens, after chopping through a field of some of the best players in the game, I did make the final table. But none of the Silly Name Six did, so that was a bit of a disappointment. Phil Ivey had the chip lead at $195,000 after he used his pocket Kings to knock out Hassin Habib. I was second chip leader with $168,000.

The table was full of aggressive players. Like Toto Leonidas, who went all-in on the button to try and steal $9,000 worth of blinds. I saw him with my pocket 7s and he turned 9-6. He didn't catch what he needed on the flop and, as one of the commentators said, 'Toto gets to go back to Kansas in ninth place.' Then I knocked out Nick Murphy when I only raised $10,000 with my pocket Kings. Murphy came over the top with a $30,000 all-in with A-6, and he went out seventh.

Among the crowds on the rail was a group of supporters with a Union Jack. It must have been a pisser for them when I went head to head with another Brit player, John Morgan. I slow played my pocket Queens by only raising $10,000, John came over the top, all-in for $75,000 with A-K. I knocked him out in sixth place.

The only player on the table playing as aggressively as me was Phil Ivey. But then he went all-in with a pair of 2s and got caught by Diego Cordovez with pocket Aces. Phil went out in fifth. I was raising, re-raising and calling and trapping everyone off the table. They didn't know where they were. At one point, David Pham turned to me and said, 'Are you going to raise every time I bet?'

I said, 'I'll only do that, son, when I've got the best hand or a worse hand. Never when I've got the same hand. Except, come to think of it, if I've got the same hand, I'll probably raise as well.'

As he was still thinking about that little curve ball, he got knocked out in fourth by Simon Zhang. Then Zhang got knocked out in third. That left me heads-up with Cordovez. I was chip leader and fancied my chances. But Cordovez had been catching the deck all day. We hit a stalemate for two hours.

We were almost level on chips when I looked down at A-A – which, as you'll know by now, is my bogey hand. Even though I'd been lucky with them against Dave Welch, no one gets pocket Aces cracked more often than me.

Diego raised. I decided to slow play my Aces to try and finish this match off before one of us grew a beard. I called, planning to get him all-in later. Wrong move. He had pocket 6s, which he might have folded if I'd shoved, but of course he caught a 6 on the flop and his set beat up my pair.

So, for the second time, I'd been pipped at the post for another WSOP winner's bracelet. I felt I should've really had those two WSOP titles to go with my first.

But there was one thing that was even more sick: who would've thought that the Devil would get beaten by his own number – 666.

My roll continued with winnings in Pot Limit Hold'em and No Limit Hold'em tournaments. And then I entered the $2,500 Pot Limit Omaha. This time there were 100 entrants and a prize pool of $487,500, the winner getting $195,000. Again I got down to the final table, which was a strong field with Phil Hellmuth, Ali Sarkeshik, Dave Colclough, Phil Ivey, Markus Golser, Amarillo Slim, Chris Bjorin and Hassen Kamoei.

On this final table the Europeans outnumbered the Yanks because at this time we were better Omaha players. Having said that, us Brits were all short stacked, and I was second shortest at only $33,000, so I had work to do.

I got some luck when I caught a card on the river and survived an all-in. Now these guys all knew about my bad-boy image, so when I hit the river I jumped up and started doing an impression of Elvis singing 'All Shook Up'. It was so unexpected everyone started laughing. I should have really been singing 'Return to Sender' considering what happened next.

I was dealt K-K-J-10 and was heads-up with Amarillo Slim. Slim raised and I called in case he had Aces. The flop came 9-9-6. I checked, and Slim bet the pot. I decided after a long study I had the best hand and raised him $37,000 all-in. Now with all the possible winning hands

I could have, Slim's Q-Q-5-2 was in terrible shape and any good player would have thrown it away. But Slim wasn't a good Omaha player and he called me . . . and the turn was another fucking Queen. I wondered if he'd got his nickname by putting in the money with only a slim chance of winning.

I suppose that bad beat was to make up for me actually getting a bit of luck earlier on. So I got bounced out in fifth place with only $21,000 in prize money.

The $10,000 Main Event didn't go any better when I got a pair of Jacks to David Chui's pair of Aces. I played bad – I should have folded.

Shame I didn't get to the final table because it was eventually won by Chris 'Jesus' Ferguson. It might have been a Jesus versus the Devil showdown.

A few months later, the WSOP Main Event's crown as the world's biggest poker game was knocked off when a new British tournament was announced – the Poker Million. The WSOP had a first prize of 1.5 million dollars but the Poker Million had a first prize of a million *pounds*, the equivalent of just over $1,500,000. Deal me in, baby.

At the end of the year I flew out to the new richest poker game in the world, the Poker Million on the Isle of Man. The bad news was I'd be getting another one of those light aircraft flights that I loved so much . . . as recommended by Buddy Holly, Otis Reading and John Denver (and any other poor fucker who's been drilled into the ground in one). At least between Leeds/Bradford airport and the Isle of Man there were no mountains to fly into.

Ladbroke's were hosting the Poker Million because, as they said, 'The recent Channel 4 *Late Night Poker* programme has seen a resurgence in the interest in poker in our casinos.' I thought, you're welcome. You'd think they would have at least sent a bigger plane for me.

The *Sun* had a big spread about the event with a picture of me next to my new mate, the snooker player Jimmy White. Jimmy was a bit of a poker player and, like me, liked a flutter on the horses. We'd met at the races and hit it off straight away. He introduced me to one of my favourite rock'n'rollers, Ronnie Wood of the Rolling Stones.

I once took another great musician, Roland Gift from the Fine Young Cannibals, to one of Ronnie's painting exhibitions. I was amazed at Ronnie's work – it's not that modern-art shit, he paints people you recognize. We went straight on to see him play in concert with Mick Jagger, and then somehow we made it to the after-party. Roland was a lovely bloke – he came all the way from London to Hull to sing at my birthday party and wouldn't take a penny.

The *Sun* also mentioned that Amarillo Slim would be playing in the event and that he would 'rely on his reputation to intimidate opponents, including British favourite Dave "Devilfish" Ulliott'. I thought, good luck with that tactic, old son, because the last time I'd been intimidated at a poker table was *never*. It also said that Slim was known for always carrying $25,000 in cash in case someone asked him to play, and that he'd been robbed at gunpoint sixty times. I thought it was quite likely that there was a connection. Personally, I'd have either stopped carrying the cash or bought bullet-proof boxers.

Any event like this can be a crap shoot because you've got four days of playing before the final, and that's four days of walking through minefields. There were good and bad players here and either one could nudge you onto a mine. But the high-profile events were good for the game. Besides, I had to hold up the nickname end of the event for British players because there was already 'The Brat', 'Jesus', 'Slim' and 'The Orient Express' playing, and they were all American.

Not everyone was happy to see a 200-strong poker-player circus roll into town. On the first day, when there was a big crowd of us stood in the casino bar, a TV programme came on showing a local Christian leader denouncing the event and generally damning all gamblers to hell and back. We listened with great respect . . . and then all burst out laughing and started cheering.

On day two I won £6,000 in a cash game, which at least meant that I'd earned back my entrance fee for the Main Event. And on day three I got another £3,000 win. By the end of day four I was sixty-seventh out of a starting field of 156.

The 2000 Poker Million final would be played using the hole-camera technology of *Late Night Poker*, but the difference was it would be transmitted live. To avoid the danger of information being sent back to the players about how the hands were being played, the final table was in a sealed studio with surveillance equipment to scan for bugs and transmitters. Promoter Barry Hearn described the final as being like a combination of *Late Night Poker* and *Big Brother*.

Soon none of this made any odds to me, though,

because by day five I was knocked out. I stepped on a landmine. In the end the Poker Million was won by John Duthie, who has since become a good mate – proving that sometimes good guys do win.

Late that year I won the FF 5,000 Pot Limit Omaha event at the Winter Poker Tournament at the Aviation Club in Paris.

The year ended about as badly as it could when my old mate Pete Robinson died. From the moment we'd met all those years ago in Armley prison, he'd been a really great friend, one of the ballsiest guys I'd met. And he needed to be when he developed multiple sclerosis. He was in bed for over a year, and I went to see him regularly. We'd have a good natter about the early days and make each other laugh, as always.

Someone so full of life as Pete dying so young couldn't help but make you think. Everything is a roll of the dice, in life as well as gambling: from getting up to going to bed. Especially the bit in between. But if life is a gamble then it's one you've got to take. What else can you do? The best thing to do with your life is to live it as best you can. I'd always been able to do that. And losing friends like Pete made me feel grateful that I could.

24. The Worst Way to Lose Money

Throw it away!

On my early trips to Paris I used to stay on the Rue Washington, which wasn't up to much, but sometimes gamblers can't be choosers. This time the hotel was obviously classy because when I asked if the room had a TV, the receptionist said no, but added that there was a cock fight in the lounge every night at 7 p.m. When she showed me round the room she said that Louis the Sixteenth had stayed there. I pointed out that there was still a Louis the Third in the toilet. She said not to worry, she wouldn't charge me extra.

I decided to take $10,000 cash to the casino with me and leave $40,000 behind. There was a safe in the room, so I put the money in a carrier bag ready to put in the safe. I got ready: the suit, the watch, the shades, the rings, the flick knife, the WSOP bracelet. Then I locked the money in the safe, picked up a bag of trash from the room to put in the bin, and marched off to the casino with my ten grand.

Two days later I'd lost the ten thousand, so I went back to my hotel room for more cash. I opened up the safe, took out the carrier bag and tipped it out on the table. And sat there looking at a pile of dog ends and coffee cartons from two days ago. I'd obviously picked up the wrong bag, put the rubbish in the safe, and then thrown $40,000 into a Paris bin.

I immediately went to the local tip and asked if I could look around for the rubbish bag – I said that I'd mistakenly thrown some keys away – but they told me that the bin wagons just tipped everything onto a conveyor belt that went straight into the furnace. So my forty grand was about to go up in smoke. I'd have preferred the thought of a dustman pulling up to work in a Porsche and drinking champagne with a car full of lap dancers than to think the money had been incinerated.

The first one to say '*C'est la vie!*' gets a punch on the nose.

When something bad happens in life, if you survive it, at least you get a good story to tell. I knew I wouldn't get a single second's sympathy from any other gambler, but I'd get a lot of laughs. Still, I'll have to keep telling the story for fifty years before I've got forty grand's worth of laughs out of it . . .

I'd been playing in London for nearly fifteen years and I'd played at the Victoria Casino more than any other casino in the world. I'd also met, and played against, characters like the gangsters Mad Frankie Fraser, Roy Hilda and Freddie Foreman, gambler Derek Baxter, people born into money like Zac Goldsmith and Alice Rothschild, snooker's Stephen Hendry, Steve Davis, Ronnie O'Sullivan and Jimmy White, footballers Teddy Sheringham and Frank Lampard, and Nelly (the rapper, not the elephant). The best thing about London is that there are so many nationalities living in it that you're unlikely to run into a Londoner there, so more likely to meet someone you can understand. Which is a bit rich coming from me, because when I first hit London I spoke so quickly and with such a broad accent that most people didn't catch what I said. Which was probably just as well, considering what I was saying to them.

My old mate from Hull, Tony Booth, had also introduced me to a game run by the Arif brothers – probably the most notorious family in London. So when I was invited to a private game of theirs above a London pub, I didn't really know what I was walking into.

When we arrived there were six people already in the game, including two of the Arif brothers, Dennis and Ozzer. Sitting in the wings was a great old gambling character, Manchester George. I hadn't seen him for a while. I sat down and after a couple of hours I was winning about seven grand and the others were dropping away. Finally, there was just me and the two Arif brothers left, which I figured wasn't a good spot to find yourself in.

But they were winning as well, so we agreed to stop and have a drink. Like most heavy-duty guys they were very polite and gracious. And I got to go home with my balls still in my pants and not hanging off someone's charm bracelet.

Another London character was George Crawley. He played in all the games in London. He came over to Vegas a few times, and I even heard a story about him taking a million quid over there and doing it all in. But you never ask a gambler about his losses.

George was a nice guy, and he'd give a lot of people a chance – meaning he'd put people in tournaments for a slice of the action. And with another pal of mine, Derek Baxter, he set up the Western Members Club. He had a nice house in London and he and his missus were kind enough to let me stay. George would sit by his desk taking bets on the phone all day long. He had a cleaver hanging on two nails under his desk, and a bull mastiff which was as big as Shergar. One night it nearly ate something of mine when I went downstairs for a glass of water and nearly stepped on the thing. All I heard was a deep warning growl from the floor.

So George would be sat there taking the bets. The cleaver on standby, the dog on alert. Now that's the kind of gambler you want to be knocking around with – a proper old-school fella with a great sense of humour, funny stories and his own booze cabinet.

Paris is called the city of lovers, but from some of the things I do when I'm there it might as well be renamed the city of idiots. It's amazing how somcone as streetwise as me can be so stupid. I got told by some people that you couldn't trust the California Hotel and that a few people had had their safes emptied there. So what did I do? I stayed there anyway.

I figured I could sort out the risk in my own way. Before going out to the casino, I put my money in the safe, switched on the TV, and made it look like there was someone in the bed – I put pillows under the sheets for a body, a scarf on the pillow for hair, and stuffed socks sticking out the end of the bed. I went to so much trouble building this figure that I nearly jumped back in bed with it.

Anyway, I was quite proud of myself and I went off to the casino. Six hours later I came back to the hotel, opened my room door and everything was still. Then I looked closer and saw that the safe door was wide open. I went over and found all the money exactly where I'd left it. Which meant only one thing – I must have forgotten to shut it.

I was always popular in Paris, especially with girls, safe breakers and dustbin men.

It was that time of year for me to go back out to Vegas for the 2001 World Series of Poker. Vegas was now a bit of a home from home for me – but a home with a much bigger electric bill.

I've never had much luck in the WSOP Main Event, and this year was the same, but my record in the other tournaments was good. I entered the $1,500 Pot Limit Omaha. In this game Gaylen Kester went on a run when he was very low on chips, and he eventually managed to knock out the other players until it was just me and him left. I came in second and picked up $83,000 winnings.

I entered the $2,000 Pot Limit Hold'em and got through to the final table. It got down to just two players – me and another guy who's been a bit of a thorn in my side, Burt Boutin. I got in a hand with him and put in all my money on a coin-flip. I'm not very good at winning coin-flips – and I didn't win this one. But $99,000 in prize money made it a bit easier to bear.

I now held the dubious record in Las Vegas of having the most second places in World Series of Poker tournaments.

My next trip was to Tunica, Mississippi. It's a town in the Deep South, near the Mississippi River, where the hotels had been breeding like rabbits until it was one of the biggest gambling destinations in America. In the late nineties Jack Binion had opened a Tunica version of the famous Las Vegas Horseshoe Casino and now they held the Jack Binion Annual World Poker Open there, and at the Gold Strike Casino next door. It was like a version of the Las Vegas WSOP but with more mosquitoes and banjos.

I entered the $1,000 Pot Limit Omaha tournament. I played my way through a field of 117 players until there were only ten of us left. I was about second in the chip count and, at that point, my mate Sam Farha was third. One player, Rick Ellerman, actually had only one small blind left in chips, so he was a dead cert to be the next one knocked out.

But Sammy had other ideas. One player raised and Sammy re-raised with a 'monster' hand, meaning that he actually had fuck-all – he had something like A-Q-7-2 – but that's Sammy, a fearless player. Anyway, it all went tits-up and Sammy managed to knock himself out in tenth position. I don't think Sammy realized what he'd done until he was walking away shaking his head.

After a few hours seven players had been knocked out and I was heads-up with Ron Rose. You could never run a bluff by Ron – he was tough to bluff. I had to bide my time and wait and wait. The heads-up confrontation went on for over six hours and turned into a proper brawl.

I finally managed to get him on the ropes and knock him out. Poker-wise, of course.

So, I was the Omaha champion in Tunica, and picked up $123,000 in winnings. And a week later Tunica was good to me again when I got to the final table of the $10,000 No Limit Hold'em championship. I was hoping to do the double and pick up another Tunica poker title but this time I could only manage fifth place and $61,000.

Englishmen can only have so much sunshine before they explode from the shock, so it was time to fly back home.

25. The Best Way to Kill a Bookie

Don't let the bastards get your money

Ever since that Saturday when I'd walked into the bookies to fetch my dad when I was fifteen years old, I'd been hooked on the horses. Of course, it helped that my first bet was on a 50–1 shot that came in and won me the equivalent of two weeks' wages in two minutes. That's like a drug dealer giving you a free hit to get you hooked.

It must have worked, because over thirty years later I was still betting the nags. For years the horses would have been for me the closest to what gamblers call a 'leak'. Meaning a weakness for something that reduces your gambling winnings. You might also include all the money spent on sex and booze and rock'n'roll . . . but I wouldn't. Remember when George Best was staying in a hotel and ordered champagne from room service? The waiter delivered the champagne, saw that George's bed was covered in casino winnings and the new Miss World. He said, 'Mr Best, where did it all go wrong?'

Luckily for me, poker players didn't need to be able to run up and down a football pitch for ninety minutes, so champagne, casinos and Miss Worlds were a normal part of the pre-match training regime.

I'd spent years putting too much money over bookies'

counters. The only things that can help even out the odds between the punter and the bookie are being able to understand the horse's form and making sure everything is in your selection's favour.

I usually bet on handicaps. Horse handicaps are like reading a book – they tell you a story.

In Stakes races or Group races you haven't got a lot to go on, and there are improving horses, so it's tough. But give me a handicap race (not sprints) and I can read the form; I will know exactly where I am. I just know if everything's right – the right draw, the right jockey, course experience. In form, the right going, correct weight, good prize money, and a horse that has had a break . . . When I say the right going, it always has to be good/fast, never soft (when it's wet, don't bet). Then an each-way bet on a 5–1 shot or better gives you a great chance of cash back or a nice win.

I also check out the statistics – you can do this by checking ten-year trends in the *Racing Post*. I try to place the bet as late as possible, because if one horse gets pulled out, leaving seven runners, then each-way is no good.

I like to watch my selection relaxed, not on my toes or sweating. It's like baking a cake – if all the ingredients are right, you'll end up with a winner. Of course, you might have to wait a week or two for the right horse, but so what? That just means you can put more money on.

So, the big change was when I became much more selective about what I bet on and when. As soon as I did that, I started winning much more.

In the earlier days I was betting too much to put it all

on myself without being barred, so I'd ask Gary or another mate, Julian, to put bets on for me. That way we could lay more money across more bookmakers. Julian is also banned from several bookies now.

One of the best tips I ever had was on a 50–1 shot. And it came by a strange route. A gambler I knew had stopped and given a lift to a fella he'd passed who'd broken down. In return the fella gave him a tip – McCarthy's Hotel. I saw that it was at 50–1 in an eight-runner chase, so I could back it each-way. Now that's a real rarity. It seemed too good to be true.

I told my mates in the bookies but they thought it sounded too good as well. So I rang some more mates over in Ireland, Don Fagan and Alan Betson, because they both liked a bet. They piled their money on, and told all their mates too. I only bet £250 each-way because I still wasn't convinced.

I should have been, because it romped home the winner by a few lengths. It made me a few grand but could have made a lot more: £5,000 spread over different bookies would have given up £250,000. Soon after, my phone rang and when I picked it up, I couldn't hold it to my ear because of all the shouting coming down the line from Irishmen, all screaming 'DEVILFISH! YER DA MAN! GO, DEVILFISH!' So at least the Irish bookies took a real battering.

I started winning so the bookies decided, one by one, to ban me from their shops. First, William Hill's in Hull banned me, then Ladbroke's, the Tote and Stanley's. William Hill's even served papers on me telling me I was banned. I was in the pawnbroker's when one of their people came in and handed them to me.

I suppose it didn't help that after the success of *Late Night Poker* I was now a known gambling face. One bookies after another banned me as word got round. I had to go through a lot of them to be banned, so as soon as the banning started I made sure that I made as much as I could off each one before they joined the list. And eventually some of the new ones that opened barred me before even taking a bet off me. Within a year I was banned from all of them, Rossy Brothers too, and Corals. They'd either serve papers on me personally, like William Hill's, or just tell me when I walked through the door. Kenny Walsh, at Rossy Brothers bookmaker's, let me bet longer than the big firms . . . but only until I had sixteen winning bets in a row.

At least I could still get a bet on a racecourse, because they could just pass it on to another bookie.

I ended up being banned from every bookies in the country, and those bans stand to this day. Which is mad, when you think about – because basically I'd been banned for using my brain. I wasn't banned for cheating or race-fixing or bribing or anything like that (although plenty of that went on in racing), but just because I could read and *think*. That's crazy. Especially for someone who did as badly at school as me.

It's the same with casinos. They'll also ban you at the drop of a hat. Or at the count of a card. Card counting isn't illegal, because it's just someone using their memory and their ability to count – but it will get you banned from any casino in the world. It's a bit like an athlete being banned from the Olympics because he's too fast.

I could count cards, and track cards too. And that's why I got banned from playing Blackjack by both the Four Queens and the Rio. Luckily they only banned me from those games, not the whole casino, because the Rio would later become host for the WSOP which is the greatest poker event in the world and not to be missed.

So, it's no wonder that gamblers have little sympathy for bookies and casinos, or that 'The Man Who Broke the Bank at Monte Carlo' became such a popular song. If they did a version now it would have to be called 'The Man Who Broke the Bank and Got Banned from Monte Carlo'.

Anyway, it didn't stop me. I just used other people to lay bets on my behalf.

Nowadays betting shops are glass-fronted, so kids walking by can see the slot machines. It's like a magnet to drag them in. And, just like when I first walked in, they'll start listening to the horses and they'll hear a name they like and they'll have a bet on it – and the next thing you know they're in there for the rest of their lives.

If people want to gamble, I'm a big believer in people *gambling against each other* and *not against the system*. A bookmaker is part of the system, a casino is part of the system – like Big Brother, basically. Any normal guy off the street stands no chance against the bookies, unless he does some miracle six-horse accumulator, which is about the same chance as winning the lottery or picking up matchsticks with your arse cheeks.

And even if you're lucky and back too many winners, you get banned! Let's rephrase that – as soon as you start to look as if you know what you're doing, you get banned.

So bookies are mostly one-way traffic for money, and it ain't coming your way. That's why if you want to gamble, I encourage you to play poker. Playing poker means you're only playing the other players, not the system. In poker, the system's not stacked against you; if you're better than the other players, you win. If you invite ten people round to your house and they all put in ten quid to play, then any one of you could walk away with a hundred and ten.

You can also try online poker – you can play as small as you want, you can play at home. Guys who stand in the bookies all afternoon aren't seeing much of their kids – listen to one who knows – but if you play on the Internet you can do it at home while they're watching TV. And you can bet as small as you want and get massive odds; you can enter a tournament for ten euros and win a few thousand. The poker site takes a rake, of course, but the beautiful thing is that basically you're only playing against each other. You can even play for free to practise. No bookie would let you free-roll.

Sermon over. Back to the action.

If you thought Frankie Dettori's seven-race whitewash at Ascot in 1996 was a miracle, listen to this. Joe Beevers, who is part of the Hendon Mob, also used to put bets on for me. One day I had my own magic run at Ascot when I picked six winners, including one horse at 20–1 and one at 14–1. Unfortunately I didn't have them in a six-horse accumulator because a £1 bet would have won me a million. But Blue Square, the betting firm, got in touch with Joe because betting one horse a race and choosing all six winners was such an amazing feat. Joe told them he'd placed the bets for me, so Blue Square contacted a news group, who put the story all over the newspapers.

But the odds of that happening are very, very slim. So my advice is to fuck the system and play other guys with the same chance as you.

That might sound strange coming from me because I took on the system and the casinos and the bookies and, in the end, I won. But that's unusual, and it only happened after years of losing. Without the poker to save me, the horses would have probably killed me. So if you learn anything, it's got to be to give yourself the best chance you can, otherwise you're giving the best chance to them.

My path is a hard one to walk down and I don't recommend it. Do as I say, not as I do.

26. Have Cards, Will Travel

Around the world in eighty plays

One of the nicest places I've played at is a small Caribbean island called Aruba. It's a tiny island, only about twenty miles long, but it's always hot and bright with blue sky, clear blue sea and beautiful white beaches. So about as far away from a casino in London as you could get. Well, apart from the fact that a few times a year the Aruba casino was full of pasty-faced British poker players. Still, even that wasn't enough to put me off.

I flew out to Aruba in October 2002 for the Caribbean Poker Classic that was being held in Palm Beach at the Excelsior Casino. There were fifteen Hold'em, Omaha and Stud tournaments being held over seven days. And I got fuck-all in every one except the one that I won – the Pot Limit Omaha. That netted me $8,000, which was nice but wouldn't even cover the pop and chocolate from the hotel mini-bar.

But I was on a beautiful island so I couldn't really moan. But, being me, I did.

Served me right, because two weeks later I was in sunny Blackpool. And by 'sunny' I mean pissing it down with rain so heavy it turned your trouser legs into drainpipes. It's the only place I know where the meat pies have ASBOs, the fishermen have two glass eyes, and anyone who has tattoos that are spelt correctly gets free parking. I'd gone to meet my daughter Kerry and granddaughter Charlie. The Northern Lights Poker Festival was on at the same time, so I thought I'd kill two birds with one stone and play the Omaha tournament. I picked up the first prize, £6,000, which just about covered the fuel bill of my Hummer truck. I was afraid they would pay me in 20p pieces from the slot machines.

A few months after that I was back in the Caribbean to play on the Turks and Caicos Islands – as close to paradise as I've found. The Turks and Caicos are a group of islands in the West Indies, sort of in the middle of Jamaica, Cuba, the Virgin Islands and Colombia. I'd never met a virgin so those islands were one place I wanted to go. I wanted to fly into Jamaica but the planes couldn't land properly – they couldn't come in low enough because the clouds of smoke made everyone too high. And I couldn't go to Cuba because the planes couldn't land through all the cigar smoke. Flying into Colombia was the safest bet because the pilots all naturally headed for the white lines down the middle of the runway. Don't know what they were thinking of.

The Turks and Caicos Islands are actually still ruled by Britain and their anthem is still 'God Save the Queen'. But I couldn't find a decent chip shop in the place.

Out there in the Turks was a guy called Mr Rami Campbell. He was a big black guy, the head of the police; Rami and a friend of mine, Bob the Butcher from London, were organizing a tournament.

I flew to Miami and from there flew to the Turks. The

Chinese girlfriend I was with, Teresa, didn't have a visa but Rami Campbell said he'd sort it out. We landed safely, but only after I'd had an argument with a certain poker player on the plane. When he found out I'd been arguing with another player, Rami asked if I wanted him put on the next plane back home. I didn't know then that Rami had the power to do those things.

I learned more about that when we were in the queue for Customs and Rami spotted us, marched right up and escorted us straight through without us having to show our passports. That was quite an eye-opener.

The Turks and Caicos Islands are beautiful, like Aruba, so you feel like you're living in a postcard. But, still, no chippy. We found out we were staying in the same room that Will Smith and his wife had been in the week before. I was also introduced by Rami to the president of the island.

The next day a band was playing on the beach and they'd put two sofas right there on the sand: one for the president and his missus and one for Rami and me and a few others. I thought, this ain't exactly normal, but it's good. I got pretty drunk and ended up sitting on the arm of the president's sofa, and the next thing I knew, I'd slid off the arm and fallen into his wife's lap. She was a beautiful American actress – I could have stayed there all night. I tried to pass it off as an old English custom – the traditional sofa arm slide. The president seemed to take it well, and I didn't get shot by his bodyguards. Which is always a good thing. Not getting shot dead always improves a holiday. Unless you're in Skegness.

If I'd managed to win any money in the tournaments on these islands it would just have been a big bonus, as I was on a complete free-roll – I'd got to stay in paradise for a while for nothing. Which beat the hell out of staying in piss-soaked London and being charged for the pleasure.

Truth is, I'm a city boy, really, and being in those paradise places for too long would probably drive me mad.

After winning the £250 Pot Limit Hold'em, Christmas Cracker at the Vic that year and picking up ten grand pocket money, my next destination was back to Tunica, Mississippi, to play in the Deep South version of the World Series, the World Poker Tour.

I started off slowly by entering the first event on the first day – the $500 Pot Limit Omaha – and I came fifteenth and got $2,600. Then for the rest of the tournament, whatever event I entered paid me exactly fuck-all.

Finally, we got to the big one. The 4th Annual Jack Binion World Poker Open $10,000 No Limit Hold'em Championship, to give it the full title. When the Main Event started there were 160 players risking their ten grand for the $589,000 first prize. There were big crowds in the casino to watch this event and cameras everywhere, filming for TV. Things didn't get off to a good start when I found out that the organizers had forgotten to put my name in the draw. So they quickly opened up a new table for me and shuffled a few players about.

Up until the day of the $10,000 Main Event, there'd been a lot of European players about in Tunica, in the casino and the card rooms and in the bars. But that was about to end. I had a good feeling about this tourney from the off, and it proved to be right because I started to build an early chip lead over the others. By the time we got down to the third day the field had been chopped down to only thirty players.

And by the time it got down to the last twenty there were only two British players left from the whole field – me and 'Gentleman' Ben Roberts. But then Ben got knocked out soon after.

So, the rest had been whittled away and it was down to the last six for the final table. After nearly a month in Tunica, everyone was ready for this. The TV cameras were there, the crowds were there, and there was a live Internet broadcast of the commentary on the action. They even had a red carpet leading past the cameras to the card table in the casino ballroom.

As we were playing in a casino not far from Elvis's Graceland mansion, I figured it was time to rock'n'roll, baby. And it's no good feeling like a million dollars if you look like sixty cents. So I put on the customized Devilfish suit with embroidered red devils on the cuffs, I put on the gold and diamond 'DEVIL' 'FISH' duster rings, the WSOP winner's bracelet, the shades, the silk socks and the handmade shoes, and I strutted down the red carpet like the heavyweight champion of the world, throwing jabs at the cameras. Don't do the talk if you can't do the walk, that's my view. And I walked it right up to my seat at the table.

Not that anyone else seemed to appreciate it. My red

carpet strut was met with a stunned silence. I think they were all gobsmacked. For one, I was a Brit, and the crowd were almost all American. And two of the final-table players were from Texas, another Southern state, and one player was from just down the road, so he was a home-town boy – so all the cheers were reserved for them. And the rest of the American crowd's support went to Phil Ivey, who was considered the up-and-coming player. One of the commentators even wondered out loud how I could be so cocky. He'd obviously never met me.

So I wasn't the favourite player at the table, no one fancied me to win, and everyone else was tipping some-one else. But I loved it. I loved stunning them into silence with my walk out. Some players like being the underdog. I don't. I'm an overdog.

There's no point in having bells if you don't ring 'em, and there's no point in having balls if you don't swing 'em. I couldn't be arsed to be a wolf in sheep's clothing – I'd rather be a wolf in wolves' clothing, who dines on lambs.

The final began with over two hundred spectators. Right from the off I built up a chip lead.

I got to the point where I was chip leader with 600,000 of the 1.5 million on the table. Phil Ivey was second, and my main threat. This was a strong line-up of players. They hadn't got here by accident.

Next up was Tommy Grimes, who was an old-school road gambler, and experienced player, and well used to big games. I know he'd been picked out by some people as a likely winner. He was also from Texas, so the crowd was behind him, especially when he raised a pot against me. Straight away, I raised all-in behind him. The crowd all ooh-ed. And Tommy folded the hand. Then the other Texan, Jeremy Tinsley, did the same to me as Grimes and came in with a big raise. So I repeated the treatment and came over the top with an all-in bet. Jeremy folded his hand. And just as I was making these plays, commentator Russ Hamilton was saying that he wouldn't be surprised if I blew the whole thing because he thought I couldn't lay down a hand.

He was wrong, I could, when I wanted to. I just didn't want to.

This was a tough table full of strong players. So I carried on playing British Bulldog: I raised nine out of the next ten pots and stole the money every time. So including the Grimes and Tinsley plays, that was eleven out of twelve hands that I'd steamrollered everyone. The players weren't the only ones back-pedalling: the commentators who had doubted my ability to play a big stack were having second thoughts. Apart from New York John – John Bonetti – who shouted out in his Brooklyn accent, 'Devilfish is the best player at that table. He can play!'

By this time I was putting the table in such a spin it was like the Whirling Waltzer out there. I was spanking these boys more than their daddies ever did.

Tommy came back in a pot with a bet of $26,000 and I went all-in again behind him. I don't know what made him call my bet with his last $160,000 with only K-5, which is worth about as much as a pinch of shit. I had a pair of magic 7s. Next thing, Tommy was out the door.

And he felt so badly about me booting him off the table that he refused to even give an interview for the cameras. I think that's called post-traumatic stress, Devilfish style. Tommy's a good friend and a gent, but this was war.

The next person I took out was Jeremy Tinsley. He had a bit of bad luck during the game – he made a great call with A-Q, but it couldn't beat Johnny Donaldson's A-10. He's a good player, but the Devilfish managed to put the bite on him. After that there were four left: me, Phil Ivey, Johnny Donaldson and Buddy Williams. And there was over $1,115,000 in prize money to play for.

Buddy Williams was the next one to move into my sights. Now, Buddy was in a wheelchair after an accident he had when he was a kid and so, of course, everyone wants the guy in the wheelchair to win. That's natural: you think if someone's already had bad enough luck to end up on castors, then you naturally want them to have good luck in other things. But it didn't make any difference to me; chair or no chair, Buddy was another poker player, and so like any other player, to me he was just potential lunch. In this case, meals on wheels.

Actually, I didn't want to knock Buddy Williams out yet. Buddy was now the short stack, so as long as he was there, the other three were playing quietly because they all wanted him out next. For that reason I wanted to keep him in. No sentiment from poker players.

Eventually it got to the point where I raised and he re-raised all-in and it was such a small re-raise he'd made that I had no choice but to call him. I had a huge chip lead by then and it was only costing me $41,000 for the chance to eliminate Buddy, so I called. And he had me in pretty bad shape, to be honest, because he had K-Q to my K-7, but I drew a 7 on the flop for a pair of 7s, and knocked Buddy out. He wheeled away from the table to groans from the front row of the crowd. Mostly because he ran over their toes.

Next in line was Johnny Donaldson. Johnny was an amateur player who had won his seat at this event by winning a $200 qualifying heat, so he was definitely the happiest guy at the table because he knew he was guaranteed at least $145,000. Johnny's a really likeable guy but I decided it was time for him to go. And it was quite a funny coup, as I had a Queen and so did Phil Ivey, but I had Phil out-kickered with a better second card. The flop came down Queen high and I decided to check it and not bet, and for some reason Phil Ivey checked it too – and I didn't know why, because it was quite a dangerous flop. But it went good for Phil because Johnny Donaldson – who had A-8 – decided to move all-in for $120,000. I snap called him. This gave Phil a chance to get away from the hand and save himself. He folded and I won with a pair of Queens. So that was Johnny Donaldson out. Which left just Phil Ivey and me, heads-up.

This was the showdown people had been waiting for: the Devil against the Tiger – Phil would later be called the Tiger Woods of poker. It didn't take him long to get all his money in after only three hands. The crowd called out and everyone rushed to the rail to get a glimpse of the action. I'd check-raised him all-in. Now the cameras zoomed in and the commentators were on their feet to see the deal. We both turned our cards over: I had 6-5, he had K-8. The flop was 8-2-7. Phil had flopped top pair and I had an up-and-down straight draw – I could win with a 4 or a 9 to give me the straight. So, I had eight cards in the deck to catch.

Phil was about a 2–1 favourite, but I was hoping to get lucky and finish it. I'd run lucky for four days.

Wouldn't you know it, I hit the straight both times – the next two cards dealt on the flop were the 4 *and* the 9 – which is what happens when you're in form and playing well. And it was a great Hollywood hand to end on and take the title with.

So that was that: I'd won it. And my wallet got $589,000 heavier with the first prize, which was my best payday so far. As well as picking up a WPT title to add to my WSOP one.

Everybody was raving about the way that I'd won it, but you know how modest I am so I'd better leave it up to others to describe it.

The World Poker Tour commentator, Mike Sexton, said: 'I truly believe that Devilfish's win in Tunica was the best, most one-sided win, and most dominating performance that I have ever seen on the tour. It was truly dominating. Don't be in any doubt, there were some top players in there, but it was absolutely a one-man show and the Devilfish was leading the charge.'

And in *Poker Europa*, poker player Isabelle Mercier said: 'The atmosphere was electric. Every person in the room felt like a part of history. Devilfish never gave away one single chip to his opponents.'

Poker journalist Nolan Dalla compared my win to one of horse racing's most famous occasions when Secretariat won the Belmont Stakes by thirty-five lengths, blitzing the field. These are some of the best compliments I've had as a player.

After the final had been won, there was a list of things for me to do: the prize-giving ceremony, photo sessions for PR and news, interviews for the TV cameras, and signing autographs for fans. As the game had grown more popular since *Late Night Poker* and begun to appear on TV all over the world, I'd started to be recognized more, which I liked, obviously, and enjoyed meeting the fans. I also enjoyed phoning home and telling my kids what their old man had won. David, in particular, loved to know how I was doing, and he was over the moon.

Later that night I went to dinner with Jerry Lee and his lovely wife. Jerry's a jeweller, so I asked him to make me a new pair of Devilfish rings, this time in white gold.

Of course, me being me, everything couldn't just go smoothly, could it? That would be too easy. Whatever heights I managed to hit, there always seemed to be some kind of drama that I could still get myself involved in. I only had a day to party and celebrate because I was due in London soon to play in the £10,000 Poker Million.

When I got to Memphis airport to check in I found out that I'd messed up the tickets and managed to get there a day early. It was obviously a mistake, because I'm a late-for-my-own-funeral type. Even though I had a bagful of over half a million dollars, the amount they wanted to charge me for the flight-change was ridiculous, some $5,000. What was that for – sitting on the captain's knee? I could afford it, but they were just taking the piss. I decided to stay a night at the airport hotel.

Airport hotels are like holding cells for hell. They're like a punishment for either missing your flight or being a tight bastard. Maybe they thought I fell into both categories because I got the crappiest room. It did have a speaking alarm clock – but it told me to fuck off. The light bulb was so dim that when you switched it on the room got darker. As well as being tiny, it was the spookiest, weirdest little room you'd ever seen: it had no windows – instead it had a funnel. That's not a joke – it had a *funnel*. It went up from the ceiling, like a chimney, and if you turned a handle, a skylight opened up above and let a bit of dirty daylight in! I mean, I couldn't believe it. It was like a room designed by a madman on crack. It reminded me of the solitary cells in Armley. But at least I didn't have to pay to stay in Armley.

One thing the room did have, luckily, was a chain on the door. And even more luckily, I remembered to put it on. I was just drifting off to sleep when I heard some noise outside, then silence, and then the door of my room suddenly popped off its lock – the door was forced open and there were three blokes trying to get in. The chain was pulled tight. I jumped off the bed, slammed the door shut and jammed my foot against it. I started calling out to some made-up mate of mine in the room to make out that I wasn't alone. I felt a thud on the door from a kick from the other side. Then nothing. They'd decided to run off and find someone easier to rob. I jammed a chair against the door and then stripped everything off the bedside lamp so I could use it as a club.

I started to wonder if I'd been tailed from the casino to the airport. The trouble with being a big winner on the news is that you're a big winner on the news – which becomes like a shopping channel for thieves. I had enough value on me in the duster rings and WSOP bracelet to justify being robbed, let alone the six hundred grand I'd won at the Main Event. That's enough money to buy all the houses in Tunica.

In the end, I figured they probably didn't know what I had on me for the simple reason that I was still alive. For over half a million, I didn't doubt that someone would've just put a bullet through the door and through me to get to that amount of cash.

Last night I'd been the toast of the town, WPT title winner and tournament champion, enjoying a champagne celebration and a juicy steak, signing autographs and doing interviews in front of camera lights. Twenty-four hours later I was in Motel Hell, fighting off a local stick-up gang, *bollock naked*.

So I stayed up for the rest of the night watching TV programmes like *America's Most Wanted*, *World's Worst Hotel Room Killers* and *Top Ten Airport Murderers*. You know, stuff that made me feel better. It also made me think that half the people featured on those programmes were working at the airport, because when I went back the next day to check in, the staff behaved like a bunch of criminals on parole. The woman dealing with me took an instant dislike to me – I guess she thought it saved time – and sent me down for a search. Which ain't good when you've got a bag full of cash.

Customs were quite surprised to find I had the half a mill, but I had proof that I'd won it and so they telephoned Ken Lambert – who worked for Jack Binion in the Horseshoe Casino – and he confirmed to the Customs guys that it was all legal and above board. And it's always a good day when you manage to avoid having a full body search by a fat-fingered security guard with a lisp.

So it was a very relieved Devilfish who finally got on that plane home with a big bag of money. I'd never been so glad to see Hull and to see my kids.

Even though it was the Jack Binion World Poker Open, the event had actually been played at the casino next door to the Tunica Horseshoe – the Gold Strike – because the Gold Strike had a bigger card room and bigger poker room. And it was really nice when I returned the following year to find a big picture of myself as the WPT winner hung up in a prime place in the Gold Strike poker room. It wasn't so good the year after when I returned and saw that they'd taken it down. But that's fame for you – here today, buggered off tomorrow. Big deal; at least I was still on the wall in Caesar's Palace in Vegas.

A couple of months later I was back in Vegas for the 2003 World Poker Tour events at the Bellagio Casino in April, including the Bad Boys of Poker tournament; and then I stayed in town for the World Series of Poker, which started in May. In those two months I got a second place finish, a fifth, sixth, twelfth and an eighth, and raked in almost a hundred grand on top of the Tunica win.

In 1999 *Late Night Poker* had changed the poker world for ever, and a similar thing was about to happen four years later in Vegas at the 2003 WSOP. I'd already had those twelfth- and eighth-place finishes but my result in the $10,000 Main Event was as poor as usual – it was the one event I could never seem to run good in.

Now I'm not one to watch poker being played. Usually when I'm at the table, if I'm not in the hand then I'll be talking to someone or stretching my legs. But two finals I did watch were two of the best – the 2002 and 2003 WSOP finals – and for very different reasons.

In 2002 I'd hung around waiting for the final to be played because of something that had happened earlier: on day three of the Main Event, a non-pro player called Robert Varkonyi had knocked out my old sparring partner, the Poker Brat himself, Phil Hellmuth. Phil's a good guy but he's such a bad loser he makes me look like Mother Teresa. When he's beat, he suddenly turns into Phil Hell-mouth. Especially in this case because Varkonyi kept playing the hand Q-10, which obviously ain't a great hand, and he kept winning with it. Which also lit Hellmuth's fuse. So when the amateur, Varkonyi, knocked out the pro, Hellmuth, Phil said that if Varkonyi went on to win the Main Event he'd shave his own hair off.

Over the years, I've had plenty of run-ins with Phil, so the chance to see him get scalped was worth waiting for. I was also in line to do some commentary on the event. Anyway, sure enough, Robert Varkonyi made it through to the final table of the last nine players. You could see

Hellmuth getting more jittery as one player after another got knocked out, but Varkonyi was still there. The final eventually came down to a heads-up between Varkonyi and the British player Julian Gardner.

This was a bit of a dilemma for me because I knew Julian and he was a great lad and a good player, so for that reason I was rooting for him; but also I knew if Varkonyi won I'd get to see Hellmuth scalped. Everybody was waiting for that. The casino brought out a chair and an electric razor in preparation. Sure enough, Varkonyi got Q-10 again and Julian was all-in with J-8; the board gave Julian a straight . . . but also gave Varkonyi a winning flush. So the non-pro had won the world's biggest poker game, $2,000,000 in prize money, and Hellmuth's hair.

Phil sat down on the chair in front of everyone in the casino who had gathered round, and Becky Binion took the razor to cut his hair. But she did it really gingerly, as though she couldn't bring herself to do it properly, and she just shaved a little patch off the back. I thought, there's no way I'm letting him get away with that, so I stepped forward, asked Becky if I could borrow the razor, and then immediately shaved a bald pathway right down the middle of Hellmuth's head. It looked as though he'd been mugged by a lawn mower. You could say that I'd put him all-in, because now he had no option but to shave the rest off. I couldn't stop laughing. The crowd was whooping and cheering. Phil had a big smile on his face. I always say that if Hellmuth was made of chocolate, he'd eat himself. But off the table Phil's a good guy.

Funnily enough, the only other WSOP final I wanted

to watch was just a year after that. It ended up with a match between Sammy Farha and another non-pro player, Chris Moneymaker (which is a good name if you're a good poker player, but a bad one if you're not). I'd been playing a lot with Sammy and I was cheering him on because if he won the money that meant I'd have a chance at getting it – even though I knew it would be great for poker if Moneymaker won because he was an amateur and he'd come from nowhere: he'd managed to get to the final of the world's biggest game by winning a $10 qualifying satellite on the Internet.

And he did win. Moneymaker won the 2003 WSOP Main Event and turned his original $10 into a $2,500,000 first prize. I knew it would cause a massive leap forward for poker. The number of entrants in 2003 was 839, but next year it would rocket up to over 2,500.

Everyone involved in *Late Night Poker* in 1999 had helped provide the first leap forward for poker; now in 2003, a qualifier like Moneymaker winning the WSOP provided the next big jump. Overnight, every poker player in the world thought they had a chance to win the big one. And it caused poker to become even bigger than it had before.

I somehow managed to resist the temptations of Blackpoo~ ~d for some reason went back to the Caribbean at ~f 2003 for the . . . wait for it . . . Aruba World ~Poker Classic II $4,000 No Limit Hold'em ~p – and by the time they'd finished announc-
~'d already lost half my stack.

There was a $1.6 million prize pool and a $500,000 first prize on offer. I survived day one but only just – I had less chips than I started with and was the lowest stack. On day two I survived two all-ins. Then I started to rock and roll. The Devil had come to breakfast and their forks weren't long enough.

I made the final seven players and I was chip leader with $700,000. The bad news was it cost $90,000 in blinds every round – which was an absolute joke – until they lost one player. The final six would be coming back to the TV table the next day. All the players were going all-in as they had no choice. Unfortunately they all kept surviving. I'd been trying to keep out of trouble, and folded most hands.

Eventually I was down to $430,000 chips. I looked down at two Queens. There hadn't been a decent hand shown in two rounds, so when a guy moved all-in in front of me, I called him. He'd bluffed before. This time he had two fucking Kings. What a surprise.

I was left with $200,000. I moved in behind the button on my mate Don Fagan's big blind, with J-7. Don looked at his hand (which was J-2), and started muttering about how he should throw it away. I thought, 'Well throw it away, then; after all, we're mates.' Don decided to call me for another $140,000, and – surprise, surprise – he hit the fucking 2, knocking me out. (When the six players made the final the next day, the TV decided to put blinds back down to $32,000 a round. Great.) At least the best player left, Erick Lindgren, won it.

But poker's bad beats are easily outweighed by life's

hard knocks. Anything good that happened this year was completely wiped out by the death of my sister, Janet. After she and her boyfriend Mick had split up, she had devoted herself to their son, Keith, and brought him up to be a great kid. I couldn't have lived Janet's quiet life but some people live for their families and for their children, and my sister was like that. And thank God some people are because they make great mothers and carers, and that's what Janet was.

Mandy rang to tell me. Janet had had breast cancer but kept it to herself, so her death, to us, was totally unexpected.

We'd been close when we were kids because there was only two years between us and Janet had looked out for me and taken me under her wing. And even though I didn't need it any more, that wing was gone now. It was weird thinking that someone you'd grown up with and known so well just wasn't there any more. Difficult to come to terms with. All that history just wiped out. I didn't even go home for the funeral because it would have just been too sad and I'm a big believer in doing things for people when they're alive, because when they're gone it doesn't mean anything. Regret is a really bad thing to carry round, it can be a real burden, and I've always tried to not get weighed down by it. But you always think you could have done more.

My son David asked me to listen to a song called 'The Living Years' because of the lyrics: 'Say it loud, say it clear/ You can listen as well as you hear/ It's too late when we die/ To admit we don't see eye to eye.'

Janet dying made me decide when I got back to England

to make more of an effort to get on with my father. We'd had clashes over the years, especially when I was younger, and we both could be stubborn – too alike, I suppose. But then I thought about how all that didn't matter, and how it didn't really matter if I had to compromise just to smooth things over and make it easy.

So, all those people out there who are in the middle of feuds that are splitting their families apart should wake up and make up. Because when death drops on your doorstep it's a really big eye-opener – once they're gone, it's too late.

27. Big Mouth Strikes Again

Lightning doesn't have to strike twice — once is enough

Poker can nail you to the spot, and it can take you places. Over the years poker had made me sit longer in one spot and in one chair than anything else. In the old days people used to believe that the world was flat; even in my lifetime there was something called the Flat Earth Society. Because poker players around the world spent so much time on their backsides, I was thinking of starting the Flat Arse Club.

Poker had also been the reason for me travelling round the world more than anyone else I knew, certainly more than anyone from my background. The thing is, wherever I travelled, I'd still end up sitting on my arse playing poker. The game can fire you through the air but it still ends up nailing you to a chair.

But there's nothing like winning at home. Ask any of my wives that I've ever lost an argument to. They'll say the same.

My biggest loss, though — the biggest loss I'd had after losing touch with Kerry and Paul, and then losing Janet — was when my marriage to Mandy finally ended after twenty years. She was (and still is) a diamond and we still loved each other but we just couldn't carry on being together. My fault, not Mandy's. She'd coped with being married to a gambler better than anyone I'd ever met.

And as I've said before, for a woman to be married to a professional gambler ain't easy – it takes a special breed.

Mandy, being a natural businesswoman, carried on running the pawnbroker's.

In a way, poker had taken certain things away from me – some relationships, a good marriage, and more time with my kids. But it also gave me things that I wouldn't have had otherwise. And the money it had given me allowed me to look after everybody in the family in a way I would never have been able to do otherwise.

My record in Britain for poker was better than for marriages. I'd had thirty-one event finishes and seven first prizes; in America it was thirty-three event finishes and four first prizes. Pretty evenly matched. Even though I'd had eleven first-place finishes in Europe – and, more importantly, won *Late Night Poker* – I'd never really had a British tournament win to match the stature of my WSOP gold bracelet in 1997.

That is until I entered the 2004 British Open £1,250 No Limit Hold'em tournament at the Victoria in London. Out of a field of 171, I managed to get heads-up with a big Russian guy called Valery Ilikian, who was a nice guy that looked like a Mafia enforcer. I'd never before seen a guy who looked less likely to be called Valery. Apart from his brother, Barbara.

But I managed to win, send him back to Russia in second place, and become the British Open champion for the first time. It was my biggest win in Britain, coming in at £90,000, and my biggest win outside America since I'd become the first *Late Night Poker* champion.

It must have set me on a roll because back in Vegas I got my highest ever finish in the World Series of Poker Main Event when I came in seventy-second. That might sound a bit crap, but this was the year after Moneymaker had won, so finishing where I did put me in about the top 3 per cent and won me $30,000. Top prize that year was $5 million, and 225 places were paid.

My roll carried on because a month later I went to Barcelona for the World Heads-Up Championship and got a third place in one tournament, a second place in another, and a first in the Pot Limit Omaha event. I was in the lucky position of being able to use poker to help me escape, and to travel to tournaments from Vienna to Vegas.

I had a nice surprise when I was given the European Poker Lifetime Achievement Award. I didn't even know I was in the running. I thought of myself as being too much outside the establishment to get any awards. I didn't think I was a safe enough bet. Though there was something about that word 'lifetime' that made it sound like I was nearer the end of it than the beginning. I'd just have to try to upset those odds.

The following year I was in Monte Carlo for a one-table No Limit Hold'em tournament. There was me, Phil Ivey, John Juanda, Chris Ferguson, Gus Hansen, Phil Hellmuth and Mike Matusow – five Yanks (one adopted), one Dane and me. Only the top three would get paid. Now I'd agreed to enter this event and pay the entry money of $130,000, because the promoters, the online poker site Full Tilt and

Fox TV, had agreed that I could advertise my new website devilfishpoker.com during my interview, but then the rules were changed and advertising was banned. Which was a joke. So when I got third place, I stood up in front of the cameras and took my jacket off. Across my back I had www.devilfishpoker.com in big letters. The event was being shown live all over the world. That went down like a sack of shite, and I got banned from Fox promotions.

Still, I did get my $130,000 entrance fee back. I ran over this tough table and at one point had trebled my starting chips. Then they put the blinds up to $90,000 and it took all the skill away – it came down to luck. My mate Phil Ivey was certainly having his share of luck that week – he'd already won $1 million in the Main Event, and then he won this too.

If you're gonna get a dose of bad luck and good luck together then it's better to get the good luck last because that might save you from whatever shit the bad luck has put you in. And that's especially true if you're 30,000 feet up in a plane. After the Monte Carlo tournament finished, a few of us players – me, Freddie Deeb, Harry Demetriou, American Dan, and another guy I didn't know – decided to get a flight up to another tournament in Amsterdam, which meant flying from the airport nearest to Monte Carlo, and that was Nice. Actually, it wasn't nice, it was horrible.

Never, ever fly out of Nice airport at night and at the end of the year. They have these lightning storms and you can see the flashes through the clouds. I didn't know this yet, so me and the boys innocently got on this small plane called a Fokker. The name should have been a sign, right there. But us lot of daft Fokkers just hopped on board.

We took off in this plane and only got ten minutes out to sea and it all kicked off big time, lightning bolts across the sky like bonfire night. You could see this electrified barbed wire cracking down. It was crazy. As if that wasn't enough, we got served up a big side order of turbulence. At least in a big plane you know it's going to take some almighty fucking bolt to bring it down. But those little planes always seemed to be on the news for nose-diving into fields.

There was a massive explosion, the plane dipped, all the lights went out, and we started rocking around wildly. Then we dropped a few hundred feet like a roller-coaster diving into a dip. The lights flickered and went out again. The guy in front of me lost it and jumped up and started screaming, 'Please God, no! Please! Oh please God, no!' It suddenly occurred to me that none of my family knew I was on this plane. I thought how this would be pretty grim shit – to die this way. I looked round at Freddie Deeb and his heart was already in his mouth but he was too sick to swallow it.

I was quite cool about it, even for me. We'd obviously been hit by lightning, and I didn't like the situation, but the only thing I was really worried about was that there was definitely something wrong in the cockpit. Because the pilot would usually come straight on the microphone and say something like, 'Don't worry, the left wing's fallen off but we'll be down soon . . .' But they didn't make an announcement. And if they were in trouble – the blokes flying this Fokker – then we were right and truly Fokkered too.

Finally, one of the pilots came through on the speakers and confirmed that we'd been struck by lightning, and they were returning us to Nice. What the pilot never told us – we found out later when it made headlines in the paper – was that the lightning strike had made him and the co-pilot temporarily blind. He'd forgotten to mention that bit in the announcement: 'This is your captain speaking. We've been hit by lightning, we've lost an engine, we're out of fuel . . . oh and the co-pilot and I are now blind. Try not to panic.'

They managed to turn the plane round and get back through the storms and land us at Nice. It was pissing down with rain and freezing cold. When we were on the ground this bloke in overalls came out with a stick and a torch and started looking under the plane for damage. It didn't look like too close an inspection to me. I wanted that plane with its pants down and a doctor's head up its arse. We were all sitting nearby on a coach like a row of condemned men, dripping with rain, and thinking about how close we'd come to being the first group booking for the electric chair.

Boris Karloff finished the plane inspection and said we could get back on. When I was younger and mad for nothing but cards, I probably would've been happy to sit on a wing. But now I was the first to say no fucking way. That plane now just looked to me like a combination of a death trap and a lightning rod with wings, with 'Rest In

Pieces' painted down the side. My exact words were: 'I'm not getting back on that Fokker!'

Talk about bad luck/good luck: bad luck to get on a plane that flies into an almighty electric shit storm – and good luck to survive and not get fried like an onion ring and dunked in the ocean.

American Dan got back on the plane, which just proved what a sick gambler he was. The rest of us decided we'd sooner stow away on the *Titanic*. If you're gonna go heads-up with Fate, you'd better know you're holding the nuts.

It was a year later that I finally managed to get up to Amsterdam, on a Fokker again. After we landed I went straight to Marcel Lüske's club. Marcel's a big friend, I've played at his place loads of times.

I was standing with Marcel by the club's door, discussing what the deal was going to be, when we heard a commotion. We looked up at the security cameras and saw that a poker player called Yanni – a German lad who happened to be partially deaf – was being attacked by some big guy who was obviously trying to rob him. Marcel immediately opened the door and leapt out to help and I went out behind him.

When we barrelled down the stairs and burst outside, the mugger made a break for it. He had about a ten-yard start but we were gaining on him, so he turned round and started to pull a gun out from inside his jacket – a Dirty Harry handgun. Fortunately for us the gun was so big that it got hooked on his pocket and he dropped it in the street. He turned and ran and Marcel ran after him.

I stopped and picked up the gun. It was a black heavy fucker. I cracked open the chamber and saw the six brass circles – the bases of the bullets.

I can honestly say that that was the only time in my life I was glad to find out a bloke had a bigger one than me. If it wasn't for that bit of luck, I think Yanni would have come round that corner and found me and Marcel face down in our own juices and probably already halfway down to the great card game in hell – both of us still debating how much percentage Marcel was gonna get out of me when we got down there. I mean, the Devilfish ain't going to heaven now, is he?

As I'd become more famous for being a player, poker had become a bit like a Get Out of Jail Free card and a VIP party invite all rolled into one. Poker got me inside the kind of places that before I'd have needed a balaclava and a gun to get into. For instance, I was invited to play in a charity poker tournament at the Playboy Mansion. I thought that a live action version of the magazine had to be worth a look, if only to see a centrefold walking around without the two staples across her belly.

So off I flew out to Los Angeles to the Playboy Mansion – which isn't something I'd ever thought I'd hear myself saying back when I was working in a timber yard in Hull. In those days it was more likely I was getting a police van to Armley Prison.

I hooked up with this pretty girl Susie that I'd first met in Vegas. She was a TV presenter from New York and she'd said she was interested in doing a story on me. We arrived at Hugh Hefner's place in a limo but the security wouldn't let any cars other than official Playboy limos through the gates. So we drove to a sort of park-and-ride down the road and jumped into one of Hefner's limos to get into the mansion.

The place was full of guests, poker players, women, Playboy Bunnies with their bodies painted, celebrities and waiters keeping everyone topped up with drinks. After a few champagnes Susie confessed to me that she also liked girls, and I thought, well, we'll have to see what we can do about that. We were certainly in the right place, and she must have been thinking that too. She sat behind me as my Lady Luck, drinking champagne, while I played the charity poker tournament.

Celebrity and charity poker games are never that gripping to professional players, and I lost interest even quicker when one of the prettiest Playboy girls there started making eyes at me. She was probably wondering who that middle-aged fucker all dressed up like a rock'n'roller was. She'd apparently decided that this Fish was a good catch. When Susie went to the ladies, the Playboy girl came over. All she was wearing was body paint. She took me to one side and after a while she said that I'd better stop talking to her because I was making her paint run. Susie reappeared, had a bit of a strop and threw a glass of champagne over the Bunny. That certainly made the paint run. I guess Susie wasn't as up for a three-some as she'd first thought.

I'd had enough at that point; I'd already been poker playing and partying in Vegas before I'd got to LA. Back at the hotel Susie decided she wanted to start messing around with the sound system and blasting music out. I was so tired by this point that I wanted to collapse flat out in bed. This is exactly why I don't like champagne – if a girl has champagne it either makes her crazy or fall asleep. And either one is not what you're looking for. You'll either end up with a black eye or a spare hard-on.

I woke up late the next morning to find that Susie had managed to get her hands on some scissors and decided to cut up all my clothes. There were suit arms and shirt arms and trouser legs everywhere. I felt lucky that my balls were still attached.

I got out as quick as I could and returned to Vegas. And that's a good clue as to how I live – I'm the only guy I know who goes back to Las Vegas for a quiet life.

28. Bringing It All Back Home (the Money and the World Cup)

It's coming home, it's coming home . . .
poker's coming home

Sometimes I'd forget how crazy my life was. I'd just get used to it. But then something would jump up and kick me in the balls, just to remind me.

For instance, at this point in my life I'd probably won more money on horses than I'd lost, but only because I'd started betting wise enough to win really big – and then doing that got me banned from every bookies in the country.

But, because of my sponsorship deals, in 2005 I was invited to present the winning trophy at the 2,000 Guineas. That was unbelievable. The Guineas is one of the oldest and most prestigious horse races in the world, one of the five Classic races run in Britain, and it's been going for two hundred years.

I started as a raggy-arsed kid in Hull with barely a spit to slide on, a lad who went into betting shops when I was too young to be there (and also went on to lose so much I starved and then won so much I got banned), and yet here I was at Newmarket racecourse on the biggest day of the year as the trophy presenter in the Guineas. There was probably more money spent on champagne and wine here in one day than the whole estate where I'd grown up earned in a year.

The sponsors had a Las Vegas-style arena in a part of the enclosure called the Hyperion Lawn. I tried to pass on a bit of advice to the punters there. Playing poker and punting on horses is similar because both need experience to spot the things you don't see without years of playing. I advised people to not back the hot favourite, Dubawi. Favourites had a bad record in the Guineas. And, in the end, the winner of the race was Footsteps in the Sand at 13–2.

So I got to present the 2,000 Guineas trophy to the winning jockey, Kieren Fallon, the trainer Aidan O'Brien, and owners Michael Tabor and John Magnier.

Two days before the Guineas I'd been in London trying to defend my British Open poker title, and a month after it I was back in Vegas for the WSOP. It turned out to be a good one for me. I won a quarter of a million dollars for coming third in the $1,500 No Limit Hold'em event, and while I was playing at the Bellagio Casino I first met the American actor James Woods. He's got a great sense of humour and we hit it off right away. Jimmy's one of a few Hollywood actors who are into poker, including Ben Affleck, Lou Diamond Philips, Matt Damon, Toby Maguire, Edward Norton and Jennifer Tilly. James was in one of the best ever films about Las Vegas, *Casino*, and also in one of my favourite films ever, *Once Upon a Time in America*.

Later on, he took me to a party in Vegas he'd been invited to. He was cracking jokes in the limo all the way there. At the party, everyone knew him, of course, but because I was his guest he stayed with me all night, which was good of him since it would have been easy for him to swan off with his actor pals and leave his new English mate stood there like a lemon. But he's a class act. I remember things like that.

One year we entered the same No Limit Hold'em event at the WSOP, and we ended up on the same table. James raised, and I called the bet. The flop came 7-high, which meant that with the pair of 7s I already had, I'd flopped a set. The nuts. But I'd got it against the one guy in the tournament I didn't want to knock out. I would've usually slow played the three 7s to trap my opponent into betting, but I just wanted him out of the pot so before he bet I told him to fold. He started fingering his chips, wondering what to do.

I said, 'Jim, throw your hand away. I've got you beat.' Now I couldn't say what I had but I did advise him to throw it away. He said that he'd got a big hand. I said, 'It ain't as big as mine, throw it away.' He showed me his two Kings and threw them away, and I showed him my three 7s. I guess that made him realize ... what an idiot I was! But money and tournaments are not the be all and end all.

Poker has brought me some kind of fame but I'm hardly what you'd call an A-lister. The thing about meeting people who are, though, is that their fame doesn't affect me. I mean, I either get on with someone or I don't. I'll talk to anyone from anywhere. I don't look down on anyone and I don't look up to anyone. I've met famous people who are pricks and others who are really good guys. James happens to be one of the good ones.

Another poker-playing actor I became friends with was

Ben Affleck. I'd first met him down in Tunica when I was in the casino playing a cash game and this young guy in a baseball cap sat down to play. I didn't think anything of it and we'd been talking and playing for a while before I realized who he was. I always like to have a drinking buddy, so after the game we decided to head out. I rang my girl, Stacey, who was in the hotel, to see if she wanted to come along. She said she wasn't really bothered about going out with me and the lads.

I said, 'It's not me and the lads.'

She said, 'Who're you drinking with?'

I said, 'Ben Affleck . . .'

Before I'd put the phone down, Stacey was downstairs, in the lobby, dressed to the nines. I'd never seen a woman get ready so quickly. Amazing what a Hollywood name can do.

When we first met, Ben was still going out with Jennifer Lopez and they were probably the most famous couple in the world at the time. But as J-Lo didn't like him gambling, drinking and smoking, then obviously hanging round with a lot of smoking, drinking gamblers wasn't exactly her ideal scenario. I can't imagine I was ever on her Christmas card list, put it that way.

So when I met these guys over poker, it was the game and the friendship that came first. The fame thing gets put to one side and guys like that are always relieved to meet someone who doesn't give a toss about celebrity. I got on well with Ben, like I did with James, because he was a good bloke.

The next time I met up with Ben was in Aruba. This

time, we went to Chicos and Charlies nightclub there, and ended up drinking late in the Holiday Inn, which also had a poker room. In fact there's a picture on the wall of the two of us playing poker there. It was the least we could do to pose for a snap because we had to get $10,000 credit off the owner, Mike, a mate of mine. Well, you don't get if you don't ask.

Last time I saw Ben was in Vegas. He's married and settled now with the beautiful Jennifer Garner. He's a gent. And a great name to use to get your girlfriend ready much quicker.

I came back to Britain for a game that would turn out to be one of the best wins of my career. But before that, someone told me that I'd been namechecked on *East-Enders*. I didn't see it because, guess what, I was playing poker, but I was told that some of the *EastEnders* cast were having a game of poker and one of them got all cocky, so a character called Garry said, 'Oo the hell d'yer fink you are, then – Devilfish?'

Then in April 2006 came the big one – the first Poker Nations Cup. Held in Cardiff, it was like the FIFA World Cup of poker. Countries from around the world were invited to send teams and all the strongest poker-playing countries were there: England, Germany, USA, Ireland, Denmark and Sweden. I was honoured to be chosen as the England team captain. Every boy dreams of playing for England. I was twelve when England won the World Cup in 1966 and I remembered how excited everyone had been.

Our boys were me, Joe Beevers, Ram Vaswani, Tony

Bloom and Julian Gardner. And each team had to have an Internet qualifier. In our case it was Scott Griffiths. It's an unusual thing in poker – for poker players not to be playing just for themselves. The winning team would split a $100,000 prize, but right from the start you could tell that wasn't the motivation.

I'm not really a big team player but as soon as all the players met up at the venue it was obvious that national pride was at stake. There were huge flags hung everywhere representing all the nations, supporters for each team, commentators for each country, and dozens of TV cameras. The event was being shown not just in the countries that were playing but all over Europe and America.

There was almost as much action off the table as on it, with everyone making side bets with each other according to which heat they were playing, and Jesse May, who was commentating, setting himself up as an on-site bookmaker. Jesse came to the event with his pockets full of pounds, dollars and euros, but I don't think he left that way.

In the first heat I threw in Scott, our Internet qualifier, so that he wouldn't be hanging around getting nervous. He did good, too, finishing third and getting us 3 points. In fact, he did better than me, because in the next heat I could only get sixth and 1 point. During the matches, the teams all sat backstage at their own tables, watching the action on big screens and cheering on their players.

Tony and Julian played next but they could only get two fifth places in the next heats, which meant we were bottom of the league with only 8 points. Germany already had 20. And there were only two heats to go.

So we didn't have much to celebrate . . . but that's no reason not to. So when we finished for the day and went back to the Hilton Hotel, I dragged all the boys out for a good night's clubbing. That might not be the usual preparation for a 10 a.m. start the next morning – and Joe Beevers did point out that it was actually my job as captain to *stop* the lads from partying, not start them off – but poker players ain't athletes and getting well-oiled might improve our play. That's the Devilfish Management Technique – 'If at first you don't succeed, don't worry – get pissed!'

Even though I was the oldest in our team, after our night out I still had to prop the rest of them up on the way back to the hotel. What a disgrace. I just hoped they'd prove to be better players than partiers.

Anyway, my plan must have worked, because the next day Joe and Ram played a blinder – they won their heats outright (Joe beat the Irish and Ram beat the Yanks) and bumped us up to 28 points. We overtook Germany and finished the heats fourth out of the six countries. The USA and Ireland were joint leaders. Those points were converted into different-sized chip stacks for each country for the Grand Final.

Each team captain had to choose three players for the final. I picked Joe, Ram and me. Joe was our opening player, with Ram and me last. Players could be substituted according to how play was going and who was performing best. Joe did us proud, but he'd been on long enough and it was time for a change, so I threw in Ram. No country had been eliminated yet and a few of the captains had called a time-out when they needed to rethink or regroup. The atmosphere backstage was getting more and more rowdy – every time we won a hand we'd cheer on Ram or Joe, or they'd cheer me on, and of course the other countries did the same for their teams. It was like the World Cup final but without the crying and diving.

Ram's a great player but he isn't nicknamed 'Crazy Horse' for nothing, and at one point he did make a crazy play and lost the hand. That damaged our chip stack. By this point only one country had been knocked out – Sweden – so I decided it was time for me to step up before Ram blew the lot. I was captain, so if the chips were going to be fucked off, I'd be the one to do it. I substituted myself for Ram. That was the last player substitution we were allowed, so from now on it was a fight to the finish.

The next team to bite the dust was Denmark, knocked out by the USA. Then the Americans fell when their captain, Robert Williamson III, was knocked out. That left only England, Germany and Ireland to fight it out for the Cup. Don Fagan was representing the Irish, and he's a strong player, but I managed to get the better of him after making a great call (revenge for Aruba). That knocked Ireland out in third place. I couldn't hear the noise from the backstage area, but I could imagine it – the rest of the team now knew it was going to be another England versus Germany final.

This Poker Nation tournament was being run by the same company that produced *Late Night Poker*, and when it got down to the final, the event seemed to grip the viewers in just the way that the first *Late Night Poker* had. Especially when it was England against Germany.

I was up against the German team captain, Michael Keiner. I'd liked the guy ever since I'd learned that he used to be a plastic surgeon but had refused to do breast reduction operations because he said it would make the world a worse place.

Michael's a good player but I started out as I meant to go on by taking him on immediately. The advantage of putting someone on the back foot is that they lose balance. I knew I couldn't lose this – I couldn't let England lose another final to Germany. It was just one of those matches where all the world was watching.

Then the final hand came down . . . and I brought the Poker Nations Cup home to England. I couldn't hear the shouts and cheers from the rest of the team and our supporters in the green room because I was in the card room – but I could feel a minor earthquake rumble from all the stamping.

So we became only the third English team, and I became only the third English team captain, to lift a World Cup – after Bobby Moore in 1966 and Martin Johnson with the Rugby World Cup in 2003. It's probably the achievement of my poker career that made my dad most proud, lifting that big silver World Cup (and not dropping it). I guess that was a pretty good thing for him to be able to tell his mates in the betting shop.

I might have had to drag the lads out to party when we were in the middle of the tournament, but after we'd won it, they didn't need my encouragement. The $16,667 we'd each won just about covered the bar bill.

*

I had to leave Britain quickly because three days later I was due in Vegas for the Five-Star World Poker Classic – where I managed to finish eleventh (big deal). Then I had to leave Vegas quickly because four days later I was due back in London for the England versus Germany match in the Party Poker Football and Poker Legends Cup. That event was exactly what it said on the tin – English poker players and English football legends playing against their German equivalent. Our team was me, my old mate Ian Frazer and, fitting in with the theme of our Poker Nations win over Germany, the footballer on our team was Alan Ball, a genuine football legend and the youngest player in the World Cup-winning England team of 1966 (he was even made Man of the Match).

So it was a real pleasure to be able to help him win against a German team again, because our players took second, third and fourth place and we won the heat over-all. Alan Ball was actually our highest placed finisher: he got second (Uli Stein won it).

That was another one of those can't-quite-believe-it moments for me, like presenting the trophy at the Guineas, because I knew that forty years ago my old man, along with the rest of the country, had watched the World Cup final on the TV and seen Alan Ball play. Weird how things can come round, and the people you can meet if you stick around long enough.

Representing my country didn't end there because then I had to be in Vegas for the Intercontinental Poker Championship. This was like another poker World Cup but this time each non-US country was represented by only one player. I was playing for England and there were twenty others playing. This time I did about as well as England usually do at the real World Cup. But the WSOP started two days later so at least I was already acclimatized to Vegas.

I'd played in some strange places in my time, but I'd never been invited to play in a completely different world altogether. This time it was the digital world. I got a call from a computer design company in California, asking me if I wanted to be in their next Xbox game, *World Series of Poker: Battle of the Bracelets*. I didn't know one end of a games console from the other and any eight-year-old could run rings round me on the Xbox, but my sons said I'd be mad not to do it.

When I flew into LA, I was on the same flight as Surinder Sunar, who was planning to play a tournament there. While we were waiting at the baggage carousel, like two sick gamblers who couldn't go ten minutes without a wager, we had a bet on whose bag would come through first. Surinder's appeared, and mine wasn't even on the plane. Which pissed me off twice – once with Surinder and once with American Airlines.

The Xbox game was based on head-up play. The other players they were featuring were Phil Hellmuth, Johnny Chan, Chris 'Jesus' Ferguson, Marcel Lüske, Greg Raymer, Phil Laak, Annie Duke, Mike Matusow, Shannon Elizabeth and Humberto Brenes. I'm surprised they could get all those egos on one game. Maybe it would be a two-disc set.

I was hoping they could have the computer version of

me jump into the Tomb Raider games so I could chat up Lara Croft, but they said it didn't work that way. I couldn't see why not. I'd have been quite happy for her to sit down and play poker on our game. It certainly improves the scenery when there's a pretty face to look at on a poker table.

I was on screen in a different way in the summer when I went to the Cannes Film Festival for the premier of a film I was in called *Poker Face*, directed by John Hales. It was the story of a guy and his guardian angel who helps him to succeed at poker. In the end he gets to play me, and gets beat – of course. When they'd first suggested me, John said he didn't think there was much chance that I'd agree, but I'd liked the sound of it and said yes – who wouldn't want to be in a film, especially if they're playing themselves? So there hadn't been much rehearsing for me to do because I already looked and sounded like me. Which was handy.

I figured I must be doing something wrong because I was invited to the 2006 UK Gambling Awards ceremony in London. It was like the gambling equivalent of the Brits. I was made Gambling Personality of the Year – and the best thing about it was that the award was voted for by thousands of punters and players. Plus I'd beaten Frankie Dettori in a photo finish.

I'd never, ever been this respectable before. It might even damage my image.

29. A Very Good Year / A Very Bad Beat

Amsterdamned – going Dutch with Devilfish

By now I'd figured out that my life would never be normal. You might have picked up on that. I don't keep a diary because I'm too busy doing all the things that keep you too busy to keep a diary. But if I did, mine for 2007 would've looked a bit like this:

January

I went down to Tunica, Mississippi and entered the Gold Strike $1,000 No Limit Hold'em event and got first place and $109,000; and then sixth in another No Limit Hold'em for $22,000. Flew back to London and went to Cardiff for the William Hill Poker Grand Prix, got knocked out in a heat, and won fuck-all.

February

Back to London for the Party Poker Premier League, where I got a fifth place, two fourths, three thirds, and all for just $14,000.

March

Flew to Austria/Vienna for the East versus West Cup and came second and got €1,000 ($1,300). Fantastic.

April

Back to Vegas to enter the $5,000 No Limit Hold'em Fifth Annual Five Star World Poker Classic, where I came fourth and got $84,000. (And I advised them to shorten the tournament title so we'd have longer to play.)

May

Back to London for the World Open III – out in the heats again – then back up to Wales for the Poker Nations Cup II where I came first in the heats and got $12,000, and then third in the final for $0. Over to Barcelona for the €2,500 World Heads-Up Poker Championship, where I came fifth and won €11,250 ($15,000).

June

To Vegas for the WSOP; came fifty-first in the Omaha Hi-Lo Split 8 event and got $3,900, twenty-second in the Pot Limit Omaha and won $16,000, and third in the $5,000 Pot Limit Omaha, winning $332,500.

July

Fly to Amsterdam and nearly get killed.

Hang on, 'Fly to Amsterdam and nearly get killed'? I don't remember that being an event on the poker world tour. Well by now you'll know that it's not all poker, there's all the other madness out there as well. Read on.

Amsterdam had always been a favourite spot of mine. You've got to love a city that lets herds of people roam free to smoke dope, and the hookers are seen as self-employed businesswomen with their own shop windows. I didn't indulge in either, but live and let live, I say. And as poker is really a game of live and let die, it's better to play it in a nice place.

Having said all that, nowhere is perfect. Two of my worst experiences were in Amsterdam in 2007. One of them scary but funny; the other not funny at all.

Me and Stacey were staying at a hotel right next to the canal. That was my first mistake. But then in Amsterdam it's difficult to avoid the canals.

We were just dozing off to sleep when Stacey suddenly snapped awake. She said, 'Dave! Dave! There's someone in the room!'

I said, 'Yeah, it's me.'

She said, 'No, there's someone else . . .'

I said, 'Don't talk daft. Go to sleep.'

Which was a daft thing to say considering the amount of money and jewellery in the room. But I'd been playing day and night at Marcel's club and I was really shagged out. Stacey sat bolt upright and switched on the light. I was expecting to see nothing but when I turned I saw two beady black eyes looking back at me – on the sideboard next to the bed was the biggest fucking black rat I'd ever seen. It was in the middle of demolishing the hotel's complimentary chocolates. The noise Stacey had heard was the rustling and the chomping.

Stacey screamed and jumped out of bed, closely followed by me screaming even louder and jumping even higher. We made a run for the door, but it was locked and being in a panic didn't make it easier to open. I looked back and saw that the rat had decided to join us. It had leapt onto the bed and was moving towards the door. I yanked the door open, we both got jammed in it for a second, and then we fell out into the hallway. I pulled the door shut and we lay there, wrapped in the bed sheet, shouting out. Doors started to open all down the corridor. I'd met a few rats around poker tables but none as scary as the real thing.

One of the guests said they'd call reception. I just hoped that the rat didn't have a taste for money and wasn't gnawing its way through a ten-grand stack of my cash.

Ten minutes later this old guy appeared at the end of the corridor: about six-foot-six tall, long white coat, a stick, a torch, about eighty years old with white hair and big black boots. He looked like Frankenstein's granddad. I asked him if he was the rat catcher.

In a deep voice he said, 'Yes, I am!' He seemed quite proud of it. I think he was the Terminator of the rat world.

I remembered that I had all my cash and jewellery inside so I ran into the room, grabbed what I wanted, and ran back out. The old rat catcher came out and said there was no sign of the rat, which obviously had an escape route. He even told me that the hotel had a big problem with rats. I didn't remember seeing that in the brochure.

When we finally got back in the room, I opened the fridge and saw that the rat had chewed its way through the back of the fridge and eaten the chocolates inside.

Which just shows you that you should never stay in a hotel near a canal. Rats like canals and rats like hotels by canals, and rats like the chocolates in the hotels by canals. Bad combination.

I thought that after that drama, things could only get better. Wrong again.

One night my mate Paul tried to out-party the Fish but he had to leave the bar an hour before it closed. He headed off in the direction of his hotel. He was so well-oiled he could have slid there.

Later, on the way to my hotel, I crossed a square where there was a young busker. The place seemed empty. I dropped some money in his tin. I asked if I could have a go on his guitar. I was singing away to the empty square and this guy, who had his hands over his ears (he must have been cold). He was sitting on a step, probably thinking I was a nutter for giving him money and singing myself. I could've done that for free. I gave him back his guitar and he started playing again. Five guys appeared and walked across the square towards us. I thought, well at least this busker's gonna get more than I'd given him. And he did – the first of the five walked up and kicked the busker in the face. Not a word said. Instinctively, I chinned him with a right duster and, after five steps sideways, he went down. The next thing I was hit on the head, the other four jumped me, and they kicked me across the square for the next five minutes. Fortunately the cops had been called and the sirens scared the gang off.

I rolled over and lay there looking up at the sky, and it was one of those clear nights when you can see every star. I couldn't help but have a flashback to the Golden Nugget beating I'd got when I was nineteen. Here I was again.

I couldn't work out whether I was fearless or crazy or an idiot. Probably a bit of each because being fearless *is* crazy, isn't it? Any idiot knows that.

I tried to get up but my body wasn't having it. I finally managed to stagger back to the hotel on these two things that were supposed to be my legs but felt more like spaghetti. My girlfriend helped me undress and I crawled into bed and either went to sleep or passed out. I don't know which but I'd have taken either.

Next day I woke up in a full plaster body cast. Or that's what it felt like. I couldn't move. The bedside phone rang and I had to try and reach for it. I just about managed to lift the receiver. It was Paul. He said he'd had a really terrible night and I wouldn't believe what had happened to him. I said that it couldn't have been worse than mine.

So he told me his story. After he'd left me he'd walked back to the hotel. Or tried to. It was more a case of a weave than a walk. Eventually he'd weaved himself right off the side of a footbridge and down into a canal.

You know when they say it only hurts when you laugh? I could see him walking blindly off the bridge into thin air, with his hands still stuffed in his overcoat pockets, and his little legs going ten to the dozen like a cartoon character walking off a cliff.

He asked me about my night and I said I'd have to show him, so we arranged to meet at the casino. Somehow I managed to get there and, apart from the fact that I was propped up against the bar like an abandoned ironing board, no one could tell what had happened because most of the kicks had been to my body and legs. My hands were aching where I'd protected my face.

Paul turned up and I finished off my story by lifting my shirt to show him my torso. Paul was appalled. He was Appalled Paul. He had to admit that my night was worse than his. My girlfriend looked at us both like the idiots we were.

I learned afterwards that there was a few eastern European immigrant gangs roaming round Amsterdam and more often than not they'd been stabbing people, some fatally. It's not often you get to say this after you've been half kicked to death but – once again, in life – I'd been lucky.

So, if I was carrying on doing the diary, here's about where I'd be having difficulty writing the next bits because my hands were aching. But anyway, it would go like this:

October

Back in Kent for the UK Poker Open IV; got a sixth and a second and won fuck-all.

November

Entered the Poker Million VI, London. That was a waste of time.

December

I managed to round off the year in even better style than it had begun when I went back out to Vegas in December and entered the $15,000 No Limit Hold'em Doyle Brunson Five Diamond World Poker Classic (glad to see they'd taken my advice about long titles). This was a massive event. The entrance fee was more than the World Series and the prize pool was $9.6 million and first prize was $2.4 million. Out of a field of 644 players I fought through to the final three. An A-J beat my A-10 and I came in third for $674,000.

That was my biggest single win yet. And this was also my most successful year ever in tournaments. Along the way I'd managed to pick up $1.6 million in winnings and plenty of high place tournament finishes. I was also honoured to be awarded the prestigious European Player of the Year title for 2007. No one was more surprised than me. I mean, genuinely – again, I didn't even know I'd been nominated.

I hadn't been keeping count over the years, but I was told that I was now the highest-earning British tournament poker player in the history of the game, with some $4.8 million in winnings.

That was quite a long journey, when I thought about it: from making my first official bet when I was a kid in 1969 and winning £25 at the bookies in Hull . . . to thirty-eight years later winning $674,000 at the Bellagio Casino, Las Vegas.

At that rate, by the time I was ninety-one in 2045, I'd be due to win $11,466,500,000. That would make me one-quarter as rich as Bill Gates is now.

Not that you'd really be able to enjoy it at that age. It would just mean that you'd be able to afford more expensive pants to crap yourself in.

Still, fingers crossed: a multi-billionaire at age ninety-one. Then I thought, bloody hell, I'd better start eating my five-a-day and having a few early nights.

I'd start that tomorrow . . .

30. Singing the 'Cocky Bastard Blues' to Lady Luck

Prime time, baby, prime time

I knew it was time for a change of image when I walked into a card room in a casino and everyone seemed to look like me but younger. The 'black suit, slicked back hair and shades' style was everywhere. I know my image had been part of the reason I'd seemed to capture the public imagination during *Late Night Poker*: The Look + WSOP bracelet + Devil Fish rings + me being a cocky bastard = the public's idea of what a poker player should be. It also helped that I could play poker, of course, and that I won the thing. That image then went round the country, round Europe even, and over the years since then I'd expanded my horizons to play all over the world.

It can happen that way. I remember reading about how the success of the *Godfather* films changed how Mafia guys dressed. FBI surveillance tapes caught them talking about the films and how they thought they should look as good.

Anyway, out with the old, in with the new. I'd got a new young girlfriend, Jade.

I went to the Irish Derby with Jimmy White and we each donated ten grand to the bookies – I guess we must have felt a bit sorry for them. People wanted a picture or an autograph with Jimmy because he's the People's Champion of snooker, and I like to think I'm the same in poker. Snooker and poker seem to have the same kind of following, and both games have followed a similar kind of path in the way that, at first, they were minority games on TV, but then just exploded. And ever since my Monica Snooker Hall days in Hull I'd been a big snooker fan. So another gift I got from poker was the chance to become mates with people like Jimmy.

I ditched the suits and the orange shades. My image change must have been more different than I thought, though, because even people who were fans of poker on TV were double-checking it was me before they came up for an autograph. The questions I was asked most often were always about the money: the most I'd ever won and the most I'd ever lost. Well, the 'most ever won' question was easily answered because that had just happened in Vegas at the Bellagio. And the 'most ever lost' question was, unfortunately, about to become easier to answer when I went back to Vegas in the summer of 2008.

Out in Vegas there were my good mates from England, Ian Fraser and Eddie Hearn. Eddie always made sure we had the best time when we went out. Jade could drink as much as me and party as hard but it's hard to play poker and party all night long. So the WSOP started off well but went downhill.

The good bit was when I was in the players' VIP room at the Rio and found a nice American pool table. I'd spent half my life hustling games at the Monica in Hull so I knew my way round a table. I started playing all the boys, Phil Hellmuth, Doyle Brunson, John Juanda, etc. I beat them all. Hellmuth, my great rival on the poker table, decided to try and pull a fast one by bringing in a pool hustler and poker player called Dewey to beat me. The first game we played was for five grand, and I beat him. He said he'd play me for another five grand as long as we could play his rules, which turned out to mean 'no rules': no two shots, no replacing the white ball, etc. I agreed to it because I thought I'd adapt.

It was a very tight game. In the end, I had one ball left to pot. I managed to roll my last ball to the edge of the pocket and snooker him behind the black on his last ball, which in normal pool would be a great shot. But this guy had some moves, don't worry about that; he didn't even think about trying to get out of the snooker, he just rolled the cue ball onto mine and knocked it in the pocket, which left the white ball right on the lip of the corner.

But because it was a 'no rule' game, I couldn't move the white or take two shots (because of his foul shot) as I usually would. The black was near the centre spot. It was difficult to get the black ball safe from where the white was, let alone pot it. I was up shit creek without a canoe. I was stood there looking at the situation, with everyone looking at me – Hellmuth, Dewey and all the other players and spectators.

So I thought, same in pool as in poker: come out fight-ing – *I'm all-in*. I hit the white like a rocket and the black banged into the opposite corner. Much to the disgust of Phil and his hustler Dewey.

I finished off the winning shot by moon-walking round the table and taking the money out of Hellmuth's hand.

I went on to take $68,000 off them on the pool table. Not a bad start. Maybe that was a sign about how well things were going to go. Wrong.

In the Pot Limit Omaha event I got a full house beat by a two-outer on the river. Typical.

I started playing lots of $10,000 buy-in cash games, which would have been plenty big in the old days, but now they weren't big enough. So I ended up trying to create all the action in the games, which led to me taking risks and getting caught out. If you're in form you can play like that and you just mop them all up, but if you're out of form and you try to make the action, they just take your money off you. I was playing so bad it was scary, and I was also running bad, so it was a double whammy. It was a good time to quit. But quit isn't a word I use a lot, whether it's poker or pool or fighting or shagging. Or drinking. And it didn't help that quite often I was playing while one part Devilfish and two parts vodka.

Add to that I was playing a lot of WSOP tournaments as well, losing $50,000 on one and $60,000 on another. You see, you can re-buy for $10,000 every time you run out of chips in some of the tournaments, so you can easily do sixty grand in. And you're always getting the right price to re-buy. So you do. And I did.

Which is why I ended up $600,000 down.

That was the worst hole I'd ever been in. I had to think back to 1997; remember when I first came to Vegas in '97 and got $200,000 down, before I managed to step out of the noose and win my WSOP gold bracelet? Well, now I was three times more than that down. The hole was three times deeper.

An example of my bad beats: in one game I had a pair of Aces against a guy's pair of Kings. Another player had already folded a King, so my opponent had only one King left in the deck to catch. If he didn't I would be a big chip leader. And, of course, he got the King. I probably should have got on a flight back home right there and then – walked straight up to my room and packed – but I didn't. Anyway, the way my luck was going, my taxi to the airport would have probably been hit by a nosediving plane.

The World Series had been a total flop for me but the World Poker Tour was being held at the Bellagio straight afterwards so I decided to stay in Vegas for that. I entered the No Limit Hold'em Bellagio Cup IV and even though I came seventieth, I still earned $19,000. Trouble was, the buy-in was $15,000, so I'd only clawed back $4,000 of the $600,000 I was down.

The real reason I'd finished seventieth was that Bobby Baldwin, the owner of the Bellagio, decided to start a cash game in the card room called Bobby's Room. So even though I'd started with a lot of chips on day three, I'd bluffed them away because I couldn't wait to get into that room. Bobby's game was half Omaha and half Hold'em – a round of each. The buy-in was $100,000. We were playing against some rich Internet players and it was all pretty lively – these guys could lose a couple of million and not bat an eyelid. So there was plenty of money on offer, I just needed to get it.

Being $600,000 down isn't the kind of position that would make most people start throwing another $100,000 and then another $100,000 at the problem. But the kind of attitude that digs you *into* that deep a hole is also the same kind that gets you out.

Fortunately, I played a blinder in Bobby's Room, won four out of five nights playing, and not only clawed my $600,000 back, but won another $600,000 to go with it. A massive turnaround.

Bobby's a good friend, so afterwards we went for a drink in the Caramel bar. Viva Bobby's Room.

I'd escaped Death Row again, just like before. It was like the old days, except this time I didn't have my old mate Gary cheering me on. I did have Jade instead, though, and she was a lot prettier.

I came home and dived straight into making the first poker-themed reality-TV show – *Devilfish Presents: How to Become a Poker Millionaire* – for ITV Wales. It featured four novice players and I had to teach them how to play online poker. I also had plenty of other friends on the show: Doyle Brunson, Phil Hellmuth, Phil Ivey, Chris Ferguson, Layne Flack, Scotty Nguyen and more. Each week, over five weeks, one of the novices would be eliminated. The prize for the winner was a seat in the World Series.

It was a boot camp for the participants and I was going to take no prisoners. We had everything – laughter and tears, good and bad poker, and viewers got to learn tricks of the high-stakes poker trade which took me years and a lot of money to learn, but they all got it for free.

I'd ended up in some strange places in my time, but one of the most unlikely was Oxford University. I was invited to give a talk to students at the Oxford Union by Joe Barnard, who started the Oxford Cup poker tournament. I drove down in the Hummer and ran up a fuel bill that would have got Apollo 13 halfway to the moon. Other people who'd been invited to speak at Oxford were President Kennedy, President Reagan, the Dalai Lama, Albert Einstein, Archbishop Desmond Tutu and Mother Teresa. When Devilfish joined the list it probably was as big a shock to them as it was to me. That's the best company I'd ever been in – and most of them were dead.

I gave a speech to over two hundred students. It was a real blast. I stood at the front and asked if they had any questions, and twenty hands shot up. I pointed to a kid with dark hair and glasses and shouted out 'Fucking Harry Potter'. Everyone laughed, including Harry.

I was also invited to take part in an ITV £60,000 pro-celebrity darts competition, all the money raised to go to charity, with people like Steve Davis and three-time Olympic medallist Steve Backley. Steve was the British javelin champion so you might say he had a head start when it came to throwing pointy things.

After filming I went to London and found a little twist to an old story. I was in Leicester Square with Jade and we walked into the Café de Paris. When I got back from the bar with the drinks I found a guy talking to Jade. He introduced himself as one of the owners of the club and said he enjoyed watching me play the TV tournaments.

He gave me his card and said anytime I wanted to visit the club to give him a call.

Then he said, 'By the way, you didn't happen to know an old road gambler who died playing at the table in Manchester?'

I said, 'I not only actually knew him, but I was in the hand that he died on. The hand he was in was against me.'

He said, 'Christ, that was my father-in-law.'

I think that even when he asked he didn't really expect me to have met the guy, let alone been in the hand when he'd died. When you think about it, there were quite a lot of poker players up and down Britain so the odds against that were slim, to say the least. Sometimes old stories came back to life, even if the people didn't.

My father died just before Christmas 2008 after being ill for a while. He'd just passed his eighty-sixth birthday, so he did pretty well. I don't think I'm going to see my eighty-sixth birthday, but then again, I could be wrong. He was a tough guy and it was really strange to think of him not being there.

The first two tournaments I entered after his death, I won. Maybe he was watching over me – my old man Stan looking down. Because he liked to gamble.

One of my wins was a big one: the No-Limit Diamond Championship at the Euro Finals in Paris. As well as $186,000, I picked up a diamond-studded silver winner's bracelet to go with my gold one. I think my old man would have been proud of that. I also liked to think that over time I'd proved to him that after my dodgy start, I'd finally come good from poker. I hope so, anyway.

Shortly after he died, on New Year's Day, I walked into the living room and the horse racing was on TV, as usual. It was at Cheltenham. I didn't have a *Racing Post*, and I don't even bet on horses over the sticks (that's jumps), so I don't know why I even had the telly on. Just as I happened to be looking up at my dad's picture, they mentioned his name – the commentator said, 'We're just waiting for Stan to come into line.'

So I rang a friend who put my bets on. It was at odds of 14-1. Anyway, the horses were already off, they'd gone, so I couldn't ask for too big a bet because the bookie would refuse it. I had £250 each-way.

Stan won by about twelve lengths. It never touched a twig.

Epilogue:
You Can't Live Like I've Lived and Expect to End up Like This . . .

. . . because if you did, the chances are you'd be broke, buried or in jail. Or all three. Which would be *really* unlucky.

This is the point in the book where I'm supposed to say something positive like, 'If I can make it, then anyone can.' But is that true? Honestly – no. Most gamblers don't make it. Probably only 1 in 10,000 is successful at just gambling. I was one of the lucky ones. It must have been strange for my mother and father to finally see me come good after all the trouble I'd got into.

So don't follow what I did unless you've naturally got it in you, otherwise it'll kill you. Don't try this at home, not without a safety net.

I'm not bragging and saying that I survived and did well because I'm super-special – the reason I've done well is because of something I didn't have a say in: the gift I have for playing cards. I've always had it in me but I just didn't take advantage of it at the beginning. So if whoever hands out these talents had skipped our house in Trinity Street and given it to the kid next door, then you would never have heard of me and you might be reading that other kid's book right now. (Then again, the kid next door was ginger, and who would read a book called *Carrotfish*?)

I grew into it all when I realized that I had a talent. I never really thought of myself as a professional. No one did. Playing poker didn't even exist as a profession. You were just one of the boys, one of the lads; you just played for fun. I kept beating everyone, and started to wonder *why* I kept beating everyone. And then I wanted to keep on doing it. And I found that I could keep on doing it. The next big step was when I went to Vegas and won the bracelet. Vegas changed everything.

Over the years, the way I play poker hasn't changed but the places I play it in have. I've gone from being an old-style road gambler – driving up and down the country to find a game – to being a new-style runway gambler: flying up and down the world to find a game. Same game, different transport. Same me, different countries.

When I first started playing poker seriously, I always wanted to find bigger games – that's why I travelled. Now I'm playing in the biggest games in the world. I like to think I've done my bit to spread the word and promote the game. I'm proud of *Late Night Poker*, and of being captain of an England team that lifted the Poker Nations Cup, and of being crowned European Player of the Year.

I'm not saying that I'm some kind of Mr Clean poker ambassador, because I'm not. Obviously. But remember this: the thing that attracted people to poker in the first place was the fact that it wasn't a Mr Clean kind of a game. I mean it ain't Scrabble, is it? Poker is a combination of cards, chess and dog fighting. You can out-play someone, out-think them, or out-bite them.

It might be better to compare it to bullfighting, because

there's a lot of dodging and feinting and luring someone in for the kill. And a load of bullshit.

People were first attracted to poker by the fact that it's confrontational and it puts you out there on the edge. And even now, when poker is on a global scale – the most played game on the planet – it is still promoted like a dramatic showdown. A gunfight with cards. That's fine by me. Fifty-two-bullet showdowns are what poker is all about. I just hope they won't be the death of me. I'd hate to check out at a poker table. I've seen it happen and it's a miserable way to go.

When I go, I hope it's when I'm on holiday, on a yacht, on a sun lounger, on a woman, and on my hundredth birthday.

Poker is now big business, but deep down it's still a back-room game. That's a good thing. It's why people are still interested. The thing about poker that can't ever be taken out of the game is the thing about me that can't be taken away. Even now I'm still in need of a buzz, that's why I still drink in bars where sensible people wouldn't drink, where there always seems to be trouble. I just feel the need for danger, call it what you like. A death wish maybe.

So I guess what I'm saying is that if I am any kind of ambassador, then I'm an ambassador for the thing that hooked people about poker in the first place. And also an example of the kind of success that it can give to ordinary people.

Even those young kids playing online are sold on the

history of poker. I get a lot of younger players challeng-
ing me. I guess they're after a scalp. If they play me and
lose, they get a story; if they play me and win, they get a
bigger story. The young guns always want to take on the
famous gunslingers. I know I did.

I've had loads of people come up to me over the years
and say they started playing poker because they saw me
on the TV. 'You're the one that made me lose my house
and my wife and my kids!'

No, they don't actually say that. But it can happen. As
they say, stock-market prices can go up as well as down.
And being a poker player is a bit like that – sometimes
you're riding high, sometimes your share price would be
zilch. Going flat broke is part of a gambler's education.

Sometimes what poker is trying to teach you is this:
give up now, you're not good enough. If that's the case,
you've got to listen. A lot of bad gamblers turn a deaf
ear to the sound of their money going down the drain,
and their wife and kids walking out the door.

If I could do it all again, would I? Yes, but I wouldn't
wear those flares in the seventies. And I'd put a lot more
money on Red Rum winning the Grand National.

Whatever talent I've got for poker must have always
been inside me, waiting to come out. But a lot of blokes
who grew up with me where I lived went down the same
path that I was going down. I'm only different from them
because I was lucky in two ways: I met Mandy, a woman
who made me want to change, and I had an ability for
cards that gave me a lifeline.

In the bad old days it was up and down the motorway

in the rain, down alleys in the dark, sitting in scruffy casinos and smoky rooms above shops. The hours were long, the food was crap, and there were a lot of occasions when you'd lose the shirt off your back or the arse out of your pants. It was tough, but exciting.

It's easier now because you can play on the Internet. You can sit and play and watch TV and talk to your kids at the same time. Play for pennies and get lucky and earn big money. But once you start playing live in cash games and tournaments, it's tough. There have to be losers otherwise there'd be no winners.

I guess I'm among the last of those guys who fought their way up through the ranks the hard way. I don't see that happening now because there's no need for it. Which is good for the younger players, but it's gonna be bad for the people who read their autobiographies.

It's been quite a ride. Some people might say that I came from nowhere and nothing, and that it's been a rags-to-riches story. In a way it has. But I still live in that so-called 'nowhere' city that I came from because Hull is a good place with good people.

I've got a great relationship with my beautiful kids, Paul, Kerry, David, Stephen, Chris, Michael and Matthew. And also with Mandy. Though I've got a real diamond in my life now with the beautiful Stacey. I can make sure they all get what they want. And I'm in the lucky position of being able to help out other people too: I donated £40,000 towards a local skate park in Ferriby for the kids and I support a local school in Brough for children with special needs by sponsoring their talent show. And, of course, I help out a lot of friends when I can. Hopefully those good things go some way to making up for the bad things in my past, and you see a better man.

When I'm in Hull, here's how my typical week goes. Usually I need rest after I've flown back from Vegas: several gallons of vodka plus a ten-hour flight take their toll. I've got steel shutters on our bedroom windows to keep the daylight out so I don't turn to dust. It's not often I climb out of my coffin before lunchtime.

If there's a good horse race meeting on, I study the form in the *Racing Post*; if not, I go to see my mam. Auntie Dot's usually there and they sit round clucking like chickens. I might go and watch Chris and Mike doing tricks in the skateboard park. Then there's movies, bowling, restaurants, and seeing Hull City play. Or I might just go for a drive with Stacey: sometimes we jump in the Ferrari, but usually the weather means we take the Hummer. The village has a post office, a café, a pub, a duck pond, and a hairdresser's where the girls look after me. I could even go down the Monica Snooker Club if I wanted because it's now been done up really nice and has new owners.

At the weekend I always go out with the same gang: Sonic, Andy Holland, Carl Martin, Stewart Carter, Rob Corman, Julian Schiberous, and my two boxing mates Raz (Ryan Mellor) and Tony Booth. We look like the wild bunch. All the doormen are happy to see us because we stop the young guns fighting.

So, as you can see, Hull ain't Vegas. When I'm home I live the life of any normal lazy bastard.

*

You know the phrase 'from one extreme to another'? Well, that's how my life feels. Coming from a council house on an estate in a tough old port town, to flying to Las Vegas in the middle of the desert and staying at a penthouse suite in the Bellagio Casino. From lying on the floor of a damp cell to lying on a white beach in the Caribbean. From winning twenty-five quid to winning six hundred and seventy-four thousand dollars. From watching TV to being on it. From twagging off school to sneak into the movies to going to Hollywood premieres. And even being in a film myself.

And from first playing cards round the kitchen table with my family, to this . . . being the most successful British poker player in the history of the game.

That's a long, long way to travel – and I don't just mean in miles. I had to make all kinds of adjustments on the way because it was unchartered territory. No one I knew had done any of that before so I was out there by myself.

Still, if you can always be yourself, and treat everyone with respect, then you'll have a happy life. I'm the same with a lollipop lady as I am with a Hollywood star. It's the quickest way of finding out whether or not someone can take you or leave you. And that way you don't waste time trying to win round non-believers.

Anyway, in life and in gambling, just try to keep the odds in your favour, then you've got a chance.

Talking about odds, did you know that the odds of you dropping dead in any single hour over a year are nine million to one. And the odds of you winning the lottery are fourteen million to one. So . . . if there's an hour to go before the numbers are drawn, you're more likely to drop dead then you are to win the jackpot. What a proper fucker that would be – dying of a heart attack as your numbers were called. I think that's what they call a mixed blessing.

What I'm saying is that you have to play the cards you've been dealt – in life and in poker. And if it's a choice between getting lucky in one or the other, I hope you're as fortunate as me. Which is also good for me because it means that if you ever play me at cards, you're screwed.

Now shuffle up and deal . . .

Appendix:
Winner Takes All – My Tournament Record

The most successful British player in poker history with over $5.6 million earnings in official tournaments alone. Including $1.5 million from twenty-eight cashes in the World Series of Poker. Top 50 of all-time WSOP cash-ins, and top 40 on the all-time money list.

180 tournament cash-ins (34 first places, 26 seconds and 22 thirds)

136 tournament final tables

24 championships

1 World Series of Poker bracelet (plus 4 WSOP seconds and 2 WSOP thirds)

1 World Poker Tour championship

1999 *Late Night Poker* champion

2006 Poker Nations Cup champion (team captain)

*

2004 European Poker Lifetime Achievement Award

2006 UK Gambling Personality of the Year Award

2007 European Player of the Year Award

Tournament championships

£100 Pot Limit Hold'em, European Open, London,
   1996 – £11,325

£100 Pot Limit Hold'em, Christmas Cracker, London,
   1996 – £8,725

$500 Pot Limit Omaha, Four Queens Poker Classic,
   Las Vegas, 1997 – $20,700

£200 Omaha, Spring Classic, London, 1997 – £13,250

$2,000 Pot Limit Hold'em, WSOP, Las Vegas, 1997
   – $180,310

FF1,000 Pot Limit Courcheval, Paris, 1997 – $10,902

FF5,000 Pot Limit Omaha, Spring Tournament, Paris,
   1998 – $30,399

FF3,000 Pot Limit Omaha, Autumn Tournament,
   Paris, 1998 – $18,936

Late Night Poker television tournament, Cardiff, 1999
   – £40,000

FF5,000 Pot Limit Omaha, Spring Tournament, Paris,
   2000 – $29,435

FF5,000 Pot Limit Omaha, Winter Tournament, Paris,
   2000 – $34,735

FF5,000 Pot Limit Omaha, Spring Tournament, Paris,
   2001 – $24,293

LIt1,000,000 No Limit Hold'em, Torneo di Poker,
   Nova Gorica, 2001 – $30,303

FF10,000 Pot Limit Omaha, Summer Tournament,
   Paris, 2001 – $53,013

£500 Pot Limit 7-Card Stud, Euro Poker Championship, London, 2001 – £36,611

$1,000 Pot Limit Omaha, Binion World Poker Open,
    Tunica, 2002 – $123,772

$500 Pot Limit Omaha, Caribbean Poker Classic, Palm
    Beach, 2002 – $8,150

£100 Pot Limit Omaha, Northern Lights, Blackpool,
    2002 – £6,090

£250 Pot Limit Hold'em, Christmas Cracker, London,
    2002 – £10,500

$10,000 No Limit Hold'em, Binion World Poker Open,
    Tunica, 2003 – $589,175

£100 Pot Limit Omaha, Midlands Medley, Walsall, 2004
    – £8,000

£1,250 No Limit Hold'em, British Open, London, 2004
    – £90,000

€500 Pot Limit Omaha, World Heads-Up Champion,
    Barcelona, 2004 – $29,672

€10,000 No Limit Hold'em, Euro Finals of Poker,
    Paris, 2005 – $50,091

€300 No Limit Hold'em, French Open, Deauville,
    2005 – $5,442

Poker Nations Cup, Cardiff, 2006 – $16,667

$2,000 No Limit Hold'em, Five Diamond World
    Classic, Las Vegas, 2006 – $266,160

$1,000 No Limit Hold'em, World Poker Open, Tunica,
    2007 – $109,192

€750 No Limit Hold'em, Irish Poker Championship,
    Galway, 2009 – $46,330

€5,000 No Limit Hold'em, Euro Finals of Poker, Paris,
    2009 – $186,382

He just wanted a decent book to read ...

Not too much to ask, is it? It was in 1935 when Allen Lane, Managing Director of Bodley Head Publishers, stood on a platform at Exeter railway station looking for something good to read on his journey back to London. His choice was limited to popular magazines and poor-quality paperbacks – the same choice faced every day by the vast majority of readers, few of whom could afford hardbacks. Lane's disappointment and subsequent anger at the range of books generally available led him to found a company – and change the world.

'We believed in the existence in this country of a vast reading public for intelligent books at a low price, and staked everything on it'
Sir Allen Lane, 1902–1970, founder of Penguin Books

The quality paperback had arrived – and not just in bookshops. Lane was adamant that his Penguins should appear in chain stores and tobacconists, and should cost no more than a packet of cigarettes.

Reading habits (and cigarette prices) have changed since 1935, but Penguin still believes in publishing the best books for everybody to enjoy. We still believe that good design costs no more than bad design, and we still believe that quality books published passionately and responsibly make the world a better place.

So wherever you see the little bird – whether it's on a piece of prize-winning literary fiction or a celebrity autobiography, political tour de force or historical masterpiece, a serial-killer thriller, reference book, world classic or a piece of pure escapism – you can bet that it represents the very best that the genre has to offer.

Whatever you like to read – trust Penguin.